Also by Lindy West
Shrill
The Witches Are Coming
Shit, Actually

ADULT BRACES

Driving Myself Sane

LINDY WEST

GRAND CENTRAL

LARGE PRINT

This book is memoir. It reflects the author's present recollections of events and dialogue. The author has changed some names and identifying characteristics of people and places.

Copyright © 2026 by Lindy West

Jacket design and illustration by Sara Deck. Jacket copyright © 2026 by Hachette Book Group, Inc.

Hachette Book Group supports the right to free expression and the value of copyright. The purpose of copyright is to encourage writers and artists to produce the creative works that enrich our culture.

The scanning, uploading, and distribution of this book without permission is a theft of the author's intellectual property. If you would like permission to use material from the book (other than for review purposes), please contact permissions@hbgusa.com. Thank you for your support of the author's rights.

Grand Central Publishing
Hachette Book Group
1290 Avenue of the Americas, New York, NY 10104
grandcentralpublishing.com
@grandcentralpub

First Edition: March 2026

Grand Central Publishing is a division of Hachette Book Group, Inc.
The Grand Central Publishing name and logo is a registered trademark of Hachette Book Group, Inc.

The publisher is not responsible for websites (or their content) that are not owned by the publisher.

Grand Central Publishing books may be purchased in bulk for business, educational, or promotional use. For information, please contact your local bookseller or the Hachette Book Group Special Markets Department at special.markets@hbgusa.com.

Map by Kadin McGreevy

Print book interior design by Amy Quinn

Library of Congress Cataloging-in-Publication Data has been applied for.

ISBNs: 9780306831836 (hardcover), 9780306831850 (ebook), 9781538783078 (large print)

For me

Consider the subtleness of the sea; how its most dreaded creatures glide under water, unapparent for the most part, and treacherously hidden beneath the loveliest tints of azure. Consider also the devilish brilliance and beauty of many of its most remorseless tribes, as the dainty embellished shape of many species of sharks. Consider, once more, the universal cannibalism of the sea; all whose creatures prey upon each other, carrying on eternal war since the world began.

Consider all this; and then turn to the green, gentle, and most docile earth; consider them both, the sea and the land; and do you not find a strange analogy to something in yourself? For as this appalling ocean surrounds the verdant land, so in the soul of man there lies one insular Tahiti, full of peace and joy, but encompassed by all the horrors of the half-known life. God keep thee! Push not off from that isle, thou canst never return!

    –Herman Melville, *Moby-Dick*

You know what, Brodfard? Maybe I'm just an art critic from Darien, Connecticut. But I resent when you made fun of me saying I liked pizza. Pizza is really yummy for me. And there's no pizza at this party. So having said that, now I can say goodbye.

—An art critic from Darien, Connecticut, *Wet Hot American Summer: Ten Years Later*

Contents

PART ONE: HOME BODY

Alarm   3
A Vroom of One's Own   6
Adult Braces   14
Mid Wife Crisis   26
Hypothetical   42
Crystal Cave of Wonders   48
BAAA   59

PART TWO: COLEMAN STOVE

Jante's Girl   65
Monsters   81
On Showering   87
Addicted to What the Pepperoni Stick Did   90
Voice Memos   103
Hwy 194, Colfax, Washington   106
Two Hikes   107
SR 272, Palouse, Washington   116
On the Edge   117
US-89, Livingston, Montana   128

Contents

Tore My Soul Open on a Lube Rack   131
Mary Tyler More-to-Love   139
US-18, Douglas, Wyoming   *153*
We Live in a Society, Bitch!   155
US-18, Lusk, Wyoming   *163*
We Cannot Open It Because We Cannot See the Bottom   164
Hwy 79, Buffalo Gap, South Dakota   *172*
Good Knievel   173

PART THREE: SEVENTEEN-YEAR BLOOM

Long Bright Noon of the Soul   181
Hwy 2, Ansley, Nebraska   *187*
Here Lies My Beloved   189
Hwy 2, Litchfield, Nebraska   *195*
Uphill Battle   197
Hwy 2, Sweetwater, Nebraska   *208*
Too Big to Fail   210
Precious Moments   221
Grenade   228
Man Cave   243
US-65, Harrison, Arkansas   *252*
Hot Chicken   253
I-40, Silver Point, Tennessee   *259*
Naked and Afraid   262
US-321, Walland, Tennessee   *272*

Contents

Cicada 274
US-321, Townsend, Tennessee 279

PART FOUR: SEA LEGS

Jingle Bells 283
I-95, Mims, Florida 289
Arrival 290
Bodies in the Sand 296
Overseas Hwy, Islamorada, Florida 322
The Key 323
I-75, Ocala, Florida 324

PART FIVE: HEAL TURN

Jeffie 327
US-98, Medart, Florida 337
Cry of the Limpkin 340
Hwy 27, Blakely, Georgia 345
Shy Marshmallow 347
US-280, Dadeville, Alabama 355
Heat Wave 357
I-65, Elizabethtown, Kentucky 362
Lost and Found 364
Horny Baddie Summer 372
Kalamazoo, Michigan 389
I Just Work Here 390

Contents

PART SIX: BEING THERE

Hwy 194, Fond du Lac Reservation, Minnesota 403
New Town, New Me 406
US-2, Wolf Point, Montana 412
Drip Droop 413
US-2, Glasgow, Montana 415
Life Finds a Way 416
US-2, Malta, Montana 422
Bird Box 424
Switchback 428
Curlew Lake State Park, Republic, Washington 437
Yay or Neigh 440
Triple-Double 443

Acknowledgments 451

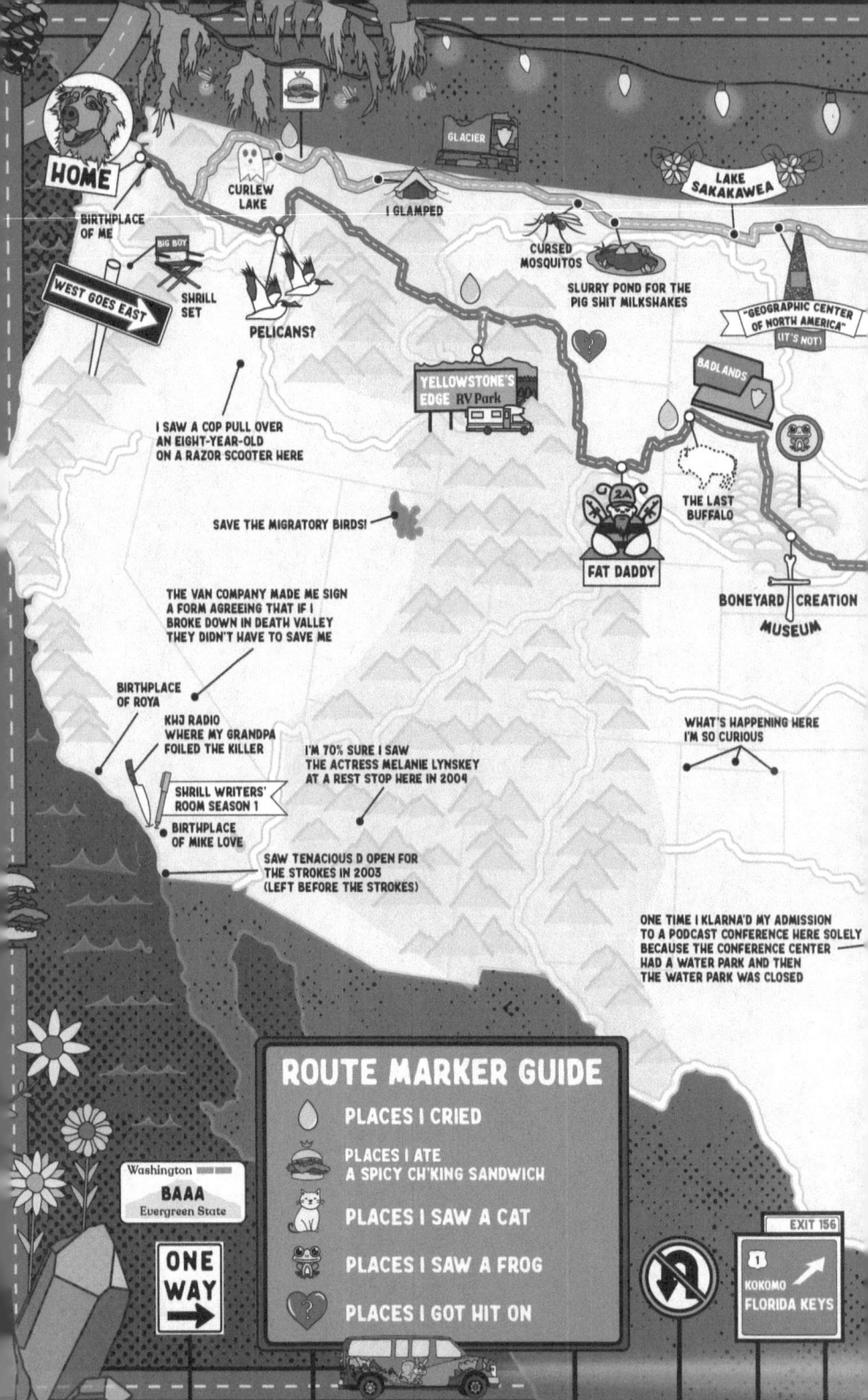

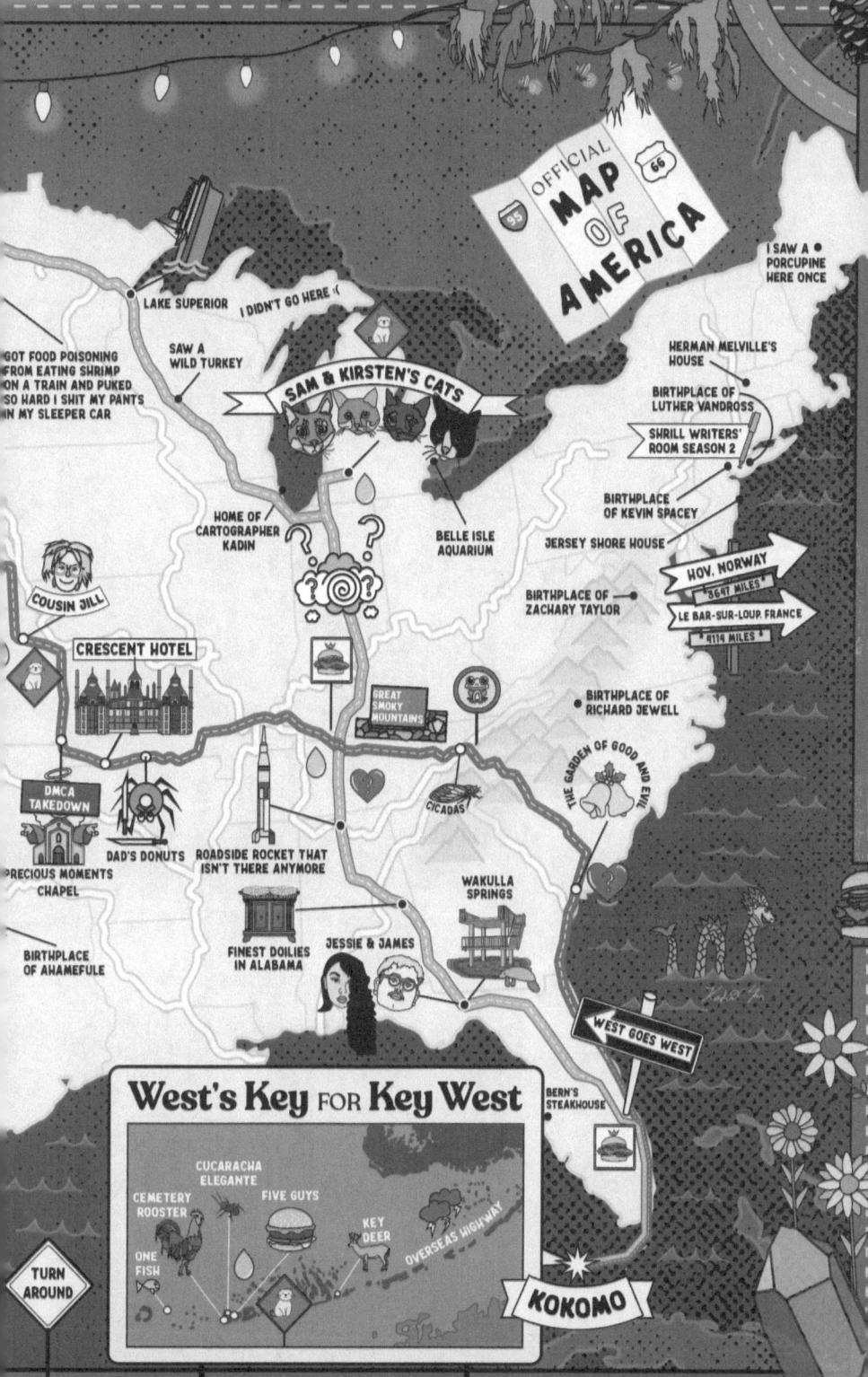

Part One
HOME BODY

Alarm

July 2, 2021

I was snoring on the green velvet living room couch, Carrots the cat purring on my chest, when a caustic beeping woke me.

It sounded like a twentieth-century alarm clock, not an iPhone—an old-fashioned, analog, gritty kind of beep. The time was 6:52 a.m. Sam and Kirsten were still asleep upstairs, and I didn't want to wake them. As I searched for the source of the noise, it changed to a slow beep for a while, then switched back to fast beeping. Did Kirsten set an alarm because she wanted to get up and say goodbye to me, but then she accidentally left her phone down here? It had to be a phone. There was a little pouch on the dining room table. I looked in there, but it was just Sam's wallet. No beeping phone. There was an iPad on the table.

Maybe Kirsten's alarm was going through the iPad? No, not that either.

I noticed a small cardboard box tossed in with the previous day's mail. It was addressed to Kirsten and the return address said, simply, *Good Stuff*, and an address in Minneapolis. That seemed like good news, because a murderer wouldn't put a return address, would they? The beeping was definitely coming from inside the box.

Okay, I thought, *it's a bomb*. Sam had been getting death threats because she worked on *And Just Like That*, the *Sex and the City* reboot. It was not impossible that a crazed *Sex and the City* fan mailed Sam a bomb because they didn't like how Miranda was treating Steve.

If there was a bomb in that box, I thought, because of Miranda Hobbes's queer awakening, and I just let the house blow up with two of my favorite people and four of my favorite cats inside, I'd be really upset. So I gingerly picked up the bomb, took it outside, and set it on the front step. Certainly a bomb can't penetrate a residential front door! I was a hero! Eat your heart out, Richard Jewell!!! I went back inside.

Satisfied with the morning's counterterrorism operation, I started on my chores, packing and organizing to get on the road. I had to leave Kalamazoo by 8:30 if I was going to make it all the way to Duluth before sunset. After about an hour, I peeked my nose around the door and found that the beeping had stopped.

Kirsten came downstairs.

"I found a bomb," I said. "I put it outside."

"You found a bomb and you put it outside?"

"Yeah."

Kirsten went out on the porch, then came back in, laughing and carrying the bomb. She grabbed some scissors and opened the deadly parcel ("NOOOOOOOOO!!!"—me, tackling her). Inside was an alarm clock. Kirsten's teenage son, Gordie, had been sleeping through his phone alarm, so she'd ordered an old, loud, vintage alarm clock on eBay and the seller had mailed it still set and with batteries in it.

It wasn't the first time I thought something was a bomb when it was actually a chance to wake up.

A Vroom of One's Own

I was holding my dog's face in my hands and singing the Beach Boys' "Kokomo" to comfort him after his neuter surgery, when I felt the first stirrings of mutiny. *It's not fair*, I thought. Women don't get to just go to Kokomo and live in a hammock and leave their worries behind and drink mai tais and become leathery beach men. Women don't get to have midlife crises. We get "nervous breakdowns" and it's not sexy and we can't even go lie down, because the countertops are sticky, and if we don't wipe them, then what will happen—some teenager comes along and does it with a PAPER TOWEL?! Not in my casa, *hermano*!

I was in the autumn of my own yet-undiagnosed midlife crisis, and I was so tired. It had been a hard couple of years. COVID, other stuff. On this particular morning, I'd woken up worrying about the dog, and the money, and my husband's upcoming trip, and whether my mom was mad at me, and the fact that my braces had worn a hole in my left cheek, and I couldn't remember the last time I'd woken up not worrying about someone else, not staring down the barrel of a bunch of shit that I had to deal with. For one day, I wanted to know what it felt like to open my eyes in the morning with an oasis in my chest and do whatever I wanted. Even as a child, I was a worrier. Even in my teenage years, my mind dragged heavy with dread. Now I was so worn down and twisted up, I wanted to disappear. Or, barring the constraints of space-time, the next best thing: I wanted to run away.

"I wish I could get in the car and drive all the way to Kokomo," I told the dog, who gazed back at me with an expression that said, unmistakably, "I have no idea what's going on. Where are my nuts???"

Then I thought: *Wait, why can't I? Where are MY nuts?*

People hate the Beach Boys' "Kokomo" because it's "stupid" and "bad" and songwriter Mike Love is "a MAGA asshole" who "kicked Brian Wilson out of the Beach Boys" and allegedly maybe according to the *National Enquirer* "refused to pay for his own daughter's cancer treatment and then she died." However, counterpoint: "Kokomo" is good!!!!!! I don't have to think that Mike Love's personality is good to think that "Kokomo" is a funky little number that gets me groovin'!

As a fictional-map fetishist,[1] I am helpless before a list of magical islands where people are falling in love and defying a little bit of gravity. Someone wants to take me to Aruba AND Jamaica AND Bermuda AND Bahama AND they think I'm a pretty mama??? Now we're cookin' with gas! I first heard "Kokomo" in 1993, when I was eleven years old, courtesy of the Muppets, and it imprinted on me for life. I don't want to get too deep into high-level neuroscience, but let's just say the spider librarian who indexes my brain spun a gossamer thread from "Kokomo" straight to the concept of adventure itself. For me, "Kokomo" always held a powerful—how do you say—Montserrat mystique? "Kokomo" represented everything exciting, beautiful, and

---

1. I've said it before, and I'll say it forever: You could write a book about donkey mucus, and if it has a map of a fake country in the front, I will spend $10,000 on a first edition.

mysterious that might happen to me in the vast unknown future.

So there I was, at a crisis point, clinically fed up, singing to the dog, and the song seemed to offer a prescription for just that moment: If you need to get away from it all, you simply MUST get down to Kokomo immediately, baby girl!

This idea—driving to Kokomo—stuck in my craw and all the Waterpiks in the world (I had three) couldn't dislodge it. You know that moment when you're driving to work and you see your exit coming up and you look at the horizon and you think, *What if I just kept driving?* I wanted to do it for real, to swim in that feeling, to take my body into my own hands and move it as far away from home as I could, physically, mile by mile, alone. For the first time in a long time, I was hungry to see what was out there. I wanted to steer. I wanted to be free. I wanted to catch a glimpse!

How long would it take to drive to the Florida Keys and back? Two weeks? I mapped it. At least a month. I can't be gone for a whole month. What about all the stuff I take care of? Who will turn the thermostat down at night and make sure all the lights are turned off except for the one light that I leave on so burglars know someone is home?

But also, I thought... I don't have a real job. I don't have little kids. I have a tiny bit of money left (ha ha, not enough!) from my last book and the third season of *Shrill*. In truth, the only thing stopping me was that long ago I'd convinced myself I had no interest in adventure because I was an agoraphobic wreck from being a fat woman in public. At some point, I'd decided that I was an indoor person, a vicarious person, that my exploration was over, that the door was shut and only home was safe.

Usually, *safe* means alive. But sometimes *safe* can mean dead. *Dead* as in still. *Dead* as in dark. *Dead* as in no longer growing.

It had occurred to me lately that perhaps I was dead. Was I dead?

I brought the idea to my husband, Ahamefule. A month... on the road... solo... Kokomo and back. I was sure he'd say he was too busy. The dog needed too many walks. Aham had his own life—he wasn't just an accessory to mine. But to my surprise, he took me by the hands.

"In ten years together, you've never once expressed any interest in doing anything by yourself," he said. "I've been waiting for you to ask me something like this. You're actually not allowed to not go."

Holy shit, I thought. *It's happening.* Hose off that double-wide hammock, Jimmy Buffett! Mama's comin'!

Giddy, I sat down to make my itinerary. The song says, "Off the Florida Keys / there's a place called Kokomo," which seemed like a good place to start, so I googled "Kokomo Florida Keys." I got a bunch of links to the lyrics of the song "Kokomo." Hmm. Suspicious. I googled, "Where is Kokomo from the Beach Boys song located?"

Google: "Although the song depicts Kokomo as a place off the Florida Keys, there really is no Kokomo in South Florida."

W
H
A
T
??????????
J'EXQUEEZE MOI?

Kokomo isn't a real place????? Kokomo isn't a real place. Of course it's not. Why would it be? I learned about it from a singing frog. Of course the big destination of my symbolic road trip, the capital of not having to deal with shit for one precious fucking moment, is fictional. Was happiness fictional too? Sometimes, lately, it felt like it.

But I wasn't going to let Mike Love, the worst Beach Boy, ruin this midlife crisis for me. Driving to the Florida Keys would be just as good as driving to Kokomo, I reckoned—better, even, since they exist. I wasn't too sure what the Florida Keys were, but soon learned that they are a coral and mangrove archipelago stretching toward Cuba from the southern tip of Florida, connected by something called the Overseas Highway, a series of reality-straining bridges hovering for miles over the open ocean, seemingly devised by dastardly murder-inventor Jigsaw from *Saw*. Sounded perfect for my purposes! I was hankering to get a little dastardly myself.

There was just one last thing to figure out. I couldn't leave Aham without a car for a month, and I couldn't afford to pay for a month of hotel rooms on top of a rental car and gas. Plus, some deep, unknowable instinct told me that to really get this growing done, I needed dirt, grime, sweat, exposure, back pain, bug bites, and the kind of scouring discomfort that only living outside can provide. Seeking comfort above all else was what had gotten me into this meltdown. If I had to rent a car anyway, let it be a van. I would drive to Key West in a van, and I would sleep in the van, and I would be afraid, but I would do it anyway. I would be uncomfortable, and I would heal.

Adult Braces

The pain was on both sides—an electric stab if I bit down on certain molars. Chewing had become a series of jump scares. Is this fun-size Milky Way going to send a bolt of lightning straight to my bunghole? What about this one? In the summer of 2020, reduced to nibbling in the front like a little weasel, I ran to my cool Gen X rock and roll dentist, Dr. Nikole, and begged for help.

I never used to have dental anxiety. My childhood dentist was lanky and twinkly eyed with a soft-spoken Scandinavian Zen that reminded me of my family in the old country. The dentist's spitfire wife ran the office and would give me little toys and gossip with my mom. I remember my dad always reassuring me, as an endorsement of this dentist's gentleness, "He has never hurt me." It wasn't that reassuring! Did some dentists HURT YOU? What the fuck?! But I did trust my dentist, and it was true, he never hurt me at all. I also never had a cavity (until my early twenties, when I suddenly had a bunch[1]), and my dentist said I had the most "perfect teeth" he had ever seen. He said it all the time. Perfect teeth. Wow, such beautiful, perfect teeth.

He probably said that to lots of kids, to be nice, but at the time, I imagined that it really made my dentist's day when he saw these chompers on the agenda. Like when a piano player gets to play the finest Steinway concert grand.

I wasn't the kind of girl who heard "perfect" a lot as an assessment of her body, so I clung to it. Not just good teeth but perfect ones. No braces needed for this *perfect tooth model*. No retainer, no headgear, not me! They just came out like this! Must have something to do with my perfect skull and *beautiful soul!* PLEASE KISS ME, JUST ANY BOY PLEASE PLEASE KISS ME I AM BEGGING YOU.

---

[1]. I read that kissing a new person can trigger cavities because their mouth biome corrupts your mouth biome, and come to think of it, this was around the time I started kissing regularly! Should have saved myself for marriage!

My dentist retired when I was in my twenties and he was in his eighties. I looked up his obituary while writing this and discovered he only just died in 2024, at age 107. Another patient in the comments on his memorial page called him an "iconic dentist." Amen, brother!

Extremely un-iconically, some random fucking guy took over his practice. Not having the first clue how to pick out a new dentist, as my family had been dentisted upon by the same man since the Nixon administration, I stayed. The first time I had to get a filling from the new guy, Dr. Glover, he drilled my tooth without fully anesthetizing it, didn't believe me when I gasped that it wasn't numb, and then told me I was being "hysterical" (literally!) when I started sobbing. He drilled my sensate pulp while I struggled to keep my panic attack as still as possible. He drilled until he was done.

A few months later, Aham and I were stopped at a light downtown near our dental office, and a dirty and disheveled man crossed the street in front of us talking to himself and swearing and arguing with no one. In our family, we call that "having a hard time." And this guy having a hard time? OUR FUCKING DENTIST. Not some dentist we once knew, but our present-day, actively practicing dentist. Not who you hope to see having a hard time in Westlake Park! (Also, later, when I first went to see Dr. Nikole, she looked at that guy's treatment plan and said he seemed to have marked teeth for drilling where there were no cavities! I was rudely being dental-tortured by a demon[2] befouling Dr. Childhood Dentist's sacred space!!!)

So anyway, I didn't used to have dental trauma and anxiety, but now I do, and that's why I sought out Dr. Nikole. She listens to me (!!!!!) and gives me gases and lets me play my little audiobooks and prescribes me Ativan for bigger procedures, and if you're still being drilled by a man, have you considered *a woman*? It's 2026! Fire all men from all jobs!

When I told her my teeth were hurting, Dr. Nikole looked at my x-rays and discovered that my molars had a bunch of big cracks in them. I was like, "Great! Sounds like an easy fix! Gorilla-glue those bad boys up so I can be on my milky

---

2. Dr. Glover…DRGOVEL…RG DEVOL…RAGE DEVIL!!!!!!!!!!

way!" And she said no—that's actually not how cracked teeth work. You just kind of have to *have them* until they get so bad that you need a crown or your tooth crumbles into dust and blows away. Sorry!

The reason my teeth were all cracked, she explained, was that I had developed what's called a *crossbite*. That's where your jaw shifts (from, say, stress-clenching and misery-grinding in one's sleep) and your molars no longer fit together snugly like LEGO bricks; they clack together violently like twelve otters smashing twelve clams on twelve rocks. The only solution for this, she said, was orthodonture.

Adult braces.

Me???????? But I literally have the greatest natural mouth of all time! Check those x-rays again, lady! You must have gotten them mixed up with A DOG.

But of course, the problem was real, and of course, I was going to fix it, seeing as the alternative was a not-particularly-appealing two-phase plan consisting of Phase One: Operation Pain and Phase Two: Operation No Teeth Anymore. I made an appointment with the orthodontist she recommended.

Orthodontists are the plastic surgeons of dentists, and I don't mean in terms of what they do—although I suppose there is a parallel—I mean in terms of vibes. My orthodontists, a married couple straight outta *Melrose Place*, run a braces empire stretching across the greater Seattle area. Their office is spangled with framed glossy magazine covers (from, idk, *Mouth Magazine*??) in which they pose like TOOTH ROYALTY, shiny hair and shark bites and power suits and erotic chemistry and $$$$$$ energy. My braces cost around $7,000 with a minimum of $1,500 down. The place is always packed, with the barreling, angry efficiency of a trading floor. You feel not so much like a customer as a product on an assembly line.

I arrived and was swept into a chair, where one of their assistants assessed my situation at breakneck speed without saying *hi* or *hello, ma'am* or *how are you* or *don't worry this won't hurt a bit*. He was, weirdly, French, and my fatty alarm told me instantly that this guy did not *j'adore* fat people. He strode over to the 360-degree x-ray machine—me jogging to keep up—and, without saying a word or even making eye contact, stuck a plastic bit in my mouth to position my head like a cart horse. He then switched on the machine, which went WHIIIRRRRRRRRR-RRRRRRRRRRRRRRRRRRRRRR and started attacking me!

Excusez-moi! Excusez-moi! Hold vos chevaux, monsieur!!!!!! ARRÊTÉ! CREVÈ!!!

This machine is like a huge gyroscope where you stand in the middle, and metal arms whirl around your head and shoulders and pump you full of beams so they can make a copy of your head. I don't know how to convey the magnitude, but it's scary! It is an industrial machine. It is inexorable. You cannot stop it. It could easily break your bones if you stuck an arm out at the wrong time. And this Frenchman had just tossed me in there without a fair warning or, as far as I could tell, recalibrating the machine that was used all day every day on the bodies of little, tiny kids. And I am a big, large woman!

The machine began its business and whacked me about the shoulders with its metal arms. I was paying $7,000 to be attacked by a robot. I said, "This is hitting my shoulders!" and he said, "Hold still, please," and I said, "PLEASE, MONSIEUR, IT'S HITTING MY BODY," and he said, "[EXASPERATED SIGH] Drop your shoulders." The shoulders—at least in *les États-Unis*—are attached to the body in a frustratingly permanent way. These bad boys were already as low as they could go. But François didn't care—he ran the machine till it was done and let it whack me over and over and luckily it didn't hurt too much or permanently disfigure me and I guess that's the best fat people can expect from the French!

Then we STEEPLECHASED back to the chair and François glued my brackets on with the reckless abandon of a *Double Dare* contestant, adding: "You will want to stick to soft foods for ze first few weeks. Like... [looking me up and down] *per'aps salades*." Famously, the softest of all foods!

And then he was gone. They drop-kicked me out the door to make room for the next 150 kids they had lined up that day (150 × $7,000 = $1,050,000???????). And then I had adult braces.

I've always had a shaky relationship with self-confidence, and in my callow twenties, I was a real bitch about adult braces. Not like I publicly bullied people who had them or anything, but I remember thinking that I absolutely, under no circumstances, could ever subject myself to anything that humiliating. Which is so condescending! Filing someone else's state under "humiliating" implies that they have something to be humiliated about, whether they feel humiliated by it or not. It's exactly what people do to me for being fat. This is no excuse, but every accusation is a confession, and at the time, I felt very much like an overgrown, sexless child that everyone was laughing at. I'm sorry!

So maybe it was karmically appropriate—a real Mrs. Piggle-Wiggle moment—that, rounding the corner into forty, I wound up getting braces myself. And not an elegant, gossamer Invisalign tray, either. Full metal train tracks, welded on. Because if there's one thing I'm even more certain of than my own ugliness, it's my incompetence and low moral fiber. There was no fucking chance in Leopold II of Belgium's red hell that I was going to keep an Invisalign tray in twenty-three hours a day, because unfortunately, I looooooooove low-stakes cheating. I love to treat myself to the indulgent thing instead of powering through the hard thing. And it's not like Invisalign is cheaper than the metal guys! I'd still be out $7,000, and my teeth would still be fucked. No thanks! Strap 'em on me, John Henry!

This was early COVID, so we were deep in Mask Culture. There wasn't even a vaccine yet. Everyone told me the same thing: It wasn't a bad time to get adult braces, as times to get adult braces go. But society didn't seem to understand that there was no good time for Lindy West to get adult braces. I was hanging on to sanity by a thread and these thirty-two little STRAIGHT WHITE MEN (all teeth are boys) had conspired to take away the one thing that wasn't wrong with me—my "perfect teeth." I hated it and I cried.

Now, "I'm embawassed to get adult bwaces" is America's #1 Next Top Champagne Problem to be sure. The actually bad version of this story would be me not being able to afford adult braces and all my teeth cracking in half and falling out.

I am indescribably fortunate to have been able to save my teeth, and I have to acknowledge that many people literally cannot do the things necessary to break out of harmful cycles, because they have to work and they have to take care of kids and they are just so tired, not to mention structurally held back by our "free" country. Unfortunately, I don't exactly have an answer to the evils of capitalism. I'm sorry again as usual!

It would take a year before I had enough perspective to see the metaphor. We think of our teeth as something fixed in place, a part of the skull, crooked or straight, but they're not. Our teeth are floating, each loose and alone in tissue, and we can shift and change them if we want to, bring them closer together or push them apart, if we're willing to move through the pain of it, if we're willing to be a little vulnerable, to look a little childish.

For many years, I thought my life was fixed in place, painful but immovable. I felt as though I had turned to stone, still and helpless, both physically and emotionally, slowly cracking while the world glided on without me. I took pride in my ability to weather any amount of discomfort to preserve the familiar and avoid humiliation. But I am not stone. I deserve more than endurance. I deserve pleasure and the good and the new.

Not perfect teeth but teeth free enough to move.

Mid Wife Crisis

I was an hour into recording the audiobook of *The Witches Are Coming*, my second collection of essays, when I got a message from a stranger (a fan, how embarrassing) informing me that they had seen my husband kissing a woman who was not me at a bar.

I stepped outside, pressed my body against my hot car, and called Ahamefule. He was silent for ten heartbeats. Then he said, "I think maybe we want different things."

I told the audio engineer that I had a family emergency and left. On the drive home, over the phone, Aham said, "You know that I am a polyamorous person," and I hung up in a rage, even though he was right, I did know that, and then I called back and pretended I'd lost signal in the tunnel. He believed me.

It was September 2019, and I had only been home, reunited with him, for one day. I'd spent the previous six months alone in New York City and then Portland, Oregon, writing and shooting the second season of *Shrill*, the TV show based on my memoir. For that first month in New York, I'd also been finishing *The Witches Are Coming* at night after working in the *Shrill* writers' room all day. I was renting a room in a mansion in Brooklyn and making enough money to take a cab to work in Manhattan if I overslept. It was the realization of every wild dream I'd ever had, and it was the worst fucking month of my life. And I didn't even know that back in the Pacific Northwest, at an artists' residency by the sea, my husband was falling in love with someone new, a tiny, beautiful bird.

Or maybe I did know. Awake or asleep, a nasty shape whispered from my guts: *You're so patient, you're so kind, you're the glue, he does whatever he wants while you work yourself to death in a strange city, he would never _____ now, or now, or now, not after this sacrifice, or that, or this, he would be a horrible person if he ever even thought about _____.* Even if I couldn't finish the sentence, I think I knew.

In *The Witches Are Coming*, I opened a chapter called "The World Is Good and Worth Fighting

For" with an ode to Aham: "My best friend, vibrating with ideas and brilliantly talented, a talent once in a generation and on the brink of everyone knowing it, wise and principled, who is so annoying, who can lift a piano, who can lift me." I went on to describe a "quiet sort of dawn ritual" we'd developed: "He is sensitive in the morning, so I am careful not to talk about bills until after 10:00 a.m.... we lie in bed for as long as we can and we talk about only good stuff."

All of that is true. But what I omitted was that we'd only developed that "ritual" to mitigate a toxic pattern we'd been stuck in for years: I'd wake up anxious, I'd vomit my anxiety on Aham, he'd snap at me for triggering *his* anxiety, I'd feel alone and unsupported, I'd stare at him with tears in my eyes until he had a panic attack, he'd zone out for the rest of the day and not listen to a word I said. We didn't implement the "only good stuff in the morning" policy to be cute—we did it because we needed therapy.

The day after I found out Aham had a secret girlfriend, I had to go back into the studio and record that chapter, make it permanent in my own voice, speak it into a microphone while a strange man gave me feedback on my diction. Only now, I could see it for what it was: an optical illusion, a conjurer's trick, an inversion, a photo negative, a prayer, a plaster cast for a life that didn't exist.

I didn't write about how often I screamed alone in the car, how erased I felt by marriage itself, yet how terrified I was of losing him. I boasted that we fought "once per year," but I didn't confess that it was only because both of us bottled up our grievances, because we'd never figured out how to communicate about anything hard. When things did crack open, he'd get angry, and I'd grovel. He'd walk out to clear his head, and I'd follow him down the street barefoot, begging him to come back and just tell me everything was fine. Eventually he'd cave and tell me everything was fine, even if he didn't feel fine at all. I didn't write that we both felt misunderstood, and we were both defensive and it wasn't getting better.

The truth is, I fell apart long before I got that phone call at the recording studio. The shift happened imperceptibly, in the two years after *Shrill* the book came out. I stopped wanting to work.

I wrote less and less. I never answered emails. I let professional relationships slip away. I fumbled opportunities. I alienated my colleagues. I stopped seeing my friends. I was afraid to go outside, because I had become a public figure, at least in Seattle. I had no privacy. People noticed me, watched me, stopped me, told me their secrets, cried. Sometimes I'd find anonymous comments online from people who claimed to be in my inner circle, saying that everyone around me secretly hated me, affirming my paranoia. I ate obsessively, just to feel some sort of tangible, reliable pleasure. I was in perpetual physical pain. I stopped moving my body. I couldn't walk. I couldn't breathe. I couldn't sleep. I couldn't imagine how I could be loved, but I also thought it was Aham's responsibility to fix me. I spent too much money. I was depressed, but I was also heightened—a frightened rabbit, my anxiety spinning at an earsplitting frequency all day and all night. Fear supplanted fun, joy, hope, spontaneity, self. I was an insatiable black hole of validation and reassurance. And that was *before* the other woman.

Aham was exhausted, resentful, and at a loss

for how to bring me back. And the whole time I was getting emails and DMs and shouts on the street, every day, from strangers who needed to tell me how much my confidence and self-love inspired them, made happiness seem possible for them for the first time in their lives. How much they *loved our love.*

~~~

My life with Aham started out a mess. It was the first few weeks of 2011. He had just gotten divorced, but I fell in love right away. I pushed him. He wanted it—if there's one impressive/excruciating thing about Aham, it's that he doesn't do anything he doesn't want to do—but I know I pushed too hard, even as he was begging me not to. We moved in together and to another state within a year, a stupid, selfish move that hurt our families and took me away from my father in the last months of his life. It was too soon and I wanted it too much and we never got our rhythm back. A month after we moved, Aham broke up with me.

When I think back on that time, I see a blueprint for all the chaos that was to come—all of my frailties in their purest form, not just untreated but unidentified. No. Not unidentified but inverted, disguised as their opposites. I thought these were virtues: obsessive, all-consuming love; desperation; agony; erasing myself to let him shine; martyring myself to earn his love; relinquishing all boundaries. My experiences with men never taught me love; they taught me manipulation and how to survive on the bare minimum.

Once, in my early twenties, I asked my big sister for advice about how to stop fixating on micro-interactions with emotionally unavailable men. She suggested I print out a picture of Jeff Spicoli from *Fast Times at Ridgemont High*, laminate it, and keep it in my wallet as a kind of anti-neediness totem. Would Spicoli care if some loser didn't text him back? No! Would Spicoli cry at the coffee shop because he was getting mixed signals from the barista? Never. Spicoli is something more than man—an earth elemental, unflappable as gravity. He is Tom Bombadil; Pippi Longstocking; Captain Ahab's uncanny harpooneer, Fedallah. If ever I found myself consumed by my feelings, I was to take out my Spicoli totem and feel the Spicoli flow through me. In retrospect, I wish she'd advised me to, I don't know, "have standards for how people treat you," but that's okay. I wasn't ready. She was meeting me where I was at.

Aham really showed up when my dad died. We got back together and stayed. I acknowledged in *Shrill* that "couples getting back together" was rare and possibly unhealthy, but, I wrote, "the only explanation I can offer is that we weren't the same people in Relationship: Part Deux as we were in Relationship: The Phantom Menace." And that's true. I certainly wasn't the same. The death of a parent ages you. But what I didn't share in *Shrill* was that a key stipulation of our reunion—insisted upon by Aham—was nonmonogamy.

Aham always knew he wanted an unconventional relationship structure; I still felt safe in the tightness of jealousy. I'm not politically conservative, but I am reserved. I like tradition, rituals, patterns, feeling like a stitch in a great weave of grandparents and great-grandparents, pairs loving each other in the same format again and again. (Which, of course, can't be true—I'm sure plenty of them were philanderers or chaotic, horny freaks—but it's not like my great-great-grandmother Bertha Brostowicz had a TikTok about her polycule. Absent documentation, we can burden our ancestors with whatever projections we like.) My Norwegian side has a family tree going back to the 1300s. Why shouldn't I deserve the same patterns of love as everyone else?

At the time, being cool about polyamory felt like a growing imperative in progressive circles. It made me defensive, particularly coming from thin people. Are you saying there's something *different* about me—some reason why I, specifically, should be obliged to seek *alternative lifestyles*? Mightn't I be happier as a lesbian separatist, or a polyamorous burlesque dancer, or an anarchic cat woman? Maybe so, but that seemed beside the point. The point was WHY SHOULD I? Why not you? YOU go be alternative! I wanted to be a teenage girl having her first kiss and her first boyfriend and her first heartbreak like everyone else, all the things I missed out on the first time around. I wanted to be someone's burning obsession. I had no interest in reinventing the wheel—I was still trying for my driver's license.

I wanted what "normal" people had because I was not allowed to have it. Stigma stole even this from me: my right to imagine what kind of life I wanted, without the poisoned lure of what I couldn't have. Monogamous heterosexual true love had always been withheld, so that's what I chased. I wasn't naive; I was furious. I had something to avenge. I craved that precious thing I'd been denied for so long while all my friends and enemies dated and married and had babies and divorced. So when I found it, even with that inconvenient caveat, I binged it.

The day Aham and I got back together,[1] in early 2012, we talked for hours. I cried for most of it. In broaching nonmonogamy, Aham said that he wasn't seeing anyone else, and this wasn't about me—it was just a fundamental part of his ethos. He believed that monogamy was, at its root, a system of ownership. I had to admit that perhaps I didn't feel it as keenly, as a white person. Aham loved me more than anyone else he had ever met in his life, I was the most special person in the world and the first best friend he'd

---

1. Relationship: Tokyo Drift

ever had, but this was not negotiable. He would not lie to me or anyone else about it, and he was prepared to break his own heart now rather than watch us decay and collapse later.

I stood at this crossroads: spend the rest of my life without Aham (impossible), or agree to a polyamorous relationship (also impossible).

We talked more. I cried more. Eventually, I got Aham to reassure me that he wasn't planning on running out to collect other wives. He wanted *me*. But he also needed to stay true to himself. It wasn't healthy to put my needs ahead of his own. *Yes, it is*, I thought. *I do it all the time. Love is making yourself disappear.*

I let myself believe this meant the nonmonogamy was symbolic. In my recollection, we negotiated down to one central tenet: Life is long, we can't see the future, but we love each other enough that *if anything happens*, it won't be a dealbreaker. The cultural taboo against cheating had never resonated with me anyway. Why was that the one thing that no one is allowed to forgive? I also extrapolated, because it's what I wanted to be true, that any extramarital funny business would be in the form of a one-night stand, quick and emotionally meaningless. I told Aham: nobody we knew, nobody in Seattle, nobody who was going to try to ruin our lives. Aham was a touring musician—the logistics seemed easy enough. Just do it on the road, bud! I requested not to be told about any such encounters. Why did I need to know? Maybe I'd even have a dalliance of my own! Just kidding, ha ha! I knew I wouldn't, because I was better than him.

I surveyed the crossroads again, and now the choice looked different: spend the rest of my life without Aham (impossible), or agree to *theoretical* polyamory that may or may not ever be acted upon (less impossible!).

This new option allowed me some illusion of control: There was a chance that Aham would never act on his polyamorous desires if I never gave him a reason to. If I could be the greatest wife of all time, forever, One Wife to Rule Them All, then maybe I would never have to have the nonmonogamy conversation ever again.

Still raw from grief, I needed my home back, and Aham was my home. People are allowed to want what they want. I told myself that I had years to adjust to the idea of nonmonogamy, or, even better, years to make myself enough for him, years to talk him out of it. Aham expressed fear (correctly) that I was only telling him what he wanted to hear because I loved him so much. He needed me to understand, really understand, that he was serious about this—he didn't want to hurt me. Yeah, yeah, yeah, sure. No problem. I promised that I would stretch and grow and be brave.

Reader, that is not what I did. I shrank into fear and calcified. I honestly don't know if I was being deceitful or delusional when I made that promise, but I used those years not as an opportunity to open up but instead to shackle Aham with guilt. I martyred myself spectacularly in order to hoard emotional currency that I could spend to prevent Aham from ever saying the word *polyamory* to me again. My nervous system fritzed if he even brought it up in the abstract, about other people, which he did a lot.

Me: Ooh, did you hear about [new celebrity cheating scandal]?
Him: We don't know what kind of arrangement they had in their marriage.

Me: (*Wishes this man would be dissolved by acid rain.*)

This went on for years. I was an animal, running on instinct, but subconsciously, everything I did fed into one grand strategy—if I pay for this expense, if I shoulder this responsibility, if I don't complain about this irritation, if I subsume myself into him, then he will look like the biggest asshole of all time if he hurts me. Because I'm just a soft baby angel who everyone loves! Time didn't unspool behind me like a ribbon; it coiled snakelike into a pile, a haystack, a mountain, immovable, never out of sight. Instinctive but tactical. A bank of personal misery that I could leverage against Aham's freedom. A prison that kept me safe.

Another neat trick that I absolutely nailed: We weren't open about our secret nonmonogamy contract. Nobody knew! Maybe I mentioned it once in a while, to a cool friend in a cool way, like, "Oh yeah, we're technically nonmonogamous but just because monogamy is *so* patriarchal" (SUCH a cool thing to say), with the implication that we loved each other too much to act on it, unlike all those other polyamorous people who wouldn't know love if Cupid himself split their tiny top hat with an arrow. I felt safe in the knowledge that if Aham ever did manage to tunnel his way out of my fortress of guilt and get laid—without my knowledge, because *I had asked not to be told*—all anyone in our lives would see was the old story of a selfish man cheating on his beleaguered, beloved, self-sacrificing, fat wife.

Which is exactly what happened.

Yay, question mark?

I won, question mark?

Cultural scripts tell us that this is a simple story. Aham is the villain, irredeemable. This other woman is a vampire, stealing my life. I am a victim, but I am also pathetic. Because I'm fat, Aham's lust for women younger and thinner than I am isn't just understandable but something deeper, the natural way of things. What did I expect? Anyone could see this coming. It's a miracle he lasted eight years. I knew other people were saying it. I knew people I loved were saying it. Maybe, I thought, even Aham was saying it.

Privately, I was contemptuous, high on my

own supply. *I do so much for you, and you're so horny that you can't even do me the small favor of not fucking other people?* It was easy and satisfying to frame it that way, even though I knew it wasn't fair. I knew it wasn't fair, but I also didn't understand. Why wasn't I good enough?

And I couldn't write about it, because I'd invested so much in this artifice—I'd made "happy marriage" part of my brand. I imagined people looking up all the passages in *Shrill* and *Witches* where I wrote about Aham and laughing: *See? We knew he couldn't really love you. We knew you were lying about being wanted.*

The shame was bigger than the pain. When Aham kissed another woman in a dark bar, he wasn't simply discarding me, he was devaluing me. Because, to the public eye, his love was the only thing that gave me any value at all. My value was never mine; it was borrowed. She won. I lost. As it should be. As I always knew it would be.

Hypothetical

The months before my road trip were peaceful. After I found out Aham's big secret, I insisted I didn't want to know any details—if I was going to try to do nonmonogamy (and I was holding on to this marriage if it fucking KILLED ME, YOU ASSHOLE!!!), it felt necessary to keep it compartmentalized. If I'm being *really* honest, I was engineering my backup plan: a total system collapse that I could blame on polyamory. COVID made it all easy, for a while. We had our intimate, insular life at home, and then Aham had his other life with whatever other stupid fucking people that was none of my business. *People do this all the time*, I told myself, like a mantra. *People do nonmonogamy all the time and they love it and it's normal and they're normal and happy.*

Then, one day, in violation of my embargo,

Aham sat me down and told me the identity of the woman he was seeing, and it turned out that I'd met her before. She was artistic director at an arts organization in Portland, Oregon, where one of her co-directors had booked Aham's stage show in 2019. That show happened about a week after I'd confronted him about the bar kiss, but I went anyway, shell-shocked and raw, looking—even I had to admit—beautiful thanks to the chemical peel of grief, and I have a vague memory of being introduced to a gracious black-haired woman in the lobby, who hugged me warmly. Her name was Roya.

In September 2020, Roya's best friend died of cancer, less than a year after his diagnosis. She was his caregiver during his illness, not a weight of responsibility or a degree of loss you expect to bear in your mid-thirties. She was smoke and ash. So, whether I was ready or not, Aham had to tell me who Roya was and where she lived, because he had to go be with her while she bore the unthinkable. Because he was her partner too. I'd resisted that reality long enough.

It was one of those hypotheticals that I'd held

up as an example of why polyamory would never work: What if one of these "other women" that you "love" has a crisis? Are you just going to run out on me at any time? *I'd be there for her, the same way I'd be there for any friend in crisis.* Well what if she has a crisis on the same day that I'M IN A HORRIBLE CAR ACCIDENT? WOULD YOU CHOOSE ME OR HER? *If you were in a horrible car accident, I'd be there with you at the hospital! Oh my god, what are you talking about?!*

I remember being reflexively unkind, yelling, "You're telling me you're this random woman's *whole support system*??? She doesn't have ANYONE ELSE?" But my higher self understood: Roya did have somebody else, and then he died. I know what it's like to love someone and lose them. I know what it means to have a best friend, that the term *best friend* is inadequate to describe the real thing. I remembered my best friend, Aham, standing in my parents' kitchen the day after my dad died, whisking hollandaise, making my mom and her sisters laugh, and cooking us eggs Benedict, a ludicrously extravagant breakfast to match our ludicrously extravagant pain.

That's who Aham is. And stretching out in softness to make other people feel better—that's who I am. I was tired of trying to turn both of us into someone else. I relented.

After that, starting in early 2021, Aham would spend a weekend with Roya in Portland about once a month. It wasn't easy. I extended the bare minimum of grace. I was prickly and miserable before he left and made him work for my smile after he got back. I wanted him to have a bad time and feel like he was doing something bad.

But gradually, imperceptibly, things changed. The more time I spent alone, the more I started to see ways that my understanding of marriage had pulled me away from myself. It's exactly what Aham had warned against in his initial pitch for nonmonogamy all those years ago. (Irritating.) He always said he wanted me to have space to be myself too. I always thought I wanted my life to be him. But what if I let my life be me?

My friend Jenny and I started going to the gym together three mornings a week; I'd pick her up, and we'd get drive-through coffee and scream and laugh and gossip and wear ourselves out; the ritual of it was soothing. I slept every night in a decadent exhaustion. When he was gone visiting Roya, I had long stretches of time to spend with my friends—the kind of time that can get lost once you're married. Hester and I watching an entire season of *Battlestar Galactica* in a day. Angela and I taking a two-hour lunch at Canton Noodle House and then going to a second location for cake. A slumber party at Aditi's parents' house, where we watched Lifetime movies and, in the morning, Rohini taught us to make upma.

Each weekend without Aham got easier, until one day he left, and I noted, with interest, that I didn't feel anything. No angst, no pain. I breathed only the air I wanted to all weekend, and when he came back on Monday, I was buoyant. It felt good to miss him.

I still never wanted to meet Roya, or be friends with her, or look at a picture of her (except when I was alone and sad and needed to press on the bruise), but she seemed like a perfectly nice person.

On one particularly grounded day, I asked Aham: What did Roya think about me?

"She likes you! She's always liked you."

He made it sound so uncomplicated. She just *liked me*. It was almost aspirational.

I pushed the thought away. Polyamorous people. *They think they're so evolved.*

Crystal Cave of Wonders

I have a relative who is a woo-woo witch queen, a real charisma monster, a dreamer who searches for the self reflexively like the rest of us breathe and makes it feel magical, not corny. She is the coolest, most magnetic person I have ever met. We were briefly close, in my twenties, but I always felt like I was tap-dancing to keep her. *What can I bring you? What do you need? Who do you want me to be today?*

    A long time ago, she got mad at me for something I said—something I thought was a compliment and she didn't, and, to be fair to her, reality is perception, not intent, but to be fair to me, I think she'd been looking for an excuse—and she hasn't spoken to me since, so I won't write about her beyond this paragraph. But when I was young, there was nothing I wanted more than this person's attention, and I never quite got it, she breadcrumbed it for reasons that I'm sure were instinctual and self-protective, the complex trauma of family, and I understand why and I don't hold it against her, but I've been thinking lately about how fucked up I am over not feeling "cool," and I think she's part of it. The coolest person in the world, who was supposed to love me unconditionally, never could. I must be *such a loser*.

At the co-op in my old neighborhood, I ran into a woman named Rainbow, who grew up with the aforementioned relative. They ran wild as teenagers—she remembers me as a toddler, and I remember them as celebrities, twin stars. When I was a teenager, Rainbow owned a shop in Belltown that sold crystals and things, and one afternoon after a stop at the army-navy surplus store to buy some bell-bottoms and a big coat, I crept into Rainbow's store, Ola Wyola, too shy to say hi but bewitched by the smell of it, the incense, the opulence, the Gen X cool, the vintage textiles and mysterious totems.

Rainbow and my relative eventually drifted apart. And then, twenty-five years later and just a few weeks before my road trip, there she was, contemplating a navel orange at my neighborhood grocery store. She remembered me, and she hugged me, and she told me she'd reopened Ola Wyola right up the street—her little magic shop where she sells crystals and jewels and does Reiki healing and chakra clearing and all kinds of things that I never knew how to believe in, and she told me I should come by.

When I started seeing my first long-term therapist, Judith, in fall 2019, she observed that I seemed to have no boundaries at all. I was blurred all around my edges, at the mercy of anyone who wanted to treat me any which way, because I'd lost track of myself and therefore had no way to calibrate what I deserved. When you are nothing, you figure you must deserve nothing. Why would nothing deserve something? It would be a waste.

At the beginning of every session, Judith told me to make a circle with my arms, like I was holding a beach ball to my chest, but palms out, like I was fending off a crowd. That circle was my pristine, private space, where I was free to breathe and the demands of the world couldn't penetrate. It worked like a spell. Judith would say, "We're here to pay close, caring attention to you," and ask me how that felt. To my surprise, it felt bad.

This made no sense—I'd always felt ignored, desperate for attention, never satisfied with the pittance of care the world had to offer me. But when confronted with the question directly—did I want this perceptive, nurturing person to pay attention to me for fifty-five minutes?—the answer was no. I was more comfortable in the dark.

I have never had much of a spiritual life, beyond the certainty that my stuffed animals have feelings and the occasional attack of OCD-adjacent superstition (the pink TUMS tablet fell out of the bottle before the green TUMS tablet, so if I don't eat the pink one first, it will become angry and burn down my house). I was a girl obsessed with fantasy books who, presented with the option of believing in real magic, rolled my eyes. The risk of embarrassment and disappointment was too large. It was safer to assume that if I couldn't see something, it wasn't real. I thought crystals were just gay rocks (complimentary). I didn't even do incense. The question of whether I "knew myself" didn't occur to me until I was sitting there in my beach ball, age thirty-seven, quaking under the kind, corvid gaze of a mom in a turtleneck.

And suddenly, I could see everything: It's not that I didn't know my self; my self had disintegrated. There was nothing to know. Could it be that I wasn't unhappy because an unjust universe had made me invisible but that I made myself invisible because I was unhappy? That I didn't want Aham to see me more clearly and love me better—I wanted him to be content with an invisible wife, a wife forever in the dark, and never ask for more?

It's a loaded phrase, *finding oneself*. It conjures images of barefoot white people acting awful in other countries—particularly colonized places where white people aren't just a tedious annoyance but a specter of rape, plague, exploitation, and cultural and physical genocide. Imagine becoming one of those dusty white guys who eat fruit on TikTok for a living and brag about their unvaxxed sperm! I'd rather set myself on fire. I'd rather move to Neptune, and I don't know if you've looked up Neptune recently, but it's a ball of poisonous ice wrapped in 1,300-mile-per-hour methane winds (PS: My culture is not a costume!).

So what do you do if it turns out that you really, really, really, desperately, profoundly do need to "find yourself," like you could bleed from the thought of it, like your teeth are cracking with the ache of it, like life depends on it?

I stepped into the new Ola Wyola and I was fourteen again, clutching my army-navy bag, and twenty-one again, in my estranged relative's apartment, a cave of wonders, every surface an altar, smelling thickly of smoke and tinctures. Rainbow was warm and funny, an enveloping gust of joy, an easy mirror of that other relationship that I couldn't fix. She pulled me inside and pressed a blue stone the size of a tangerine into my palm: "This is for your throat chakra," she said, "for speech and getting out the things you need to say."

"Can I book a treatment or something?" I asked impulsively. I didn't have the vocabulary to conceive of what a "treatment" entailed, but I knew I was in a transitional moment in my life, and I knew I wanted to spend more time with Rainbow. This felt like an answer to the question

I'd begun to ask with Judith. "Whatever you think I need?"

"Rainbow Soul Journey," she said. "I bring the ancestors in, diagnose your blockages, we go on a trip through your Crystal Cave of Wonders, clear all your chakras, it's a little bit of everything."

"Yes," I said. "Everything is what I want."

I booked my Soul Journey for a week before my road trip. I was nervous that I wouldn't do it right—I didn't know what any of the words meant. What if Rainbow told me to abracadabra my cornholio chakra, or expected me to chant, or float, or scream, or transmit communiqués from the Mushroom Kingdom?? I felt like I was about to be exposed as a fraud who didn't belong here and, worse, hurt Rainbow's feelings. I couldn't believe I'd gotten myself into this, just because Judith wanted me to open up more. JUDITH was FIRED as soon as I found the emergency exit from my Crystal Cave of Wonders!!

I lay on Rainbow's treatment table in her warm storefront, and she covered me with a blanket. It was cozy. So far, so good. I certainly knew how to lie down. Maybe I had this in the bag. My jitters subsided. Rainbow invited the ancestors and the angels to join us, and I felt something right away—perhaps it was merely a thrill at entertaining the forbidden idea that dead people weren't really lost, that my dad and all my grandparents were still within reach, still thinking about me, close instead of far. Rainbow moved up and down my body with the singing bowl, then placed the necessary crystals over each of my chakras. Every rock from Vishuddha to Manipura tumbled into my cleavage, an avalanche of concentrated meaning aimed straight at my heart, which I chose to take as a good omen.

Rainbow kept up a steady patter about my "quantum future self" as she worked, and I tried to imagine who that could be, this version of me who somehow contained every possibility yet scoffed at the notion that her self, her *herness*, was anything but glass-sharp, obvious, and innate. At once infinite and singular. Meanwhile, in the real world, I had a hard time remembering my own face. Could she really be me? My quantum future self felt like a cool older sister, someone who was like me but better, wiser, who could see reality from an extra axis I didn't even know was there—laughing like a good witch at my worst fears, not because they were foolish but because she knew I was worrying over an un-losable game. *Don't cry about that boy; high school isn't real. Don't worry about "finding" yourself; being lost is an illusion.*

I learned the function of each chakra—crown, third eye, throat, heart, solar plexus, sacral, and root—and everything Rainbow described felt like something I needed. Grounding to the earth, creative abundance, pleasure without shame, personal authority, self-love, clear communication, intuition, integration? Two of each, please. We did some breathing exercises and vocalized trauma release (moaning and bellowing like a yak), exactly the kind of emotional nakedness I'd been dreading and exactly the kind of emotional nakedness I needed.

Rainbow took me on a guided meditation to the much-hyped Crystal Cave, where I built myself a shimmering shell-pink cottage and planted seeds for the future: three wishes. All my wishes were variations on the same thing: an image of myself as I knew I could be. Just me, but strong. Just me, but brave. Just me, but alight with self-certainty. She told me to remember the "rivers of abundance" that flow up through my legs from the earth itself, energy that is mine to harness, to nourish my seeds. By the end of the journey, I didn't have to force myself to stay open. It felt easy.

Rainbow hugged me and sent me out the door with a box of crystals—one for each chakra—a mnemonic to remind me what I'd learned. Amethyst for trusting my instincts. Black tourmaline for protecting my boundaries. Rose quartz for self-love.

Whatever you believe to be true, it is objectively healing to spend an hour or two being lovingly tended to by a deeply perceptive person, to open yourself up to close, caring attention from a therapist, a healer, or a long-lost star. If a crystal helps you in any way, then its power is "real," whether the effect comes from some mystical quality in the mineral, or because the physical stone provides a locus for you to channel your attention toward whatever you need most. And isn't it true that the dead are with us whether you believe there's an afterlife or not? Isn't grief another manifestation of closeness, of reaching out and touching a person's indelible image, even if only inside yourself? Isn't it possible that there is some astral plane, some time out of time, where my estranged relative and I are both our healed quantum selves and can love each other without pain?

For too many years, I worshipped the dark magic of control, convinced that if I could force certain details into place and hold them there, happiness would follow. What are any of our sacred cultural recipes—monogamy, capitalism, thinness—but happiness spells sold by feckless profiteers? Entertaining the possibility of something larger than myself, even for just an afternoon, released me from that airless chamber where I was my own sick god and the people I loved were psychic opponents instead of free, beautiful beings. Spiritual exploration lets in sunbeams of chance: the flip of the tarot, the softness of asking, the opening up to the unknown, the intact self rippling to infinite horizons instead of collapsing inward, impossibly dense and fatally heavy.

I left Rainbow's better than I'd arrived—ready for the road—and I definitely believe in that.

BAAA

June 7, 2021

The van had a queen bed in the back, which folded down into a table with two benches like a little diner booth. When you opened the rear doors, there was a kitchen—a refrigerated drawer powered by solar panels, a Coleman stove[1] on a pullout shelf, and a pump sink. The rental company's gimmick was that each van was custom painted with a different "fun" mural, and each van had a name. You cannot request which van you

---

[1] One of my dad's favorite jokes: A guy goes skydiving for the first time. He jumps out of the plane, pulls his parachute cord, and it doesn't open. Same with the backup parachute. The guy's panicking. *Well*, he thinks, *this is it. I'm dead.* Just then, he sees a guy coming toward him in the opposite direction, shooting straight up into the sky. "Hey!" he calls out as they pass. "You know anything about parachutes?" "No!" the guy yells back. "You know anything about Coleman stoves?"

want—it's a surprise! My mom drove me to the office, a ramshackle building on the side of a highway outside Seattle, and I caught my first glimpse of my van and its one-of-a-kind, non-changeable, nonnegotiable, permanent, bespoke mural.

It was butter yellow, gold, and pink, the colors of a desert sunset. Purple palm trees waved in the distance, while in the foreground, a sexy, dark-skinned, beautiful Black queen in a strapless white bathing suit lounged next to a swimming pool with pastel-pink water. She had high cheekbones, large jugs, and a martini. She lay on her stomach with her curvaceous butt just below the hole where you stick the gas in, and she stared into the viewer's eyes with a look that said, "Under no circumstances should a white lady drive this van across the Deep South."

I'm not trying to say that a Black lady should never be painted on a van! Representation matters on novelty vans FOR SURE. But should a white person drive from Seattle to Florida and back in a van upon which is painted a mural featuring a very sexy but objectively objectified Black woman? A mural of unknown provenance?!!? If a Black person painted this van for the purposes of spreading...Black joy(?)...across the nation, and the artist said, "Lindy, please drive my masterpiece far and wide, for the culture," I would say OF COURSE, as I strive to be not just an ally but an accomplice in liberation. But I had no way of knowing who painted this vision on the side of this van!

With me behind the wheel, it's giving "horny DEI training," you know? It's giving, "I only watch DIVERSE pornos!" It's giving, "I changed my name to Nkechi." It's absolutely screaming, "I studied sex-positivity at an HBCU and I'm comfortable in my own skin, sista!" Which I most certainly am not!!!!!

I turned to my mom and whispered, "I cannot drive this van, what am I going to do," and she said, "Ha ha ha ha ha ha ha ha ha ha ha ha ha ha ha ha ha ha ha ha.

"Ha ha ha ha ha ha ha ha ha ha ha ha ha ha ha ha ha ha ha ha ha ha ha ha ha ha ha ha ha ha ha ha ha ha ha ha ha."

I went inside and gave an employee my name and nervously asked a few things that I really should have checked in advance: Was I even allowed to drive one of their vans as far as I was planning? Wouldn't the van need an oil change at some point in the seventeen thousand miles I was about to put on it? Would I get reimbursed for that? Could a theoretical person who theoretically only had a $500 credit limit put their deposit on a debit card, and, if not, could they use their mommy's credit card?

The teenager at the desk tossed me the keys and said, "Yeah, that's fine! Your van's right outside! You're in BAAA! She's one of my favorites!"

BAAA? What did that mean? Why was the van called BAAA? Was it an acronym? Black Asses Are Awesome??????? Help me!!!

I walked outside. And...where was my van? Some jive turkey had stolen Foxxy Cleopetrol and replaced her with an impostor!!!!! This new van featured a pastoral scene—green fields and blue sky and a white picket fence, with a deranged cartoon rabbit screaming homicidally on one side and a bug-eyed sheep frozen in terror on the other. *Ohhhhhhhhhh*, I thought. *BAAA*. Like the sound a lamb makes when her jackrabbit husband tells her he's polyamorous.

And then BAAA was mine, my home for a whole month.

Part Two

COLEMAN STOVE

Jante's Girl

My dad always told me that I was special. And my mom always told me that I was not special. But what you have to understand is that my mom has a chronic condition called "being Scandinavian," and in Norway, where her parents were from, they live by a code called the Law of Jante:

1. You're not to think you are anything special.
2. You're not to think you are as good as we are.
3. You're not to think you are smarter than we are.
4. You're not to imagine yourself better than we are.
5. You're not to think you know more than we do.

6. You're not to think you are more important than we are.
7. You're not to think you are good at anything.
8. You're not to laugh at us.
9. You're not to think anyone cares about you.
10. You're not to think you can teach us anything.

The Law of Jante isn't a real law; you don't go to prison if you catch yourself thinking that anyone cares about you. It's a set of mores, encouraging small social sacrifices for the greater good. The point is that the individual is never more important than the collective, which is quite beautiful and true to my values. My mom devoted her life to taking care of people. She was a nurse through the AIDS epidemic; she performed abortions when other nurses refused; her feet hurt every day for thirty years; I doubt she ever got a full night's sleep. She lived Jante's Law like her parents taught her, and like she taught me. And the world would be kinder and more functional (if a little austere) if everyone else thought that way too.

On the other hand, from the day I was born, my dad was in my face being like, "Listen, kid, you GOTTA LEARN THE BLUES." He always seemed to see some spark of genius in me, and he was exuberant when I'd do my crappy piano recitals and sing quietly in the back row of the choir and adequately execute the bass clarinet part on the *Jurassic Park* theme. I hated every second of the attention, but my dad reveled in each performance like I was the Luther Vandross of eighth-grade concert band.

I suppose it's normal to want your kids to follow in your footsteps, and my dad was a multi-hyphenate charm machine, a star from a family of stars. In 1932, his parents were both featured in a publication called *STARS OF THE RADIO*. They were glamorous and fun and had drinking problems and were friends with famous people and famous enough themselves that there was a gossip item in the *Daily News* (a Los Angeles paper that ran from 1923 to 1954) about their courtship:

Dear Ken: In regard to a rapidly spreading rumor concerning a so-called romance between

Mona Lowe[1] or Winnie Parker and myself, a rumor which I have just learned is causing the young lady in question a bit of discomfort, it is all, shall we say, premature. We are friends, good friends, but as far as I know I have not been fortunate enough to believe that it can be called, rightfully, more than just friendship yet. Still, she is a marvelous girl.

—MY GRANDPA SPANKING THE GOSSIP COLUMNIST ON HIS NOSY ASS!!!

Eat shit, Ken!

My Grandma Winnie was a singer employed directly by NBC, which was a profession in 1932 (job title: alto). My grandfather was a radio executive who helped open the first West Coast office of CBS. One morning in 1934, a man named Clarence Walter walked into the studio—interrupting a live broadcast about caramel raisin pudding—and said that voices on the radio had told him he needed to "put a ring around the moon and produce beautiful colors

---

1. My grandmother's stage name—STAR behavior!

in the moon." Then he pulled out a knife and stabbed a newsman in the brain! It would surely have turned into a killing spree had not MINE OWN GRANDFATHER "brought the attacker down with a flying tackle."[2]

So for most of my youth, I was leaning Jante. If you're nothing special, you never have to try, and if you never try, you never have to take anyone down with a flying tackle. I was a shy, chunky kid who loved dragons and often went to school wearing the ugly felt hat of a Tudor peasant. The Law of Jante is an invisibility suit. When you Jive, Jaugh, Jante, nobody can see your hat.

Dispiritingly, I wasn't sure I could cut the mustard with the Norwegians either. My mother's people were self-sufficient, rugged, working-class. Generation after generation, they lived in

---

2. Real headlines:

CRAZED MONTANAN AMUCK IN STUDIO—*The Helena Daily Independent*

MURDER HEARD OVER RADIO: UNSCHEDULED DEATH DRAMA AT STATION KHJ—*The Portsmouth Herald*

REAL LIFE DRAMA UPSETS LECTURE ON PUDDING: RADIO PROGRAM "RATHER NOISY" AS WILD MAN KILLS PERFORMER—Santa Barbara *Morning Press*

the same Norwegian village, farming the same land, fishing the same lake, marrying the same neighbors, as far back as the records go. In my genealogical research I found one guy who came up from Germany and married my great-great-great-great-great-great-great-great-great-great-great-great-great-great-grandmother[3] in 1504, and it was huge news.

My mother's father was active in the Hjemmestyrkene, or Home Forces, the Norwegian armed resistance under Nazi occupation, and in February 1945, he and eleven other guys skied out at midnight to retrieve packages of weapons and ammunition dropped by an RAF plane. There's a whole plaque about it in the village.

---

3. This guy named Claus Berg (1470–1532) was a sculptor born in Lübeck, Germany, and he was invited by Queen Christina of Saxony to run her sculpture workshop in Odense, Denmark, where he made a bunch of crazy altarpieces that are famous enough to have earned Claus a Wikipedia page (his relation to me is somehow not mentioned!?!?). Claus didn't make it past Denmark, but his son, Frants Berg (1504–1591), got elected(?) bishop of Oslo and HE married my great ×13 grandmother, and then THEIR granddaughter somehow met and married a guy from the village and all my other ancestors were like *TAKK ODIN, some new DNA up in here!!!!!!*

Grandpa Ole was a war hero, which, later in life, he NEVER MENTIONED,[4] and I act like *that's* the less intimidating family legacy? If I don't know how to be a Star of the Radio, I'll just fall back on being an anti-fascist superspy? I hope the guns and ammo drop is at the top of the bunny slope!

Thus, I found myself in a bind from a young age: I wanted to make my dad proud by being spectacular, and make my mom proud by being humble, but all I actually liked doing was watching TV and making my Barbies kiss.

My first big break came when I was seven years old. One of our neighbors was kind of a stage mom, and her daughter, who was MEAN, wanted to go on *Star Search*, and they asked my dad if he would coach her on her song. I remember the song was "Under the Boardwalk," a song my dad hated because he was born in FDR's first term and thought pop music was a crock, but he was a pro, and this girl came over and they rehearsed it at the piano in our living room until

---

4. "Nice."—Jante

she had it down pat. And that girl's name? *Was Kelly Clarkson.*

No, I don't know what her name was or if she was actually mean or if she ever went on *Star Search*. She probably auditioned and sucked so bad that that's why Ed McMahon died!!!!!!!

I'd sit at the top of the stairs during these lessons and feel relieved, because I would rather be dead in a coffin than go on *Star Search* and sing "Under the Boardwalk," but also jealous, because this bitch was living up to *my* potential and giving my dad the razzle-dazzle showbiz daughter he never had!

In a fog of jealousy, I approached my dear, sweet father. *I'M READY. I WANT TO BE A STAR NOW.* It wasn't true, but I needed to defeat my nemesis, who was [shuffles notes] either that neighbor girl, Jante, Kelly Clarkson, or Hitler. I'm losing track. I'm not sure what I thought my dad would say—maybe I could be understudy to a sleepy snail in the backyard?—but, to my horror, he said, "Killer! You can audition for this commercial I'm writing!"

Nooooooooooooooooooooooooooo!!! *Hjelp meg, Pappa Jante!*

Adult Braces

My dad was a copywriter at a big advertising agency in LA called Dailey & Associates, and at that time, in the mid-'80s, he was working on a TV spot for Hunt's Snack Pack Pudding. The plot of this commercial was that a child gets to school, opens up their lunch box, looks inside, and sees… a sandwich, an apple, a juice box…and then… nothing. AN ABYSS. Nothing where—in a just world tended by a loving god—their Hunt's Snack Pack Pudding ought to be. And this child is immediately struck dead (figurative) by something called…THE HUNT'S SNACK PACK PUDDING BLUES. And then her corpse reanimates, and she sings a modified twelve-bar blues about it, which goes like this:

*Hey, Mom, it's not what's in my lunch
 box / that's bringin' me down.
It's what's not in my lunch box / that
 could turn my world around!
I work hard all day / just to bring
 those good grades home,
But my mojo just ain't workin' on
 a sandwich and apple alone!
I need that Hunt's Snack Pack Pudding!*

I practiced really, really hard. I gave something my all for the first time in my life, and a couple of weeks later, I heard back: They'd decided to go in a different direction. I did not get the part. I was coached by the guy who wrote the commercial and I still could not get cast. And I did it Method! I personally infected myself with the Hunt's Snack Pack Pudding Blues, an affliction I struggle with to this day! (My therapist calls it "depression," but that's just because the Hunt's Snack Pack Pudding Blues isn't in the *DSM* yet.) Can you imagine being a big enough genetic dud to cancel out being a nepo baby for something as low-stakes as a pudding commercial callback?

The Hunt's Snack Pack Pudding Blues became part of my narrative of who I am—someone unremarkable destined for unremarkable things. Someone who just isn't that special.

I managed to avoid the limelight for a few more years, until I went to overnight summer camp for the first time. The camp brochure mentioned that there would be a talent show, and my dad—who could smell one drop of show business in a million gallons of bug spray—said, "You know what'd knock 'em dead, kid? You and your little friends should sing 'The Elements' song by Tom Lehrer." *Ah yes*, I thought, even then, *a brilliant combination of children's two favorite things: chemistry and novelty songs from the 1960s.*

"The Elements" consists of the entire periodic table of the elements (as it stood in 1959—sucks to suck, dubnium!) set to the melody of "I Am the Very Model of a Modern Major-General" by Gilbert and Sullivan, another huge hit with the fourth graders of 1992. Not even Kevin Spacey as the negotiator in the 1998 movie *The Negotiator* could have convinced my father that this was a bad idea!

So I went to camp, I handed out the lyrics, and my cabin-mates were like, "Um, we have archery, and Brooke C. fell in the sea urchin touch tank, and Brooke N. just ate a whole thing of Dr Pepper ChapStick and she's barfing," and I said, "Okay," and they said, "Okay," and Brooke N. said, "BLLLLLLLTCHCHCHCCH," and Brooke C. said, "HELP!" and so we didn't do it. We did not compete in the talent show, we did not delight the children of Camp Orkila with antimony, arsenic, aluminum, selenium, hydrogen, oxygen, nitrogen, OR rhenium, and I'm sure my dad was disappointed.

However. Do you think that this shrewd showman *did* or *did not* force me to learn the song before I left for camp so that I could "teach it to all my little friends"???? Forever after, Tom Lehrer's "The Elements" was no longer just my dad's party trick—it was *our* party trick. For a chubby girl who enjoyed neither parties nor tricks, and who had not yet experienced anything actually difficult or sad in her soft, safe little life, this prospect was only slightly more appealing than an acid attack. Every event, every dinner party, every family gathering, my dad would sit down at the piano and say, "Come on, kid, let's sing 'The Elements'!" And I'd resist, the ghost of Jante glaring from the cold air return, but it's my dad. I loved my dad *so much*. I would have preferred to be coated in the highly pyrophoric element cesium (Cs) and allowed to spontaneously ignite than to get up in front of people and perform musical comedy, but I did "The Elements" every time, of course. I want to say it got easier, but it didn't. This went on for the next twenty years.

In 2011, my dad died of prostate cancer. As I was struggling to write his obituary, to capture on paper this blazing sun of love and talent, his friend George Lowe reached out by email. George had written an oral history of their group of friends, one chapter apiece, each in their own words, and he thought it might be useful. There was so much detail in my dad's chapter that he'd never shared with me, probably because I'd never asked (Jante told me that prying is rude):

> Mother sang and recorded with Meredith ("The Music Man") Willson's orchestra, and then, when I was about three or four, she sang as Winnie Parker with the Anson Weeks Orchestra in the Saint Francis Hotel in San Francisco, so I didn't see her very much that year. She was back and forth, but I do remember the preschool where I boarded a fair amount because Dad was away in New York at the same time. I remember the nice lady at the school having me into her room in the evening so that I could hear Mother

sing on the radio with Anson Weeks. I thought that was pretty wonderful.

I don't know what it does to a three-year-old to be put in BOARDING PRESCHOOL for a year and only hear your mother's voice when it floats out of a radio box like a ghost, but I know that my dad was desperate to make people happy, felt most comfortable behind a piano, entertained so he didn't have to be vulnerable, and carried a permanent shimmer of sadness, even in a room crowded with friends.

Could that be why I always feel unwanted, even when all evidence indicates otherwise? Can melancholy hide in the DNA? Can a person be congenitally too soft for this world?

At some point during the great sifting that occurs after a loved one passes, my mom found a handwritten poem in my dad's things, an elegy for his own father, who died of a heart attack in 1953, aged forty-four. The poem isn't dated, but I wonder if my dad wrote it toward the end of his own life, when things become simple again: a final accounting of right and wrong, a surrender to the mystery that lies beyond being.

Dad gave his life to generosity, hard
  work and caring for his family.
He told me why the truth was
  always better than a lie.
He taught that being free was more
  the stuff of life than slavery.
He believed that knowing was a
  better thing than ignorance.
He owned the trust of those who
  heard his words—and little else.
He obeyed and respected a law that he
  saw in the atoms and the stars—a rule
  above hope or sentiment or prayer.
Then one day his great heart
  burst and he was gone.
Without a nod to heaven or to hell.
I hope I do as well.

I sang "The Elements" with my dad one last time at an old cocktail lounge in Seattle called Vito's, which was a hot spot in his glory days and has since burned down, where Aham had booked what we didn't know would be my dad's final show. Aham and I had only been dating a couple of months; my dad took a turn soon after that night and died within the year. Songs I'd heard him play a million times—"Here's That Rainy Day," "Django"—became something new with Aham on trumpet. Aham always turns heads when he plays, always says something beautiful, brass clear as speech. It was the only time they ever played together, the star who raised me and the star I married, the two most crucial men in my life overlapping just once. Tectonic plates colliding, forming a new continent, my past and my future briefly united. Brutally unfair, unfathomably lucky. But, if we honor the metaphor, my dad isn't gone. His great heart burst and he became the ocean floor.

And then I got up and sang without having to be coaxed, songs that, perhaps, my grandmother used to sing—"My Ship," "Blue Room," "The Boy Next Door"—her deep voice gliding out of the radio while her little boy listened, wonderstruck and lonely.

Monsters

June 8, 2021

I left Seattle late, around 4:00 p.m., and drove east on I-90. I passed all my usual exits—the Mercer Island dog park, I-405 northbound for Chinese food, Snoqualmie Falls, where Aham and I spent two nights after our wedding—and just kept driving, nothing in front of me but nothing, blank space to be filled, and it felt as good as the dream. I stopped for a cherry dipped cone at the Dairy Queen in Cle Elum, then took a wrong turn, and ended up on State Route 10, a dusty old highway that hugs the Yakima River for sixteen miles, tracks laid in the 1890s by the Northern Pacific Railway snaking below in the canyon, the freeway parallel but out of sight. I was already behind schedule, but there was no one to apologize to and nothing to apologize for. Escaping the thick scar of the interstate to waste time on scenic byways was exactly what I'd aimed to do, and for the next month, I was the only person who mattered.

As I sped kitty-corner across Washington, I felt disturbed by the foreignness of the eastern half of my state. Washington is bifurcated vertically by the Cascade Mountains, with the liberal urban elites to the west, making the police illegal and forcing veterans to use neo-pronouns, and the right-wing agricultural hicks to the east, electing a horse as mayor and agitating to become part of Idaho so they can legally shoot the mayor if he tries to enforce seat belt laws. Real reality is variegated, of course, with plenty of scary Nazis within a half-hour drive of Seattle, crunchy artist colonies peppering the eastern desert, over sixteen thousand unhoused people in "liberal" King County, and billionaires (Washington has thirteen!) sucking the life out of us all.

It was after 10:00 p.m. when I pulled into the Snake River KOA—a small, neat cul-de-sac at the base of a cliff just below the Lower Granite Lake Dam—and the office was closed. I parked the van by the registration building and sat in the dark, unsure of what to do. I hadn't been camping in years, and even when I used to camp, I was never the point person. I thought there'd be a little guy in a hut who would greet me and say, "Long drive?" and "Cool van!" and "You're in campsite number three!" and give me a bundle of firewood and a map and explain how the showers worked. But any such person had gone home hours ago, and the handful of RVs and tents around me were shut up tight for bed.

I tried to search for my confirmation email to see if it had a site number on it, but my bars read "SOS"—no service. How had I become this person, helpless without an email to tell me what to do? Did John Muir need an email to figure out where to camp in the Sierra Nevada? Did Grandpa Ole need an email to find two and a half tons of guns parachuted from a Short Stirling bomber by Allied pilot Harry W. Wilkie, a Canadian, in the snowy hills above Randsfjorden????

I hopped out of the van and circled the dark building, looking for an after-hours phone number or an envelope with my name on it or a big sign that said, "LATE? STUPID? JUST CAMP WHEREVER!" What I didn't want to do was pick a random site, go to sleep, and have the person who lawfully reserved that site show up even later than I did and knock on the window and cause me to piss the bed, after which I would have to *talk to them*. I was not going to spend the first night of my big, brave, beautiful road trip at the nexus of breaking rules, being wet, getting in trouble, and being woken up by a person who was mad at me.

Eventually, I found a clipboard labeled "After Hours Check-In," shrouded in darkness in a wooden tray next to the office door. I did a little *entrechat quatre* when I saw my name. I'd done it!!! I drove to my campsite, set up my bed in the van—down comforter, fairy lights, too many pillows, battery-powered fan—and lay there vibrating with the pleasure of self-sufficiency, only a little bit afraid of knife crime.

I slept hard enough to dream. Two round white egg sacs, cottony bulbs the diameter of pencil erasers, had attached themselves to my finger and I could not get them off. As I scraped and scrabbled, they hatched, sharp white spiders bursting out two by two. It was a nightmare, and I am an arachnophobe, but somehow I wasn't scared. The spiders were beautiful and I wanted them to live. They were just being born and I didn't want to kill them even though they were very close to me and I felt vulnerable. I let them burst out and sail to the ground and run off and start their lives. I knew they didn't want to hide in my things and bite me—they just existed and they were pretty, pure white with long, pointy legs and little, white, pointy feet, and they were scary, but they were beautiful.

I jolted awake at 4:00 a.m. to the loudest, *biggest* sound that I have ever heard—an encompassing roar that saturated the air and shook the van. I wasn't hearing the sound; I was inside the sound; I *was* the sound. My first thought was natural disaster: avalanche, landslide, earthquake. Had the dam failed? Were BAAA and I being devoured by the river? But no. Something bigger. Nuclear apocalypse? Alien invasion? Kaiju? It sounded like being inside the birth canal when a fighter jet was born. It sounded like a god.

My terror was tempered, slightly, by confusion. I knew without a doubt that something was about to kill me, but how? What was it? What was I supposed to brace for? Crushing?

Chewing? Asphyxiation? Drowning? If a woman is killed by a noise at a KOA but it doesn't make any sense, is she really dead?

Abruptly, the roar faded, and on its tail end, I was able to discern some component parts. The screech of steel on steel, a few thousand horsepower of diesel pulling a few thousand tons of freight, the now-obvious *ka-chunk ka-chunk* of the rail joints.

It was a train. The same train I'd watched from the canyon rim that afternoon as I drove State Route 10, the same train that out in the sunlight had been a charming companion, a moment of pleasure, set dressing for my Great American Midlife Crisis. I hadn't been able to see it when I set up camp in the dark, but the train tracks skirted the base of the cliff, about ten feet from my van.

A monster stays a monster forever if you never turn on the light.

On Showering

Did you know that taking a shower is good, actually? One of the ways I can tell that taking a shower is good is that when I am in a bad mental state, I avoid it like a dirty diaper. A shower is a gateway, a threshold from one module of life to the next. Everything before the shower is preamble; everything after the shower is the Day. If you stay forever in the pre-shower, you can stay forever in limbo, in the estuary between sleeping and doing. It's the same reason I sometimes get stuck in the car outside my house for hours—it's taking a transitional moment and making it a home, floating in inaction, forever on the way, never arriving.

Here are all the reasons I avoid showering:

1. I do not believe that I deserve pleasure.
2. I believe that I am a stinky pig.

3. I do not believe that anyone wants to look at my body or be near my body or touch my body or smell my body, and therefore, nobody cares or will ever notice if it's clean or not.
4. I do not feel sexy, and not showering is a good way to avoid sex.
5. When you shower, you are alone with your thoughts, meaning, yourself. You can't even hear the radio that well, even if you put a speaker in there! Gross! I don't want to know what I'm thinking!

Maybe you're asking, "Lindy, if you can't get in the shower, then *how do you get in the shower?*" Well, when I'm struggling with an impossible task set by an asshole (me), I try to shut off my brain and think of said task not as a deeply symbolic feat of willpower but simply as a value-neutral physical action. This technique actually works for a lot of things, including writing. Don't tell yourself, "Sit down and write your masterwork today." Tell yourself, "Move fingers make words tappity tappity." You can make it good later.

If I can use my muscles to make my body step into the shower stall, one foot, then another, turn the faucet, hot water in my hair, down the back, a fistful of suds, a fluffy towel waiting for me if I can muster it, that doesn't magically make me a Person Who Showers, but it does make me a Person Who Has Showered Today, which is one step closer to success.

Addicted to What the Pepperoni Stick Did

I have always eaten for comfort. I don't eat until I'm sick or compulsively consume huge quantities of food. I simply always want the best thing, the most special thing, in every moment. When I am at my mental worst, the thought *What will I get to eat today?* is the only thing that gets me out of bed. I want indulgence and pleasure. I want to go to a different restaurant for breakfast, lunch, and dinner, every day, each one a stepping stone luring me to stay awake and alive just a few hours longer, and again, and again. I want pancakes and bacon, Baileys in my coffee, Cantonese noodles with *sui kau*, Caesar salad with extra anchovies, dessert after lunch, a Coke AND a Diet Coke, a warm almond croissant, spicy Laotian sausage with sticky rice, Ethiopian ful, matzoh ball soup, three carnitas tacos, Chinese broccoli with oyster sauce, spaghetti Bolognese, charcuterie, cashews, kefir with granola, an apple with peanut butter, a vanilla malt with real whipped cream, fish and chips, a perfect little cheeseburger.

For the first twenty years of my life, I almost never ate what I wanted, and I punished myself when I did. The deprivation made me feel dead. So, once I started to wake up to the profanity of diet culture, I ate everything I wanted. I thought that would feel like life. It didn't, but I kept chasing it, certain it'd work on the next bite. I understand my logic—what is life but a scramble for resources? I watch a lot of survival TV (*Alone*, *Naked and Afraid*), and a human being stripped down to nothing is just a feral little scavenger. Get food, stay warm, get food, get food, get food, make fire, boil water, eat seaweed, eat limpets, eat berries, eat fish, eat worms, eat bark, get food, get food, get food, save food, store food, eat food, munch, munch, munch, sleep, munch. There is nothing more natural than dreaming of calories, gorging on protein, licking slick fat from your lips. Eating, swimming, and sleeping are the only sensualities that come naturally to me.

When I was a child, I was not aware of my body as something separate from myself. One by one, the people around me let me know that my body was bad. They were varied in tone but unified in message. I fractured and began to leave my body. I grew older; I let men treat me terribly because I believed a body like mine held no value and therefore deserved no respect (as though respect is conditioned on value—eat my butt, capitalism). I treated myself terribly. I treated other fat people terribly, in my head. Thin people too. I was self-hating and jealous.

One day, I learned that I didn't have to live like that. I followed other fat people, braver and smarter than I was, to a thrilling place. We declared that we had as much value as any thin person, and by declaring it we made it truer—not all the way true, not to society—but truer, incrementally, to ourselves and to the other fat people watching. We joined together, pushing, healing, eating, growing in solidarity, finally sating our hunger for life. I stopped apologizing and dieting. I got married. I wrote *Shrill*. I was no longer public property to be controlled by the aesthetics of mean, insecure strangers. I felt, occasionally, beautiful.

And then, as body-positivity went mainstream, that became my career: Loving myself where other people could see. Insisting that I was healed—that I no longer cared what anyone thought, no longer fought against my body, no longer wanted to lose weight, was no longer touched by shame and fear and unlovability. I knew that other fat people needed to see that this was possible, because I had needed to see it. So that's what I became. People were so, so hungry for it. All we had ever had was nothing. Finally, there was something, and I got to be part of it. Modeling defiance became a 24-7 project that I could not put down without betraying my people. I had to love my body unequivocally, forever, exactly as it was, or else. We couldn't trust the wider world with any nuance. We couldn't say, "Sometimes I feel bad in my body." The thin people would only slip in through the cracks with their skinny little knives and say, "See?"

Before this reclamation, I would never have dreamed of eating a cupcake in public—of confirming all the worst biases that the world holds against fat people. After, it felt powerful (and I saw no other way) to simply flip the binary—to *only* eat cupcakes, as publicly as possible. But that isn't enjoyment. That isn't listening to your body. It's reactionary—I was still letting cruel externalities control me. Constant indulgence ceases to feel indulgent. When everything is a treat, nothing is a treat. The fulfillment of desire is the death of desire. My fixation on food didn't just take the satisfaction out of food, it distracted me from other indulgences: dancing, sweating, fucking, dreaming.

Is it diet culture to *want to want things* again?

To fat people, fat women especially, I became theirs—an investment born from love, need, shared trauma, relief, belonging. I was owned by a different segment of the public now. Ones who loved me instead of hated me, but still. I felt, in a strange way, parental: devoted and awed and flooded with love, but also flattened and erased and eaten up. I took this step, I made myself mean something, I offered my relationship with my body as an example and a lifeline. And I profited from that. Why would those fat people, who mean so much to me, who are RIGHT, not wrong, about themselves, not feel some stake in what happens to this body? I gave it to them and consumed theirs, in turn, for my own inspiration.

But it became difficult not to feel penned in by that gaze. To feel that any hardship or change in my body was a betrayal of people I'd never met. When I finally started going to therapy and noticed my clothes becoming looser, I could no longer avoid the obvious: I comfort eat the most when I need the most comfort, when I am at my most anguished and disintegrated. I am at my biggest when I am at my saddest—not because being big makes me sad, but because, I suspect, being sad makes me big.

Sometimes, when I am doing better and can find the will to cook and think and move and live, I get smaller. Once, when I posted a selfie on the far side of a particularly epic depression, I received this comment from a stranger: "Can we not watch another fat positive body shrink?"

I understand why she said it; I am also suspicious and, frankly, triggered when famous fat people lose weight. It feels like a rejection of *my body*, a blatant projection that's also perfectly rational. How can any fat person credulously assume good intentions when our society worships and rewards weight loss above all else? When the tradwife 2020s seem determined to drag us back into 1990s-style body fascism? When our rancid culture can examine its own abuse of fat people and prescribe conformity, not culture change—weight loss, not *treating fat people better*—as the solution?

But there has to be a middle way, for the complex individuals inside these bodies. Is that all I am to people? "Another fat positive body"? Is that the kind of "support" I'm obligated to accept? *I liked you better when you were sad?*

Sometimes it feels like I only mean something to people if I am a mirror.

Here's the truth: Sometimes I feel bad in my body.

I'm drawn to addiction and sobriety stories—or maybe what you'd call addiction and sobriety "content," because I don't just mean narrative. I mean the nuts-and-bolts stuff, the therapy-speak of recovery, the section in online addiction spaces where they list all the AA and NA Zoom meetings for that week. I like thinking about the people going to the meetings. I imagine them greeting one another, being together without judgment. I'm drawn to the warmth. I am disfigured by judgment, the pressure to change and perform, and I breathe easier thinking, vicariously, of the freedom of surrender.

Sometimes I picture the Zoom windows of the meetings, and it's like a hundred glowing portals into other people's Christmas mornings. From my imaginary voyeur's POV, that's the quality of love that emanates from the recovery process. It's what family is supposed to be. Unconditional. Communal. People who see you clearly as you are in that moment, not an idealized version of you, not a construct. People who get you a present whether you've been bad or good.

Recently, someone dear to me told me she's getting sober. I've had addiction on the periphery of my life—it feels familiar and I don't stigmatize it. Both my dad's parents died, more or less, from alcoholism. I used to drink a lot socially, seeking the confidence to flirt with men, but alcohol didn't chase me past my twenties, when I fell in love with Aham and found I had no more need of it. But while talking with my friend about her sobriety, I felt an affinity that surprised me. Not an equivalence but a parallel. We both had feelings we needed to bury—her with drugs and alcohol, me with food. "We're all using something to manage the pain of being alive," she told me over teriyaki.

You're not supposed to say that you're addicted to food. Firstly, because it trivializes what addicts are going through. People overdose and die. They die from withdrawal. They lose their families. They lose themselves. Food simply doesn't work the same way. But secondly, because "you're addicted to food" is what diet culture says. All my life, I have been abused with this idea. "You're addicted to food" is something thin people tell fat people when they *hate us*. As self-respecting, self-loving fat people (or trying to be), our only logical posture is unyielding opposition. That's one thing thin people do really well—they rob us of nuance.

You're addicted to food.

No, I'm not. My relationship with food is perfect.

You're addicted to food. You're helpless before

it—a glutton, a child, a sinner, a drooling animal, a rapist, a war machine, a sad case, eating mindlessly like fire eats the forest, living luridly for pleasure you haven't earned. You are the worst thing in the world.

No, I'm not. I know myself, and I know I'm not that. I think I'm not that.

Their implication is that we don't, in fact, know ourselves. Only they can see us clearly. Diagnose us. "Help" us. We are theirs to play with, to define themselves in contrast. Such accusations manage to contain all of society's disgust for addicts with none of the glamour. They say "heroin chic" is coming back. They say, "At least drug addicts are skinny." There's no "upside" to a so-called food addiction. Call me when "Cool Ranch powder chic" takes over Fashion Week.

It doesn't make sense anyway—aren't we all addicted to food? How can you be "addicted" to something that you need to survive? We literally cannot stop seeking, hoarding, and consuming food, or we'll die. It is our life's work. As the saying goes in fat circles and eating disorder circles, you can't "quit" food.

This is part of the monster's game: to draw

you into the question in the first place. Why do we have to explain to you why we're fat? It is violent—needle teeth ripping the soul—to demand that people justify their physical existence to you, incessantly, day after day, all our lives. Fat people are spent. And the people who say that—they're the ones wrapped up in fantasy, not us! They're the ones self-pleasuring to the only thing that makes them feel like they matter—the thought that there is a hierarchy of humanity and they're at the top, they're the ones doing it right and they deserve everything they've stolen.

I will never give them the satisfaction. The rage that I carry inside me—for thin people who think I'm nothing, for every beautiful dogshit mediocrity who has ever looked at me and felt superior—is scary. They ruined my life. They took everything from me. My relationship with my body. My relationship with food. My relationships in general. My sexuality. Every tangible thing too—money, time, opportunities, joy, ease, rest.

I am a star, on some level I know it, and it was beaten out of me. What could I have been? How much more successful would I be if I were thin? What could I have done with the warmth, the trust, the benefit of the doubt, the assumption of competence that we afford the beautiful? Anti-fatness is a plague, and when I'm at my best, I can find my way to empathy—"We're all struggling! It is hard to have a body!"—but if I'm honest, that's me performing grace for the optics. If you think thin people are better than fat people, then FUCK YOU. I hate you, and you deserve nothing.

Anyway, if all fat people were "addicted to food," that would be perfectly fine. We are all just trying to stay alive. We're all "held together with string," as my newly sober friend said to me. An uncountable number of things can affect the size and shape of a person's body—genes, illness, injury, trauma, gut bacteria, politics, geography, culture. It doesn't matter. All people deserve respect and care.

So maybe the word wasn't *addiction*, but I did find myself needing language for my relationship with food. In the simplest terms, I have no idea what people eat. My relationship with food has been so warped for so long that I no longer have any instincts. Balance nourishment and pleasure? I could sooner pilot the space shuttle. Sitting across the table from my friend, I started to wonder: Could the word I'm looking for be *disorder*?

Not every fat person has a disordered relationship with food.

But I think I do.

When I allowed the idea "I have a disordered relationship with food" to settle over me, I felt calm. Is that it? Is that what's wrong with me? Often, I'll buy food that I don't even want because the thought of going home without it causes me panic, because I have not developed any other mechanism for regulating pain and stress.

That's not hunger; it's fear.

But I'm also afraid to heal.

What if healing changes my body?

How will you ever trust me again?

Voice Memos

June 9, 2021

I woke up at the crack of dawn to a soft drizzle. I'd done it! We now officially had proof of concept—I *could* and *did* and *would* sleep in the van! I hadn't been murdered. I hadn't frozen or roasted. I'd successfully held my pee until sunrise. No spiders had gotten in, as far as I knew, besides the ones in my dream. The lumpy, segmented foam mattress challenged my spinal fortitude, but I could work with it.

I went for a run along a concrete spit that stuck out into the river, more industrial than scenic, then took a quick shower (success!!!) in the communal bathroom. Before the trip, I'd worried about public showers and road hygiene—I was afraid I'd be uncomfortable and slide into my signature crusty depression—but I made myself go and found I loved it. It felt like summer camp and kept me connected to the outdoors. I didn't live in a house or in a van; I lived in the world.

I tried to make a romantic instant coffee in the wet morning air, but I couldn't get the kettle to work and gave up. I needed to get on the road. I was a busy van woman! I had a nine-hour drive to Yellowstone and didn't want to set up camp after dark again in grizzly bear country. This meant that I didn't have time to write in my journal like I'd intended, a small failure that punched through the morning's triumph. I had stuck to my planned road trip routine for... zero days.

I pulled out of the KOA parking lot, crossed the now unmissable train tracks, then stopped. Right or left? I still didn't have cell service, and I hadn't had the foresight to download directions in advance. I did have a physical map, but there was nowhere to pull over and look at it. Not even a shoulder. I'd have to wing it. I trusted my sense of direction, heading vaguely east.

As I wound my way through the golden heaps of the Palouse toward Idaho (I hoped), I had an idea. Maybe it wasn't the end of the world that

I hadn't journaled. I pulled out my phone, hit Record, and free-associated for a couple of minutes about my morning. Then I played it back and laughed. Was this something?

I thought about how often I catch myself lying in my journal, trying to convince my present self of what I want to be true instead of what's actually happening to me—retrofitting my honest thoughts and reactions with more evolved perspectives, as though I can trick ME into thinking I'M cool. But dictating into a phone while driving a van on a winding two-lane highway? Overthinking wasn't possible. One time, my friend the actress Martha Plimpton told me that some people can only act when they're holding a prop—the distraction transforms them somehow, distances them from their affectations. She called them *prop actors*. Maybe that was me? Was I a prop journaler?

There was something about rambling aloud to no one, alone in BAAA, sleep-deprived and a little raw and activated by freedom and an outdoor shower, without the hard-copy finality of paper and ink, that made it easy to be honest, to get skin-to-skin with myself.

HWY 194, COLFAX, WASHINGTON

Okay, I'm leaving the Boyer Park and Marina / Snake River KOA RV park in the van. Lights are on. We're in drive. I got all my stuff. I got my breakfast. I'm having some, uh, almond cake, yogurt, and some cheese wrapped in salami. I have—what is going on? There are these huge white birds here, and I just do not know what they are. They're so beautiful. They're so big, and they're flying around in these huge flocks. And the birds are huge. They look like pelicans, but they're pure white. I don't know, do we have pelicans here? I'm just captivated by these birds. It was too cold and rainy to swim here. But I did put my fingers in the water. These birds, there's something biblical about them. They're so big. They're so beautiful. I'm sure that I'll eventually look it up and they'll be called, like, the fucking, you know, the Scraggled Shit Stork or something.[1]

---

1. I did look it up, and they ARE PELICANS! They're the American white pelican! According to Wikipedia, they are "very large and plump," just like me, and were most likely road-tripping from northern Saskatchewan to Costa Rica, just like me!

Two Hikes

On our belated honeymoon in 2017, Aham and I stayed at a B&B in Le Bar-sur-Loup, a mountain village in the South of France, population... eight? Somehow, this impossibly picturesque place was just one of a thousand impossibly picturesque villages dotting the Maritime Alps, not the crowning glory of this region but its basic furniture. The cutest village I have ever seen is barely in the guidebooks, not because it's a well-kept secret but because it's kind of so-so as French mountain villages go!

Our hostess was a gracious German woman who had retired young from a marketing career and moved to Le Bar-sur-Loup to live out her dream of being a flawless ~*aesthetic*~ innkeeper. She looked like someone who was made in a lab at the Malibu Colony to become Rod Stewart's ex-wife—tall, ash blond, linen—and her house was exquisite. In the mornings, at a wrought iron outdoor table on the lip of a cliff, she served us coffee, berries, Mimolette, and croissants amid red tile roofs and undulating valleys, the Mediterranean a haze at the edge of sight. She had a distressed leather couch and a Persian cat. Our room offered a sculptural bathtub ONLY, no shower. Neither Aham nor I fit.

On our second day, we asked her about hiking trails, and she said there were two that left from Le Bar-sur-Loup. She looked at my body appraisingly and said that one of them was short and easy—we should do that one. I was immediately red hot. Could she tell us about the other one, please? At this point, she could have said anything—an eighty-mile army crawl across the bottom of the Atlantic—and there was no fucking way I wasn't doing it. Dubious, she gave us directions to the trailhead for the second hike, which, she said, was "about one mile" but "quite tough" and would take us up through the mountains to Gourdon, the next village over. Who was she calling a *gourdon*??????? This bitch thought I couldn't hike ONE MILE? Why I oughtta.

The trailhead was at the village cemetery, which would turn out to be prophetic. Aham and I walked for a time through scrubby forest, in and out of the sweltering sun, hopping over little streams and checking out a couple of spooky concrete bunkers. At one point, the canopy cleared, and we could see the dizzying slopes stretching almost vertically all around us. In the far, far distance, almost too small to see, a walled, turreted village straight out of a fairy tale perched on the summit of the highest peak. We oohed and aahed and tried to get a picture, but it couldn't be captured. It was too distant and much, much too high up in the sky. A supernatural beauty, a castle in the clouds.

"Ha ha," I joked, gesturing at the castle, hilariously far away, "what if that's Gourdon? What if that's actually where this hike goes. Ha ha ha."

"Ha ha ha," Aham agreed.

LOL, the clown woman wheezed. *Le morts qui rient.*

As the hike was only "one mile," we had not brought any water or food. After a quarter mile of flat meandering, the switchbacks began, and if you don't know what switchbacks are, they're when the trail goes in a tight zigzag straight up a mountainside that otherwise only a Spider-Man could traverse. As the trail kept climbing and climbing, winding in and out of the trees at an increasingly steep grade, the sun's heat magnifying with each foot of elevation gain, we started to wonder: Did she mean one mile as the crow flies? Is it one *vertical* mile?? Do Europeans even use "mile" as a measurement? What if this woman knows that a mile is 5,280 feet but she thinks that "foot" is the same as "kilometer" and this hike is actually 5,280 kilometers long and is taking us to Gourdon, Pakistan? What if Alana Stewart of the Alps simply wants me dead for eating all her Mimolette and getting my butt-crack sweat on her couch and this is her revenge?

There's this passage in *Shrill* that people quote a lot, and I was extremely proud of it when I wrote it:

> Maybe you are thin. You hiked that trail and you are fit and beautiful and wanted and I am so proud of you, I am so in awe of your wiry brightness; and I'm miles behind you, my breathing ragged. But you didn't carry this up the mountain. You only carried yourself. How hard would

you breathe if you had to carry me? You couldn't. But I can.

It sounds nice in the abstract. But I didn't write that passage when I was halfway up a French mountain, with no food or water, in the act of hauling said body! On the trail to Gourdon, I had to ask myself—did I lie when I wrote that in *Shrill*? CAN I CARRY THIS UP THE MOUNTAIN?

Later, I managed to find this hike on All-Trails, and apparently, it's 5.4 miles long with 1,958 feet of elevation gain. The only thing that saved my life on the road to Gourdon was that halfway up, there's some sort of medieval Catholic water fountain that squirts ice-cold God-erade (that's what I call wawa, a.k.a. God's Gatorade, because I'm Catholic now after finding the fountain) out of the side of the cliff to refresh weary pilgrims. I put my mouth to the mountain's teat and drank and drank and drank.

At last, we reached the top, and WOW—Gourdon is the kind of French village that *does* make the guidebooks. It's the *Beauty and the*

Beast town except on the top of a mountain—stone buildings with timber beams, winding alleys, striped awnings, hanging flowers, mustaches, aprons, antlers in all of their decorating—and let me tell you, my friends, I was ready to eat five dozen eggs!!!!!! I needed sugar. I needed salt. I was dangerously weak and lightheaded. It was honestly probably a genuine medical emergency. I couldn't believe we had made it to the promised land: out of the wilderness and back into commerce. Bonjour! Bonjour! *Bonjour bonjour bonjour!!!*

I stumbled up to the nearest storefront, a shimmering mirage of an ice cream shop, and slid my debit card across the counter. "*COCA-COLA, SIL VOUS PLAIT!!!!!!*" But much like the town from *Beauty and the Beast*, this entire fucking village was cash only. And *sacré bleu*, no ATMs.

There is no sweet rescue here—no kind shopkeeper willing to give a fat woman a free Coke, even as a prize for sweating out half her body weight (what do you people WANT from us???). I had to walk all the way back down that mountain, switchback after switchback, in a full fugue state, Aham cheering me on and keeping a firm grip on my hand, until we came around a bend and there was the cemetery shining in the moonlight. The sun had set on our way down, and this was high summer, so it was nearly 10:00 p.m. The first restaurant we tried was closed. The other restaurant (the village has two) was closing, but they took us in and I can't recommend this because it's extremely not safe, but you've never felt more alive than when you've almost died of heatstroke and exhaustion and dehydration and then a Frenchman seats you at a crisp, white table in a cool, ancient stone room and brings you steak and potatoes and Coca-Cola and water and wine.

~~~

Just a quick ferry ride from the Washington mainland, Lummi Island is not a tourist destination—it is a remote community of vacation homes that should belong to the Lummi people but doesn't for no doubt sinister reasons. There is a grocery store and a pizza place and formerly a fine-dining restaurant and one hike, which is called Lummi Peak.

The day we attempted Lummi Peak, it was fall 2019 and Aham and I were at our lowest. We'd had the trip planned for months, and it seemed like a convenient opportunity to "reconnect," so we didn't cancel. We'd committed to couples' therapy, and we were still in love, blah blah blah. I said something like, "Why don't you take your *girlfriend* to Lummi instead and I'll pay for it?" and to his credit, he let me have my anger.

I was not in good shape. Why I thought I could climb 1,600 feet up a mountain when rolling over in bed was excruciating is a mystery. But Aham wanted to do this hike, and I wanted him to think I was worth loving. Could it really only be two years since Gourdon?

I dragged myself up, switchback by switchback, while my lower back screamed and my lungs bled. Like a nightmare version of the Gourdon hike—which was physically horrible, but at least Aham and I were on the same team, buoyed by love—the crawl to Lummi Peak was tense and mean. In the years of therapy since, I've come to understand that Aham resented how much I'd let myself deteriorate—not how I looked but my life force, as though participating in our marriage and our future was no priority for me at all. He wanted to live life with me, not just watch me sink into depression until I died. But at the time, the only framework I had to understand this dynamic was the one I'd been indoctrinated into: I'd gotten fatter and he hated me for it.

That's the thought that nettled my brain as I trudged up the hill, stopping to catch my breath every ten steps while Aham watched me from two or three switchbacks up. I was defensive, sure that he was judging me. He was distant and impatient, offering no encouragement. It felt so ungenerous of him. Why couldn't he just love me? Is it really so bad to have a slow, fat wife when she offers as much as I do?

The sun started to set before we got to the summit and its promised view, and Aham said angrily that we should just call it. We stopped in the dark, in the woods, then walked back down in pitch-black silence, phone flashlights draining our batteries too quickly for comfort.

SR 272, PALOUSE, WASHINGTON

There's this thing where you're driving and it's beautiful and you're in a rural place and then there's a weird metal building reminding you that you have no place here and you don't even know what it's for and what they do here. Like, *Oh, you thought you were just someplace pretty? This is a working place and we know about things like irrigation and we do things in metal buildings that you will never understand. Stop enjoying it. Stop acting like you own this place. You never do anything in a metal building!* From here I can see two metal buildings that are shaped like silos, I think? Which hold...grain? Like I said. I don't know. Passed a bunch of signs that were bragging about wheat in this area. Most wheat, most wheat in the country, most wheat in the world. It was like, attention please. You are in the county that produces the most wheat in the galaxy. Please show some respect.

On the Edge

June 10, 2021

My first full day on the road revealed a flaw in my plan. In my obsession with the *symbolism* of driving all the way from Seattle to Key West and back, I'd failed to consider the *practical physical real reality* that Seattle to Key West and back is really fucking far to drive, even if you allot yourself a month. One of the signature joys of a road trip is spontaneity—choosing beautiful but indirect routes, stopping for lunch at the scariest diner you've ever seen, or taking an impulsive detour to "THE REAL NOAH'S ARK" fifty miles off the highway. I didn't leave myself time for any such high jinks. To make it to Florida and back in time to return the van, I would have to drive at least six hours a day, often nine, sometimes more. You'd have to genuinely love driving to enjoy my road trip. Fortunately, I do.

Fat people love being in the car. Ask any fat person! I bet you a hundred billion bacon burgers they'll agree with me. In the car, you're as mobile as everyone else. You can be alone. You can get chicken nuggets from a little window and eat them without anyone looking at you. You can listen to your tunes (the blistering sax solo from Mike Love's "Kokomo," maybe??!?!!!) and grab a moment's peace, and if anyone sees you through the window and makes fun of you for being fat, you can run them over. They make a whole pedal for it!

Fat people have so little privacy. The world wants us to stay home. When I'm driving, I can be alone and be anywhere all at once. On the one hand, abolish fossil fuels and invest in transit immediately, this is for sure what I believe, 1,000 percent. On the other hand, though, the car is sacred to me and telling me not to go in the car is both fatphobic AND violates my religious freedom! Something to think about!

So I don't mind a nine-hour-drive day, I just prefer to do it on roads with character, where sometimes you're stuck behind a combine and every fifty feet there's a haunted barn. But once

Adult Braces

I made my way to Pullman and had cell service again, it was clear I'd have to take I-90 all the way from Coeur d'Alene, Idaho, to Livingston, Montana. I-90, the interstate that started in my hometown. Another disappointment. It felt like a leash. But even that depressingly familiar and un-photogenic route would take eight hours, not accounting for gas and food and peeing and pooping. The cute country byroads I'd dreamed about would get me to Yellowstone at approximately—tip-tap-click-clack-abacus—*tomorrow*. Oh well.

I drove straight and fast through Missoula, Butte, Bozeman, and pulled into Yellowstone's Edge RV park in the late afternoon. It was fancier and more populated than Boyer Park, with white gravel, manicured grass, a little store selling branded YETI tumblers, and a DVD lending library instead of a VHS lending library (okay, Elon Musk!!!). A little old flirty cowboy man in a golf cart led me to my campsite, a gravel rectangle and a picnic table sandwiched between two million-dollar fifth-wheels, the Yellowstone River a stone's throw away, robust and wild and in a hurry.

I ate some pastrami in bed and watched the

sun set over Paradise Valley out the rear windows of BAAA, swiping through Yellowstone hikes on my phone until I fell asleep.

It was around midnight when Aham called from the hospital. I jolted awake. He'd been having severe constipation for a few weeks before I left, and on my first full day away, the pain had become excruciating. He'd finally gone to see his doctor, and they threw him in an ambulance to the hospital. The doctor thought it was diverticulitis, in which case, Aham might need surgery. He sounded scared.

"I'll come home," I said. "I'm eleven hours away. I can leave now and be there by noon tomorrow."

"Don't come," he said. "Don't ruin your trip. Roya is going to come up early from Portland. I'll be fine. DO NOT COME."

Roya was coming up from Portland early. But I was *me*. Didn't he want me? My less evolved self told me to milk the moment—wallow in the unfairness of being usurped at such a vulnerable time for my family. MY family. I was the one who should be there with Aham in the hospital—just like he said he'd be there for me in the hospital if I got into a horrible car accident on the same day that his STUPID GIRLFRIEND had a STUPID CRISIS!

I'd known Roya was going to come up to Seattle while I was away. It was the logical plan. I'd asked if they could get an Airbnb—the two of them together in our house of ten years felt a little too much like being replaced. Of course, Aham said, with an edge of *Do you think I'm a monster?* They were already planning on it.

The day before I left, Roya asked Aham to ask me if it would be okay for her to send me a text. I said sure. It came almost immediately:

> Hi Lindy! I think you are leaving on your big trip tomorrow, and I just wanted to say, sincerely, that I hope you have an incredible trip, and that you stay safe! And that you and Aham and your family have a really nice time together before you leave. I hope it's okay to text you this—that it doesn't feel intrusive. Sending my best wishes. <3

I tried to be mad at this text, but it was like

trying to be mad at getting catcalled by a lesbian. I wrote back:

> Hi! Thank you so much! That is really sweet of you and I deeply appreciate it. Not intrusive at all. You can text me whenever you want. <3

I was being performative again—I wasn't going to let my rival beat me in a niceness contest. My first night on the road, while dozing off in the van, I'd thought about this woman who would soon be in my hometown with my husband. What neighborhood would they stay in? What restaurants would they go to? What activities did they have planned? High-fiving because I was gone? Having a Wife Replacement Ceremony with all my friends? But then…Roya likes me? She's always liked me? What does that mean? Sounds fake!

And now Roya was coming up early from Portland to take care of my medically-full-of-shit husband, usurping my wifely duties just moments after my departure. But Roya liked me. Roya hoped it wasn't intrusive to send me a sweet text wishing me safe travels.

I told myself I'd wait until the next morning and see how Aham was doing. When I woke up, he called and told me that inflammation in his gut had gone down and the doctors were taking surgery off the table. I stifled the martyr instinct that said I should rush home as a power move—*that'll show them*—and checked in with myself. What did I actually want to do? Me, Lindy. If I was the only person who mattered. If I loved myself more than I loved Aham.

I said I was going to stay put. I was going to hike Yellowstone, and then I was going to keep driving toward South Dakota.

"That's right, baby," he said. "Go do it."

A dust storm picked up and sandblasted the van all morning—it was no weather for hiking. I sat at my little fold-down table in the van and tried not to fixate too hard on home, hoping that the wind would relent so that I could experience the natural wonder I'd driven two days to see.

That afternoon, Roya texted again:

> Hi Lindy! I wanted to let you know he's doing really well! I have been thinking of you, I know it must be so

hard to be at a distance right now. I am really glad I can be here for him and for you. Things are looking really good. I'm glad he can have a visitor. It feels good to be here. I'm sure Aham will stay in touch, he's not on meds or out of it at all, but feel free to text me anytime. I hope your trip is going well!

Was this bitch for real? Was anyone actually this nice?

Me, I thought. *I'm this nice.*

Shut up, I thought. *Not anymore. No more Mr. Nice Me.*

The wind never stopped, so I gave up on hiking and drove into Livingston, the closest town, printed out some photos to decorate the van, and watched the NBA playoffs (Bucks versus Nets) in a bona fide saloon. A guy with a goatee and a Bass Pro Shops hat sat down next to me at the bar and tried to flirt. I couldn't remember the last time a stranger had flirted with me, and, update: I hated it.

I'd forgotten that feeling of being mined,

extracted from, in a one-way transaction. I was the locus of this man's attention, but not his focus. You could have swapped me out with any woman. There was a time in my life when just the confirmation of a man's desire—however idle the desire, however mediocre the man—would have fueled me for days, and as this be-jorted loser began explaining to me why Giannis Antetokounmpo was "arrogant," I was impressed to discover a change in myself. I was not grateful for the attention. I was annoyed. He was not offering me one single thing. He did not shut the fuck up, he was boring, he didn't ask me any questions, he disrespected Giannis, and he distracted me from the game. What the fuck was in this for me, dude? Your jizz??

Not for the first time, I wondered what polyamory had to offer straight women. Multiple men? No thanks!

Roya texted again as I pulled into the campground:

> Hi! I just left the hospital. I know
> Aham is in regular touch, so I'm sure
> you're up to speed, but just wanted

to let you know he's doing really well! Zero pain, w/o being on any meds, more appetite, doctors are feeling good about things. There is a strong chance he'll be discharged tomorrow. Hope that can put your mind at ease a bit. I know it's really hard to be away in times like these. Aham's health scare aside, I hope you are having an amazing trip!

No, as a matter of fact, Aham was not doing a good job of keeping me up to speed, nor had he ever, at any point in our ten years together, done a good job of keeping me up to speed about things such as "What did the doctor say about your exploding colon?" Aham likes to text about things like "Did you know Genghis Khan invented the post office?"[1] and "All citruses are a hybrid of the three foundational citruses." He is adept at tuning out things that he finds boring, such as doctor paperwork, and there's

---

1. When I showed him a draft of this chapter, his only comment was, "Actually, the Persians invented the post office."

nothing that shuts him down quicker than having to rehash doctor paperwork that he's already suffered through once. So, no, I did not know what was going on with Aham in the hospital.

But now there was a thoughtful, fastidious woman there taking notes on everything the doctor said and sending me updates in real time while I got to stay on my dream vacation. I thought about Roya while I taped up my photos and wriggled into my pajamas and lit my fairy lights, and it occurred to me that polyamory might have practical benefits after all. Not more men, but…a bonus woman? My Virgo moon was intrigued. Is this what it feels like for a man to have a wife? And meanwhile, monogamous women are out here marrying that fucking guy from the bar? What a racket!

US-89, LIVINGSTON, MONTANA

I am leaving Paradise Valley now, leaving Yellowstone's Edge RV park, driving next to the river. It's so fucking beautiful. I didn't actually go to Yellowstone. I stayed on the edge. That's where I like to live, you know, on the edge.

I'm thinking about the ways that out of fear I have closed off huge sections of my body and my sexuality to myself because it felt safer to be closed and to be deflective, to not let anything in. And I wonder if there's a metaphor there for America. I am traversing these parts of the country where people are scared and angry. Terrified white people have tried so hard to close off parts of the country to people who aren't like them, people who they don't feel like they know. They literally legislate love. I saw a bumper sticker that said MARRIAGE EQUALS MAN PLUS WOMAN. I mean, what a psychic fucking load to care about that, you know? To care about limiting other people's love. It's so sad. Don't you want to put it down? Wouldn't you rather know them instead?

Part of the reason I wanted to do this trip is like, I just feel like I hate not knowing things. I hate not knowing. Maybe it's part of starting to get into all the truth of my life and my marriage and everything. This trip is the kind of thing where in the past, to the old me, it would've seemed like a good idea in the abstract, and then once it started, I would have been miserable and terrified. And here I am on day four and I just feel curious and grateful and, like, glowing. I just feel a glow. And it's so beautiful here. It's so beautiful. I'm still driving by the river, and there's a little island in the river. You know, when I was a kid, I just, god, everything always felt so magical. And if I could have lived in a little tent on a little island in a river, that's... here's me crying at the scenery. This is literally the boring landscape of some people's everyday lives. But it's worth crying over.

   I just want to touch every fucking place in the world, you know?

Tore My Soul Open on a Lube Rack

If I had anything resembling a dream growing up, it was to be a stand-up comedian. I wanted to tour in a van with my friends and get bedbugs in a nasty flophouse. I wanted to master the alchemy of transforming a roomful of strangers into one rapt organism. I wanted to be part of a community of people who loved what I loved. I wanted to be seen and adored, to define myself onstage, and to reinforce, night after night, that I was real. I wanted to be 50 percent star and 50 percent invisible and, in that regard, live comedy is ideal.

It's taken me a long time to admit that, because I didn't do it, which implies that I couldn't do it, which makes me sound like a blowhard, or a coward at best. But at the time I finished college and moved back to Seattle, self-esteem ragged and bleeding from four years in Los Angeles, there wasn't much of an on-ramp for women to prove ourselves in comedy. Fat women, especially, were nothing but a punch line, and there was room for one girl comedian at a time. Not on a bill—in the world. This was normal. When Christopher Hitchens published his essay "Why Women Aren't Funny" in *Vanity Fair* in 2007, the public response ranged from "At last, an intellectual weighs in" to "A scallywag to be sure, but he has a point!" In two thousand and seven!!! Anno Domini! Needless to say, I was scared shitless, and I never gave stand-up a real shot.

In those days, it was de rigueur to tell edgy, misogynist, "shocking"[1] rape jokes, which often made comedy clubs feel hostile to female patrons and comedians alike, and then sometimes male comedians were telling edgy, misogynist, "shocking" rape jokes *while also sexually pestering/assaulting people* in clubs where owners and bookers were sometimes *also sexually pestering/assaulting people*, and if anyone complained about any of

---

1. Raise your hand if you're shocked.

this, everyone said it was just a joke and, "You don't get it because women aren't funny," even though it wasn't just a joke and they knew it.

In lieu of doing comedy, I started writing about comedy. At first, I just wrote fun stuff: profiles of my favorite comics, reviews and previews, silly Q&As. But as edginess ascended to define the mid-aughts milieu, my feminist consciousness unfolding apace, it felt important to say, you know, "Women are funny, and it's not funny to rape us." I didn't like writing seriously about comedy, but I had a platform, I wasn't a working female comic who risked losing precious stage time, and so I felt obliged to say something.

My most notable contribution was a piece for Jezebel in 2012 called "How to Make a Rape Joke," which went viral and got me branded a moral scold, despite containing, in fact, a list of rape jokes I thought were good, including a *positive citation of pre-cancellation Louis CK*. In retaliation, thousands of comedians and comedy fans spent the next four-to-ten years letting me know that there was no such thing as misogyny in comedy you fat fucking pig bitch I hope you choke. Lest you think I'm exaggerating, the trolling was so extreme that *Monica Lewinsky reached out.*

I don't regret writing about rape jokes, but it changed my relationship with comedy forever.

At the time, people treated internet trolling like the weather, a natural and inevitable by-product of mass communication. I kept all the receipts of everyone who ever trolled me, especially famous people and comedians I'd previously admired. (Some of you are very woke now! But I remember!) I screenshotted everything for years. Thousands of images. I said it was for safety, and it partially was—people were threatening to kill me—but mainly, I wanted a witness. No one but me was going to read all these comments. No one but me would ever understand the breadth and the intensity of it, how much these strangers hated me and what that felt like. There was no individual language for it, and there was no cultural language for it.

I still don't have the language. But at least now there's some communal awareness that trolling was about more than hurt feelings—we've all watched internet trolls coalesce into a white supremacist militia. We've seen men's rights activists become MAGA bootlickers, and edgy comedy boys become Joe Rogan vax skeptics, and Elon Musk buy Twitter and then a presidential election, and free speech warriors become cheerleaders for fascist censorship, and Jay Johnston from *Mr. Show*[2] literally storm the Capitol on January 6, and all of the above pollinate each other with disinformation while the media that might once have fact-checked them grows more frail, more corporate, and less diverse.

Most regular people probably didn't follow those threads closely, and there's no reason why the ones who did would remember the Trolling of Lindy West in particular, but the paper trail exists if anyone ever wanted to look. I have it. And maybe that's what this is—maybe I'm the person that's looking, because I need to write the story, because even though I was relentlessly self-serious about the politics part, I didn't take the feelings part seriously enough.

I thought of being trolled as something external: bad people acting out their moral failure on

---

2. My Bible.

me. I laughed. I feigned strength. I doled out vulnerability with tactical precision. I admitted that it hurt only inasmuch as I could use that as a rhetorical cudgel. *See? You can tell how bad they are by how much they hurt my feelings!* But I didn't really look at what it was doing to me. Ten years onward, I see that I am not fine.

Before the rape joke thing, I was still young; I still thought I'd make a serious run at comedy someday. I had just started going to a few open mics in LA—not to perform but to take the temperature. Could that be me? I was shy, but I had the brazen confidence of the soft and untested. Nothing had happened to me yet; I was all potential. I didn't know if I had what it took to be a comedian, but I knew I could make people laugh, and I knew I wanted to be near comedy people. If I could just get in the right room and get comfortable enough to be myself, I could win over anyone. It's not the internet trolls' fault that that never happened; maybe it would never have happened; I have plenty of faults of my own. But, still, thinking about it makes me sad. I wish I had been strong enough to try.

I wrote about those years in *Shrill*, but I didn't

get it right. Looking back, it's obvious that I was writing from the thick of things. It's performative, posturing, like I'm still trying to prove that I'm a real comedy person. It's embarrassing. I list my favorite shows like they're credentials. I name-drop comedians I've come to know. Who cares? This is mass-market entertainment. I'm not special for growing up watching *SNL* and that Paula Poundstone special about the lady who tore her face open on a lube rack. It doesn't make me funnier to have met some of my heroes. Not to blow your mind, but it's actually not hard to meet comedians in LA.

God, there's nothing less funny than writing seriously about comedy, and here I am doing it again. That's part of why those people hated me! Why am I always trying to prove something? There's nothing to prove; this is just the truth: Comedy was the only thing that ever really mattered to me. It was my identity, my obsession, my purest joy. I was lonely in my teens and twenties, and comedy was what I had. I wasn't beautiful, but I could make people laugh. I have always struggled to find a sense of self; I am a sentimental person; I find it difficult to differentiate myself from the things that I love. What I loved was comedy and so I was comedy. And then comedy told me to go kill myself.

I became the archetype of the humorless feminist, shorthand for a scolding bitch whose goal was to destroy laughter itself. I still stumble across comedians and their fans invoking my name over ten years later—"Nobody tag Lindy West." "Lindy West's head would explode if she heard this joke."

Have you ever seen a hunter dress a deer? Emptying the body cavity, stripping the skin, scraping the flesh, applying the flame, stretching it tight? They did more than just hurt my feelings. They hollowed me out. And it was nothing to them.

Anyway.

I guess I asked for it.

Eventually, *Shrill* got optioned for TV, a half-hour comedy on Hulu, and I thought: *Here it is. Validation. Here's my chance to show them.*

Mary Tyler More-to-Love

On the third day of the biggest week of my life, I stepped on some uneven pavement in Palm Springs and turned my ankle. Just a twinge—nothing serious. I didn't even consider going to the doctor. I didn't have time! I was intoxicated with the promise of the moment. In a few days, I would be relocating to Los Angeles to work in my very first writers' room on a TV show that I created based on my very first book. This Palm Springs trip was a celebration. My grandparents had moved to LA to chase their dreams in the 1930s; my dad had done the same forty years later. Another few decades, and now it was my turn. My life was changing, right then. How important are ankles anyway? That's why they give you two!

Shrill had gotten picked up out of the blue a few weeks before, straight to series, condensing our timeline from "see what you come up with and maybe in a year we can talk about you having a show but FYI nobody gets a show" to "move to LA tomorrow, you have a show NOW and FYI you're already behind." My cocreators, Aidy Bryant and Ali Rushfield, and I hadn't even finished writing the pilot, but Hulu had a last-minute hole in their lineup and they tapped us to fill it. (I never found out where the hole came from, but it was 2018 and peak #MeToo, so if you're a man whose show got canceled due to your wiener... thank you?)

As exciting as it was, the accelerated timeline didn't set me up for success. I am pretty much incapable of guile, a real Ned Stark–ass bitch, a trait I take pride in but one that objectively makes my life harder. I inherited my dad's moral code, a DUPLO-simple equation of being nice to everyone you ever meet and trusting that they will repay you in kind (see: freedom is better than slavery, knowing stuff is better than ignorance, and so on). I arrived in LA with a naive positivity, hungry to learn and to contribute. But all the seasoned TV people were working flat out to meet our deadlines. They didn't have much time or patience for Take Your Author to Work Day, no matter how nice I was.

Still, I told myself, I might not be an experienced TV writer, but I knew how to write a story—this story in particular, because it was my story, and some magic in me had brought us all to this moment. No one could deny that, right? Well, it wasn't long before the story of my life began to change, piece by piece, my own Ship of Theseus. The lead would no longer be named Lindy. The show would no longer be set in Seattle. The character written to represent Aham would no longer be a love interest. At least Theseus ended up with a ship.

It's extremely corrosive to an already weak mind to be making a show about the most vulnerable and embarrassing parts of your own life, sitting in writers' rooms listening to skinny white guys from Harvard debating, "So what season should we have the dad die?" Your actual dad, who's actually dead. Only for it to be decided that he shouldn't die at all, because it isn't funny when dads die. Yeah. I know.

There was always a reason that made sense on paper—the studio wants it this way, the lawyers say that would protect us from litigation—but taken altogether, I couldn't escape the fact that my input seemed to be largely a courtesy. And I don't mean that I was overruled in the normal ways you hear about in Hollywood—noted to death by executives or forced to dumb down and chase ratings—I mean that as the weeks went by, I began to sense that I was being *handled*. I would show up at a meeting and get the feeling that everyone else had spoken privately already.

In one meeting, the marketing team presented us with their season 1 concept, which was that when you got to the *Shrill* landing page on Hulu, you'd find a picture of a refrigerator, and when you clicked on the refrigerator door, it would open and you'd find all the episodes inside. And they said, "See? It's a play on binge-*watching* and binge-*eating*!" I was already so lost, I didn't even know if I was allowed to say no. (Blessedly, Aidy had no such compunction.)

Navigating the opaque machinery of Hollywood made me anxious and paranoid. Whatever charm I'd managed to haul with me from Seattle went immediately on the fritz, and once it was gone, there was no chance I could win these people over. I became a quivering freak, vacillating between prickly defensiveness and desperate people-pleasing. I wasn't a person, and I certainly wasn't a boss. I was an electrified puff of steel wool. I was a collapsing barn. I was negative space only. I was a balloon on a string hovering one hundred feet above the Hollywood Business Park.

I had one lifeline. I'd had to fight for it, but they let me hire my friend Samantha Irby as a writer—besides me and Aidy, she was the only other fat writer in the room. Sam and I rented Martha Plimpton's house, a pretty white cottage on top of a mountain. In addition to being a genius, there's no one in the world who makes me feel more at ease than Sam. I don't have to perform for her. Which meant that outside of office hours, I didn't have to feel self-conscious about soothing myself with food.

At home in Seattle, I pretended not to be a dysfunctional eater. I ate in secret, often in the car. A glazed old-fashioned on the way home from the grocery store. A Blizzard on the way to the dump. To this day, I can gauge my mental health by whether or not I'm able to leave a

Walgreens without whatever seasonal Reese's shape they have that month (ranked best to worst: tree, pumpkin, egg, football) clutched in my hot little hand. I'd swing by the gas station to toss my wrappers so I didn't get caught.

But at Martha's house, with Sam, that self-consciousness was gone, and just in time—the TV show kept my anxiety idling at a scream. I shambled through each day from treat to treat. I worked and ate and sat. At night, Sam and I watched *Catfish* and died laughing and shopped for makeup online. Best of times, worst of times, et cetera.

I'd also come in with all this baggage about comedy. I thought *Shrill* was my chance to repair that part of my identity, to prove to the comedy people that I was funny and that I belonged. I know this sounds narcissistic and deranged, but once I got there, I couldn't stop wondering if anyone in the show's orbit (writers, producers, execs, cast members, friends of cast members) had been part of the 2012 rape joke pile-on, or the 2013 rape joke pile-on, or the 2014 rape joke pile-on, or the years that followed when I was meme-ified as a fat bitch joke cop.

It turns out that having thousands of people make fun of you and threaten to rape and murder you can make you feel unsafe in certain spaces for way longer than you expect. Your nervous system doesn't know it isn't a real threat. When I think back to my time working on *Shrill*, that's exactly what I felt—*unsafe*. Not unsafe in a *Dateline* way, but somatically unsafe. Survival-mode unsafe. I didn't know who I could trust and who actually liked me and who thought I was an idiot who didn't deserve to be there, and the more awkward I made things, the harder I spiraled and the further away I got from myself. I never calmed down, not for three years, and I never righted my ship.

The corporations that made *Shrill* paid me well for all this angst, but, in retrospect, the choice to option my work was largely illusory, the terms opaque. What career freelancer can say no to a few years of six-figure income? I didn't truly understand what I was selling, and nobody could warn me, because they didn't truly understand what they were buying.

Have you ever had all your dreams come true and then you hate it? Or maybe you don't hate it, but you've previously fumbled so many other parts of your life (cumulative, stacking) that when the dream is ready for you, you're not ready for it? And as you freeze, you watch the dream slide away from you, confirming your meanest internal monologues about how you suck and never deserved anything good in the first place so *of course* this was the natural end point of your career, your life, your sanity?

My ankle kept hurting through the summer as we decamped to Portland to shoot season 1. It was even harder than the writers' room. I was learning another new set of skills on the fly in a high-pressure situation that cost thousands of dollars a minute, and I didn't have Sam with me anymore. I didn't have anyone.

The cast and some of the writers and producers would hang out together after hours; I saw the pictures on Instagram. I wasn't invited. At this point, my sense of self had been so eroded that I was incapable of basic social interaction, let alone meaningful conversation, let alone charisma. I truly don't blame anyone for not inviting me to the arcade or whatever. They had never really met me.

There's no big catharsis here, no resolution. We got picked up for a second season and then a third. Sam wasn't asked back for the season 2 writers' room. I tried to keep her, but it was like fighting sand. I became the only significantly fat writer in the room. I wrote a role for Martha, but when I'd pitch her name, the words would vanish like I hadn't spoken. "We" cast somebody else. The power structure wanted simplicity, and having "my" people in the machinery was a complication. When I finally got the guts up to complain—sobbing on the phone to producers who didn't have time—I found that even the origin story had shifted under my feet: It was some magic in Aidy that had brought us all to this moment, because the show would never have gotten made without a star attached. A real star. Not me.

It's not like if you watch *Shrill* you won't see me in there. I was writing scripts, attending castings, approving props, choosing background actors, interviewing post-production crew, getting hugged by the CEO of Warner Bros. Television. I personally got to cast the dog. Despite all the psychological torture—self-inflicted and otherwise—I did learn how to make TV, and I'll always be grateful for that.

But *Shrill* was never my show, and in the ways that matter to me, I was never really there. My real personality wasn't in the room and didn't often make it onto the screen, and while I loved my coworkers, I didn't become close with people in a way that made me feel at home or might have gotten me more TV jobs after *Shrill* was canceled. I was given the illusion of power while the real deciders had private calls without me, and you can only be undermined so many times *on an adaptation of your own life* before you start to question whether you even know who you are.

This was particularly disorienting because in most of my life leading up to that point—my real, private life as a friend / family member / colleague—I wasn't just popular. I was beloved! I remember it! I remember embodying that power. Sometimes I wonder where I lost it, how my life and career would have been different if I'd managed to keep my grip. Sometimes I wonder if my last couple of years at *The Stranger* (2007, 2008, 2009) were the very best of my life—if it would be worth it to go back to the smaller world of

Adult Braces

a Seattle alt weekly, a big fat fish in a pond I loved and understood, where everyone loved and understood me. I was broke and lonely, but I was myself; I was great at what I did, and I never second-guessed it.

The best way I can describe that time at *The Stranger* is that I was always "on" if you're into show business or "in the zone" if you're into sports or "out-pizza-ing the Hut" if you're into pizza. My personality could not miss. If I wanted people to laugh at something, they laughed. I swanned around the office trailing fairy dust. I held my own charisma in my hands, glowing warm. I knew just how to do it. Saying so doesn't feel like bragging to me now because that feeling is gone. It was a psychological trick of the light, and as soon as I didn't believe it anymore, it disappeared. Maybe I wasn't ready to evolve floppy little legs and crawl out of my pond; maybe I was never suited for it. Maybe I'm just a local girl after all. Nothing wrong with that.

One of the most surreal parts of *Shrill* season 1 was shooting in the office of *The Weekly Thorn*, the fake paper we made up to mirror *The Stranger*. Our genius art department did such an impeccable job, a supernaturally accurate job, down to the tiniest details, that it gave me a strange whiplash—like I might be able to reach out and catch a ghost of myself. My chest ached for my home paper, which wasn't my home anymore, and the girl I'd been when I worked there, who wasn't me anymore.

Shooting *Shrill* was my highest point professionally and my lowest point mentally. And my ankle still hurt. I limped around set, trying to stay out of the way. I limped to my car. I limped up to my apartment, then back down again to the lobby to pick up my food delivery. I ate a lot. I was making a lot of money. Sometimes I would Uber Eats sushi from one restaurant and cake from another on the same night.

Production very kindly got me a special extra-wide, six-hundred-pound-capacity director's chair that was literally called BIG BOY CHAIR. Which, frankly, was awesome—the kind of accommodation everyone deserves—but drove home to me every day that I was something else, an outsider in this industry, a big boy in a small world. I was the fattest person on set by far. Aidy didn't need Big Boy Chair. She was literally the Hollywood version of me—the smaller version, the more successful version. I sat in Video Village in Big Boy Chair and I ate small bags of Cheetos from craft services and I said less and less. By the time it was all over, I could barely walk.

Back in Seattle, shortly after season 1 wrapped, I finally got myself to the hospital to have my ankle x-rayed, and was so disassociated that I drove head-on into a concrete pillar in the parking garage. I pulled around a corner, looked straight at the pillar, and accelerated into it. The pillar seemed undamaged—did I exist?—so, unsure of what else to do, I parked and wobbled my way up to the imaging department, a purple-black bruise from the seat belt spreading across my breasts.

The X-rays were clear: I had developed a bone spur from my stumble in Palm Springs, an untreated injury that healed itself into a monstrosity.

Some months later, a podiatrist fitted me with custom orthotics[1] and explained that to walk again without pain, first I had to walk. The walking was the healing. The orthotics would do

---

1. The braces of the feet.

their work, step by step, teaching my eager tendons, my loyal bones, to realign, to carry me forward in stronger, healthier ways. Unfortunately, as usual, the only way out was through.

Shrill was canceled in early 2021. When the call from the network came, I didn't pick up. I was strangely relieved. I stood in the silence and surveyed the wreckage of the previous few years. Even then, I doubted myself. Had I overreacted? Could it be possible that it was all in my pathetic, self-pitying head? Was I really as weird and invisible as I'd felt on this production?

Not long after, I received a package from the *Shrill* production office with a few keepsakes from the show, including a hardcover book of photographs from our three years on set, in which I *literally do not appear.*

Stuck on the cover was a Post-it that read "Linda West."

US-18, DOUGLAS, WYOMING

Is it unethical, according to my politics, to buy a small jar of raw clover honey from the Buttfuck Nowhere, Wyoming, truck stop, from an old man named Fat Daddy who is selling them from a folding table with his friend, and Fat Daddy's wearing a hat that spells out 2A—as in "Second Amendment"—in, um, rifles? And then his friend is wearing a hat that has a big rifle on it, and it says, WE WILL NOT COMPLY. Is it unethical to give these absolutely certainly virulent racists my ten dollars for some honey? What do we think? I think it's okay. I'm making connections! We're building bridges. I just realized that Fat Daddy—Honey Daddy—probably has really bad views on abortion. What if he uses my ten dollars to print a sign to go harass people at the clinic? This is what I don't get. Sir, why don't you just, like, live your life being a nice bee man? You're clearly into bees, which is very tender. He's into bees, but not industrially. He said he can't sell his honey commercially, because he doesn't make enough, because he doesn't have five thousand beehives. Sir, that's cute! You're a bee hobbyist, for the love of it! So now apply that. Apply that. Please, please apply it. Fat Daddy, please!

We Live in a Society, Bitch!

June 11, 2021

The Douglas KOA Journey in Douglas, Wyoming, has a pool, a basketball court, and a little coffee shop that will blend ANYTHING. Douglas lies on the western edge of the Great Plains, and the landscape indeed feels great, and plain. Hot, scrubby grasslands stretch out of sight in every direction, empty but not without flashes of interest—a low mountain, a gentle slope down to a bright blue stream, a beckoning copse of trees—Wyoming is an understated lady who knows to shed a few accessories before she leaves the house.

"Nice van!" the campground host yelled over her shoulder as I followed her golf cart to my campsite. She was about my age, short and chubby with curly blond hair under a visor. She was in her element—Miss Social

Butterfly—waving to everyone and doing little bits where she pretended to dRiVe cRaZy!!! We arrived at my spot, and she hopped out.

"I've seen a van like that before," she said.

"Oh, really?" I said. "You mean a painted van?"

She nodded. "They started showing up a couple years ago. The first one I saw pull in here, it was crazy. It was like, 'Peace on earth, man!' Like, 'Flower power!!'" She threw up two peace signs and swayed back and forth like Janis Joplin.

I laughed. "Sounds pretty cool!"

"You expected when the doors opened for it to be a cloud of smoke!" she said. "But then the doors opened, and it was just two totally straitlaced people! I couldn't believe what I was seeing!"

"Wow," I said. "Well, if it was this company, they don't let you pick your van—"

She interrupted, eyes narrowed: "That stuff's illegal here, by the way."

"What?"

"Marijuana."

"Oh, I don't smoke pot," I said.

"Well, you know, a lot of people think that it's

legal here because it's legal in Colorado and they think, *Oh, Wyoming's a part of Colorado.*"

"I don't think Wyoming's a part of Colorado."

"I'm okay with medicinal," she continued, "but I've seen what people are like when they're on that stuff. I've seen what it does to people."

"It's totally legal where I live, and nothing bad really happens."

"Hmm," she said, unconvinced, or possibly disappointed.

I hadn't seen anyone so titillated by the idea of getting high since myself in the mirror in seventh grade—absolutely terrified but would have leapt at the chance. Colorado sure was a long way from home.

I shot around on the basketball court for a while in the punishing sun, then went for a swim. It was twilight and the bugs were out, so I had the pool to myself. I floated on my back and stared at the fading blue sky and pictured Aham and Roya back home. She was still in Seattle, and he'd been firm with me that he couldn't maintain constant contact for the next few days. They were out doing things. She didn't get to visit very often. Roya's a person too, he said. She deserved his time and attention too. He had an annoying habit of using that phrase: "I'm a person too," "Roya's a person too." Like I couldn't say it right back about myself. I didn't really suck up all the personhood in the room, did I?

I'd been pissed off when he first asked for that space, but floating on my back in the pool, gnats and mosquitoes swarming, just my eyes and nose breaking the surface, some part of me was grateful for the imposed distance. I'd felt closer to myself all day, less preoccupied, and now I was suspended in cool water watching the sun set fuchsia over the hayfields. My cells thrummed with pleasure, muscles tired from use instead of sloth, skin toasted and freckled, and I thought: *This is better. To be in a pool in Wyoming surrounded by bugs. Not groveling at a man's elbow for a life that doesn't fit either of us anymore.*

I showered and went back to the van to eat dinner. A family towing an RV pulled in next to me and started setting up camp. I waved and then turned back to my journal. I'd vowed to talk to strangers on this trip, hear their stories, find deep meaning in brief connections, but so far, I'd stayed shy, and as the days went on, I felt myself sliding inward. I hated myself for it. Great road trips are about the characters.

The kids noticed BAAA and tumbled over to me while I was housing a gas station hard-boiled egg.

"Is this your car?"

"Yes."

"Did you paint it?"

"No."

"Why does it look like that?"

"Great question."

Ice broken, I went into my schtick about the homicidal rabbit mural, not being able to choose my own van, et cetera, and then their mom came over. She said they were road-tripping from Wisconsin to California and back, and her husband worked in public health—enough bluish signifiers that I felt emboldened to bring up something that had been bothering me since I crossed the Rockies. Had they seen anyone in a mask lately? It was peak Delta variant, and in Seattle, people were still masking outside to walk their dogs. But once I left western Montana, it was like COVID had never happened. A few years later, COVID denialism would become mainstream policy and we'd all be habituated, but in 2021, the trauma was fresh, and seeing vast swaths of the country living blasé pre-COVID lives felt fucking insane.

"OH MY GOD," she stage-whispered, hyper-attuned to the elderly Wyomingites all around us, "literally not since Minneapolis."

That's right, I thought. *Look at me go. I do know how to connect with people.*

I let the kids climb around in BAAA while their mom and I gossiped about how strange it is to traverse two realities, how sad and alienating to be in one's home country and a different world at the same time. My gracious hosts, my vicious tormentors, my people, not my people, my family, my enemies, myself, my opposite—all connected, and all apart. I wrapped a piece of pastrami around a pickle spear and took a bite. A bird flew by and shat on my head.

The kids went nuts. This bird's huge dookie in my freshly showered hair had anointed me the greatest comedian of all time (finally). I thanked their mom for the conversation—truly cathartic—and went to shower again.

An older lady entering the bathroom saw me

over her shoulder and slammed the door in my face so that I couldn't slip in behind her without entering the code. Like I was a bathroom thief! Ma'am, I did not drive to the middle of Wyoming to steal a shower! I punched in the code defiantly—got her—and then showered in the stall next to her while she passive-aggressively complained about me to her friend: "There's all this water coming in under the door! My feet are wet!"

Ma'am, you are in the shower!

"I brought my flip-flops, but now my flip-flops are wet."

Well, get over it! We live in a society, bitch!

The next morning as I was packing up to leave, a white woman in her sixties drove past my campsite in a minivan. She rolled down her window and pointed at BAAA. "Do you like that?"

I assumed she meant the paint job, so I started my routine *again*—well, it's a rental, they didn't let me pick…

"No," she said. "Do you like traveling in the van?"

"Oh, I love it!" I said. "I'm driving from Seattle to Florida and back all by myself."

"I'm alone too," she said. "Isn't it wonderful?" She scrunched up her nose conspiratorially, like we had a secret no one else could understand.

"People always ask me if I'm scared," I said, "but I'm not."

"Me neither," she said.

Her name was Sara. She was an ICU nurse, but COVID had finally beaten her—after watching so many people die, she just needed to get away. A few months ago, she'd retired early, bought this minivan, and converted it herself. She took out the rear seats, built a wooden platform for a mattress, and headed west, no real destination. She had a couple of adult children who she planned to visit, one in California and one in Oregon, but didn't mention a partner. She needed her own space to be herself, to spend some time with life instead of death, to reclaim her identity now that she wasn't taking care of other people anymore.

Sara said that being out in the world and close to the land made her feel closer to God. I wasn't here for God, but I knew what she meant.

US-18, LUSK, WYOMING

Sorry for this graphic information, but I was pooping at the truck stop just now, and someone else came into the bathroom and I thought, *Oh my god, have I been in here too long? What if someone else needs this stall?* It wasn't even the only stall! And that's a thing that I regularly do. Like if I'm pooping, even at home, I'll get self-conscious that someone else deserves the bathroom more than I do and I'll stop. I will interrupt my pooping and think, *Oh, I'll come back and finish pooping later.* That's not good! You're allowed to finish your business, your bodily function! Why do I have this weird idea that I'm not worthy of the toilet?

We Cannot Open It Because We Cannot See the Bottom

June 13, 2021

Nestled in a grove of cottonwood trees in a bend of the White River, just ten minutes from the entrance to Badlands National Park, the White River KOA had more of a festive, family vibe than my previous campgrounds—kids running wild, dads barbecuing, Bluetooth speakers blasting Dave Matthews. After a few nights feeling like a scruffy interloper in Retiree Disneyland, the energy was a fun change, even if the basketball court was occupied 24-7.

On my day off, I got up before sunrise and drove to the national park to hike the Castle Trail and Medicine Root Loop, an eight-mile trek through the Badlands' Martian crags. If you don't know what the Badlands look like, imagine the place where Captain Kirk fought the Gorn, or that Joy Division T-shirt times a billion, or a topographical drawing exercise designed by a sadistic cartography teacher. An unaccountable web of ridges and pinnacles erupting from the mixed-grass prairie, striated orange and gold and white.

As I drove, I marveled at how comfortable I was starting to feel outside of my comfort zone. The idea that I would get up at 5:30 in the morning at my campsite in my van where I slept alone and go and do an eight-mile solo hike in a semi-dangerous place I didn't know anything about? 2018 Lindy would not have believed it. I get hung up on barriers to entry—being forced to engage with the unknown. What if I can't find the trailhead? What if I need a special pass? What if I get stuck? Will I be able to physically do this? Will it be embarrassing?

I had no context for what eight miles at ninety degrees would feel like. I wouldn't know until it was too late whether I'd brought enough water. I for sure had brought the twelve essentials, though: sunscreen, phone, pepperoni sticks, a small box of crystals, braces rubber bands, queso-flavored Ruffles, and a laptop. I think that's all of them. I couldn't leave my laptop in the van—what if it got stolen? The lands are famously bad! Had to hump it with me through the Badlands, like normal!

I parked at the trailhead and found the sign. So far so good. It was 6:30 a.m. when I strode forth into the chalky white wilderness. About ten yards up the trail, I had to scramble up a crumbling bank, probably three feet high, and I realized it'd be easier with my trekking poles. I turned back to get them and ran straight into three hot young male hikers right behind me. They'd just watched my fat ass start the hike, walk thirty feet, and then turn around. A nightmare. After I passed, one of them made a comment and another one laughed. I didn't know if they were talking about me, but as a fat person, you never know they aren't.

The trail took a wide loop through the green and lively prairie, affording some distance to admire the rock formations, then turned and plunged into the maze. I pushed ahead, occasionally pausing to rest in a scrap of shade. I felt like a big, strong animal. By 9:00 a.m., I was over halfway done and I still had water, but the sun was already feeling dangerous. In such an extreme landscape, the veil between life and death is close—closer than I'd ever experienced. I wasn't going to die, but I could feel, mechanically, how you would.

At last, fire-engine red and soaked with sweat, I rounded a corner and saw BAAA waiting in the distance. *I'm doing it*, I thought, picturing the frat boys from the trailhead. *I did it! Fuck every man who ever laughed at me! I'm a fucking god!*

I drove BAAA back to the KOA, red and wet and triumphant and weak and exhausted and exultant and immortal, ready to swim for the rest of the day. There was a sign on the pool gate:

POOL IS CLOSED.
WE CANNOT OPEN IT BECAUSE
WE CANNOT SEE THE BOTTOM.
WE HAVE A NEW PUMP ON ORDER.
WE ARE SO SORRY.

But... I hiked eight miles? I'm a fucking god? Plan B was to spend the afternoon writing romantically at my campsite under the shade of the tall trees, but unfortunately, it was noon, so there was no shade. I'd brought a canopy, but I was too tired to set it up. I tried to sit in the van, but dogs die in hot cars, and I couldn't keep the doors or windows open, because it would fill up with mosquitoes and it was also my bedroom. Writing at one's campsite was a better Pinterest visual than a practical reality, I realized. I went to the camp store to get a Popsicle.

I was sitting on a deck chair in the shade by the closed pool enjoying my second Popsicle when Roya texted:

> Hi! I hope your trip is going well! I dropped Aham at home a little while ago and am headed back to Portland. Before I get on the road, I just wanted to text to say I know we are both so glad he's going to be okay, and to thank you for your openness toward me being here at a critical time. I understand how hard it is to be apart from the people we love most in emergencies—all we want is to be

> by their side. I'm glad I could be of
> support, given the circumstances, and
> it felt good for me, too. I really look
> forward to meeting you sometime
> soon, and I hope you continue to stay
> safe and have an amazing trip!

Maybe it was the endorphins from the hike, but I felt serene. Content. Relationship is closed. We cannot open it because we cannot see the bottom. Relationship is open. We cannot not open it because we know the bottom is a part of life. Roya understands how hard it is to be apart from the people we love most in emergencies.

By this point the pool deck had amassed a cohort of would-be swimmers making the best of things, strangers united by adversity, batting a dry beach ball back and forth with a forbearance worthy of Dorothea Lange. A shy, skinny girl in her early twenties said she was driving from college in Minnesota to spend the summer with her boyfriend in Utah, but confessed that she didn't want the road trip to end; she thought she might love the road more than the boy. A couple from Missouri with a pair of rowdy sons said they were trying to hit every national park in their RV before the kids grew up. I said I was driving to Key West and back in a van, alone, just because.

"I felt like I couldn't breathe," I explained. "So I abandoned my family and came here."

"I wish I could do that!" the Missouri wife laughed. She jerked a thumb at her husband. "He can't handle anything without me."

"Hey!" the husband said.

"I bet he can!" I said. "I bet you'd be surprised."

"I don't know," she said. "Aren't you scared?"

I gestured around us at the drooping cottonwoods, the swallows diving for mosquitoes, the fireflies winking into life in the creamsicle sunset. It was the first time I'd ever seen fireflies. "No," I said. "It's just this."

"You have to do it," the college girl told the mom.

"I'm not stopping her!" the husband said, throwing up his hands.

A KOA employee came out and announced that they'd gotten the old pump to work long enough to clean the water currently in the pool. Because it was so hot, they were reopening it, and we were allowed to swim "until it gets milky." Hell yes, brother! I jumped in with my fellow wanderers, and we swam until the moon was high.

〜〜〜

On paper, not much had changed in my relationship since 2019. I had one husband. My husband had one wife and one girlfriend. But two years earlier that configuration had me screaming wordlessly into my pillow. Why did today feel so different? Why was I so calm? Was I acclimating to the will of a con man, or experiencing—huge if true—personal growth?

If you freeze a moment in time, it's impossible to tell whether you're falling or flying. A place that was a triumph on your way up looks like a failure on your way down. The selfsame moment—both progress and regress, depending on perspective. Maybe the only metric we can trust, the only thing that really matters, is how we feel in the now. We all smash into the ground in the end.

Do you know anything about parachutes?

Do you know anything about Coleman stoves?

HWY 79, BUFFALO GAP, SOUTH DAKOTA

A weird thing in the Great Plains is that there will be a sign that's like, "The last buffalo was killed here!" and it doesn't, like, feel like they're saying, "We're sorry." It's more like, "Yeah, can you believe it? We did it!" You guys, why'd you do that? Like, at the last rest stop where I stopped and put my rubber bands back on, this plaque was like, "The last straggler of the great buffalo herds was killed nearby recently." What do you mean "recently"??? What are you talking about? Don't say "straggler"! Fuck you! I think I have to become a vegetarian after this trip because every cow makes me cry. Every cow. I just want them to live. Oh my god. And there's these weird little—I wish I knew what they were. These funny little, like, kind of football-shaped antelopes I keep seeing. What's it called? A curly horn? That's not what it's called. Springhorn? Well, I don't know, but there's these cute little antelopes everywhere and I need them to live!!!!!!

Good Knievel

Do you ever watch videos of peak Luther Vandross outshining even Whitney herself and feel utterly baffled by the concept of a net closing around a wild baby orca, dooming him to a life of claustrophobia and madness? How can the world be so good and so bad at the same time? How can the climate be collapsing around my dog? It makes no sense, and the tension is overwhelming. The overwhelm is immense. The immensity is crushing. The crush, sometimes, feels not worth surviving.

Disappointment is an issue for me. My own, other people's, strangers', fictional characters'—if someone has an expectation about something (or, god forbid, is excited) and then that thing doesn't happen (or, god forbid, is a catastrophe), I am ruined.

And I needlessly extrapolate—if I see an Instagram video of a fox that got hit by a car and is now living a happy life at a wildlife sanctuary eating blueberries, my brain will say, HE HAD BIG PLANS IN THE WILD. HE MISSES HIS WIFE. I switch ponytail holders every day to make sure the ponytail holder I didn't pick yesterday doesn't feel bad. Aham can literally take, like, a straw and show it to me and say, "Did you know that this straw's parents died?" and I'll cry. I'm crying as I type this. The world can never be idealized enough. No matter how nice a thing is, I will always invent a way for the sadness to get in.

In service of this impulse, paradoxically but not, I possess an optimism that does not quit. I'm a fixer. If something goes wrong, I can't let it stay wrong. I am always dodging, patching, reorienting. A plan falls through, someone gets sick, all industries collapse under a global pandemic—before reality has even sunk in, I'm pivoting to soften the blow so I don't have to sit in the brokenness for even one second.

Maybe that sounds helpful on paper, but I'm sick! People need to feel sad things, let the bad feelings pass through them and find themselves still alive, affirm their resilience despite the way that life just sucks sometimes, or so I'm told. I myself don't partake. My MO has always been to float in the blank middle of things, an energy field between me and hard realities like opposing magnets. At my shallowest, I hate it when plot complicates a nice scene. I hate it when I'm absorbed in a beautiful landscape painting and someone tells me it's about the Industrial Revolution. I want the landscape to be the meaning. I hate that a pretty picture isn't enough to make a story.

    I do a lot of intellectual caring and emotional avoidance. I say the right things, send money to the right places, but my meaty heart is a billion miles away. I avoid listening to music. I fill the silence with audiobooks day and night. High-fantasy argle-bargle. Commercial thrillers where a British person is murdered by their long-lost son. In every moment, I need something distracting me, pulling me away, telling me a story, anything but the bubble of tragedy below my rib cage that expands and contracts without warning like a sneaker wave. Music is too close to pure emotion and pure emotion is too close to me losing my mind. Are you aware that some people listen to sad songs on purpose? Okay, Evel Knievel!

It's the same driving impulse that makes me a "people pleaser," a hideous misnomer for a hideous behavior. "People pleasing" is never about pleasing people—it's about the pleaser avoiding discomfort, confrontation, accountability. It's a manipulation, a rot that threatens all my relationships, not because it makes me "too nice" and vulnerable to exploitation, but because it makes me a liar who isn't willing to do the hard work of love. It's actually cruel to not want to know how people feel.

I have always been adept at oozing my way through life from comfortable place to comfortable place, avoiding conflict and embarrassment, which sounds like a form of chillness but is really a form of control. Even what people perceive in me as "bravery," my candor and vulnerability, is a form of control. You really think I'm telling you everything? I decide which parts of me you see; I curate the way you understand my pain with sharp precision. I am not clumsy. I do not drop things, I do not fall down, I do not blurt the wrong thing, I do not take big swings, I do not publicly fail. I do not like to let go. I like to hang on! Hanging on rules! Letting go drools!

I can recall no clearer reality check, no binary more symbolic, than the airtight choice between keeping control and keeping my teeth. I chose teeth. I forfeited comfort and forced myself, gnashing and drooling, to let go.

This might read like an overstatement to you, if you do not identify as a woman warthog bieste so foule the merest glimpse of her brings certain death to mortal men, but to me, giving in to adult braces was giving in to the destiny I always knew was mine: to be revealed as a pathetic pretender to the throne of beauty, desirability, elegance, and grace; a child we all mock; an old woman making a farce of youth; a lisping clown whom it's illegal to love.

It was scary. And then I took my braces on the road and... it was fine? My braces were strangely disarming. If anything, people were warmer. Aside from the obvious drawbacks (this is a dirty cheese grater that you wear in your mouth), I kind of liked having braces. It made me feel unusual, singular. It was a conversation starter. People told me about their insecurities about their teeth, or how they never wear their retainer, or the time in seventh grade when they pried their braces off at home with needle-nose pliers. I suddenly had carte blanche to brag to every single stranger about my number one favorite subject: *I was actually born with PERFECT TEETH.* Nobody stopped loving me.

Getting adult braces sucks, but it's not as scary as sleeping alone in a van next to the train tracks, or hiking solo when you're fat, or trusting Lorne Michaels with your life rights, or telling somebody how you feel.

Part Three
SEVENTEEN-YEAR BLOOM

Long Bright Noon of the Soul

June 14, 2021

As I sped deeper into the Great Plains, my tether to home got so slack I almost couldn't feel it. My thoughts were overflowing, but fewer and fewer of them were about Aham and Roya. It helped that the Nebraska interior had obliterated my phone signal. I was alone with myself, and I hadn't turned back when things got complicated. The hospital was my first big test, and I'd passed. New territory. Everything was flat, and everything was gold.

It helped being in the van—I had to stay present, because there were always a million things to do. Put the table up, put the table down, make the bed, move the suitcase, put the suitcase back, put the screens on the windows, take the screens down, check for spiders, make sure the stuffed animals were happy, collect the garbage, fill the tank, wipe the windshield, pour out melted ice, buy new ice. BAAA had become an extension of me, my exoskeleton, my private beach ball bubble, and in caring for her, I was caring for myself—not traditionally my forte.

I had a reservation to camp at an RV park called Prairie Oasis on Interstate 80, about an hour outside Lincoln, whose Yelp page swirled with rumors of home-baked muffins. But the longer I drove through the empty white heat, the more I fixated on a real bed, an air conditioner, a pool, not necessarily a vegan coffee shop but a coffee shop staffed by a vegan. I decided to press on to the city.

A roadside attraction called the Boneyard Creation Museum materialized before me through the dust and heat haze—an educational facility and gem emporium that purports to "scientifically connect young earth creation, Noah's Flood, the Ice Age, dinosaurs, and more to the Bible." Exhibits depicted on the museum's Tripadvisor page include a *Tyrannosaurus rex* cavorting in front of the Tower of Babel and a family of velociraptors watching as three men dressed like Indiana Jones, Young Indiana Jones, and Indiana Jones's friend flee from a biblical flood in the American southwest.

I yearned for more context, but the Boneyard was closed. A smite to my immortal soul! What was the point of being on this road trip if I couldn't stop at the Boneyard Creation Museum? I wondered how the Boneyard Creation Museum stayed in business. Was there a steady influx of tourists coming through Broken Bow, Nebraska? Do the locals go to the Boneyard Creation Museum again and again to bask in the pleasure of knowing that Jesus might have cured a *diplodocus* of leprosy? Maybe that's worth it, actually—a small entry fee to have all your feelings validated anytime you want, to have the stories that make you feel safe confirmed by an institution as incontrovertible as a museum. It must be devastating to discover twin passions for geology and Christian fundamentalism—two-hundred-million-year-old dinosaur bones on a six-thousand-year-old Earth—only to find them irrevocably at odds. It could break a person.

What's my Boneyard Creation Museum? I

wondered. Where did I go to feed my confirmation bias, to rest unchallenged? Could that be the purpose of all this? To tear it down, rid myself of comforting myths, and learn to move forward without them?

Earlier that morning, I'd passed through the Rosebud Sioux reservation and was stopped at a COVID checkpoint. A cute, chubby guy in a mask asked me where I was headed. He seemed a little nervous, and I imagined that white people in RVs had been evil to him all day. I told him I was going to Lincoln, and he said, "Lincoln, okay. Well, that's really all I need to know. This is the reservation, but you're allowed to drive through it."

The Rosebud hospital has thirty-five beds and, at least as of 2020, only two ventilators, so the community was taking special precautions to keep outsiders—unmasked and unvaccinated in the name of "freedom"—from infecting and killing their most vulnerable. And so that sweet man stood on that shimmering asphalt, protecting his home one car at a time.

Some might accuse me of Orwellian doublethink here: *So, the people opposed to restrictions and mandates are insular and controlling, but the people literally closing their community to outsiders are open-minded and free?*

Well, yeah. The first group has constructed a false reality to avoid having to extend compassion to anyone outside of their immediate family unit, regardless of how many millions they kill; the second group has looked reality in the face and taken reasonable action to mitigate large-scale harm. One is craven individualism; the other is brave collective care. One prioritizes people's freedom to not wear a mask; the other prioritizes people's freedom to live instead of die.

It's the same as digging up a dinosaur bone and instead of thinking, *What is this?* you think, *How can I fit this into the story that I want to be true?*

Modern conservatism is so sad—the way people wall themselves off from the rest of the world, too afraid to identify as members of a global collective, convinced that receiving care isn't worth it if you also have to give. But we are connected. I can put my body in a car and drive it from Seattle to Key West—mountains giving way to desert giving way to mountains giving way to prairie giving way to jungle giving way to swamp giving way to that miraculous coral archipelago.

The empty highway stretched on and on. It felt like it had been the same time all day. The light never changed. The sun never moved. The bars on my phone never flickered to life. Sunset seemed impossible. I wondered if I was caught in a time loop on this highway, transported to the beginning again and again to drive and drive and drive in the eternal noon of Nebraska.

HWY 2, ANSLEY, NEBRASKA

I listened to *Parable of the Sower* a couple hours ago, and there's this thing that she touches on right away that I have been thinking about and struggling with for years, which is the claustrophobia of, like, there's nowhere to run to. There's nowhere to go. Once we use up Earth, there's nowhere to go. Mars is not gonna save us. This is it. You can't move on to the next place. Why the fuck would we terraform Mars? Terraform Earth!!! Terraform Earth, man!

It's actually a great metaphor. Terraform Earth, emotionally! That's a good metaphor. Fuck off with your Mars. Have you seen Mars? Mars sucks! I want to be Earth!

Colonizing Mars as a solution to climate change? The wastefulness of it! It's like that *SNL* fake commercial about the disposable toilet, Will Ferrell era. Single-use toilet. The wife throws a Kleenex in there and the husband has to install a new toilet and haul the old one to the dumpster. "Because when something's dirty, just throw it away."

Now this is a weird landscape. It's sand. There's sand. Why are these sand dunes? Why am I driving through sand dunes in the middle of Nebraska? What the fuck is this? All right, apparently I'm driving through the Great Nebraska Sand Dunes. That's weird. Sucks to only have the worst part of the beach. Sounds like Mars! They're beautiful, though. Everything is.

I think my heart is starting to settle.

Here Lies My Beloved

There's a part of my marriage story that I haven't talked about, because it's harder to forgive. I'm scared of what you'll think of me. I told you Aham was secretly seeing one woman in 2019. He was actually seeing two. The first one was Roya, who lived out of town, was queer and nonmonogamous, had good boundaries and her own busy life, and thus fell within our relationship parameters.

The second one was younger. She lived in our neighborhood. She was tall and thin and blond and fun and wild and she knew people that we knew. She was the exact woman your husband leaves you for when you look like me. I always think about this thing Kim Gordon said after Thurston Moore cheated on her: "It ended in kind of a normal way—midlife crisis, starstruck woman." There is a normal way of things. I knew that. I'd been bracing for it for years.

A lot of bad stuff happened during the months they were entangled. They were, without a doubt, the worst months of my life. But all you need to know for the purposes of this story is that Aham violated my trust badly, there was a period of utter chaos, and I had every reason to leave him.

On the worst night, after we'd fought and he'd stormed out, I sat on the couch, perfectly still. Our old house popped and cracked. I stopped crying. Some time passed, and I noticed a shift inside—the stillness of a fawn replaced with the stillness of an empty cathedral or a great tortoise. I examined this new self curiously. Was she me? If she was me, then who was I? What was I doing? How had my life turned into this? What was I clinging to?

I realized that I was still thinking about him. I was sick of thinking about him. Forget what was "fair" or what I "deserved" as a martyred dishrag of a wife—what did *I want* as an adult, a woman, a person?

───

The documentary *In a Dream* chronicles the life and work of Philadelphia mosaic artist Isaiah

Zagar and his wife, Julia. I reviewed it when I ran the film section at *The Stranger*, in 2009. The Zagars' son, Jeremiah, directed the film, and at first, it seems the kind of predictable but sweet hagiography one might make about one's beloved parents: tiny elfin couple in lifelong love, a perfect match, making art and meaning in their city. Julia kept their mundane life running so that Isaiah, the great artist, was free to focus on his higher calling, his Magic Gardens, his mental illness, his difficult genius. Her gift to the world was making his gift to the world possible, and that made her happy.

About halfway through, I wrote in my review, the film becomes something else entirely:

> Julia notes that Isaiah is becoming more and more detached from actual life. Then, almost off-hand, at a coffee shop, Isaiah mentions on camera that he's having an affair and the film transforms into the disintegration of a love—one that is physically manifested all over Philadelphia.

I'd forgotten all about it, but *In a Dream* surfaced in my consciousness somewhere in the darkness of 2019, the ghost of a memory. I didn't remember the Zagars' names, or what city they lived in, or the name of the movie, or that I'd written about it. But I knew that I'd once watched a documentary about a couple in love whose story takes a hard turn at the midpoint, I remembered how brave I'd thought it was to commit so much pain to film, and I remembered that the wife was angry, but the wife stayed.

Imagine my surprise, then, to discover my old review—written two years before Aham and I even started dating—and in it a mirror of my own marriage:

> Julia looms immense in Isaiah's work. He has done thousands of portraits of her, he says, some several stories tall. Her face is everywhere, and when he speaks of her and how she loves him it's with a guileless, silly exuberance. "He can't function, you know, too well in this world. He's kind of a rare flower. A thistle, maybe," Julia says. "I was his reality base, and he was my bird. He flew around."
>
> What an honor, Julia seemed to say, to be

entrusted with the care of the rare flower, to subsume yourself into the earth so the magnificent bird has someplace to rest. Women are expected to be honored to care for the great man. How many times had I told myself the same thing? How much had that factored into my determination to stay—some noble duty to forgive the erratic passions of my fragile, tortured artist?

I knew Aham loved me as much as the bird loves the nest. But was that enough?

"I don't want to be the support system for the great artist," I told my therapist Judith.

"That's right," she said.

"I AM THE GREAT ARTIST."

Judith smiled and pumped her fists in the air. "Yes, yes, yes!"

~~~

You are predisposed to sympathize with me. This is my book, and you're reading it. Presumably, you like me. At the very least, you're stuck in my head, and I control the aperture. In many ways, my side of the story is easier to understand than Aham's—mine hews to cultural norms about heterosexual love and relationships while his challenges them. Also, he was a big asshole and put me through hell. I could write this book in a way that would make you hate Aham's guts and pity me for staying with him. Or I could write it in a way that makes him sound tortured yet wise and makes me sound like a codependent freak. It's all true. All nonfiction is actually fiction.

Aham came home around dawn. I was still awake, sitting in the dark living room. I reached for my adult voice and she was there.

"I will leave you if you don't stop."

"I know," he said, hanging his head.

"I might leave you anyway."

"I know," he said.

"You don't just get to have everything you want."

"I know," he said. "I'm sorry."

I watched the wheels turn in his head as he stared into my eyes. He knew me better than anyone. He peered inside me, and I saw him break. What had he seen? How much strength had I been hiding away?

HWY 2, LITCHFIELD, NEBRASKA

I'm finding that I really didn't understand how much open space there is in this country. It feels endless, and living in the city in the twenty-first century, you feel like everything is over. Like we used it all up. But this is all here! Why is it just here? Surely there's some kind of hope, if all of this is here? But anyway, the thing I keep thinking about is the idea of infinity. Maybe I'm remembering this wrong, but there's this idea that inside of a cell the distance between things is so vast. It's as big as the universe.

I mean, isn't that true? Because you can always cut something in half and half again, and half again and half again. There's no point where the space between ceases to exist. You can always go half again. You know, infinity's easy to understand in the opposite direction, relatively. Space goes out and out and out forever. But the idea of zero?

America feels so small sometimes, so crowded and so angry. But then there's infinite space inside of us, you know? Infinite space for me to be apart from my emotions and infinite space as a refuge. I feel comforted by this space, by the emptiness of it.

Uphill Battle

I snore. According to Ahamefule, I snore so violently that it is a federal crime. According to my doctor, I do not have sleep apnea and do not need or qualify for a sleep apnea device. According to my dentist, I have the strongest and beefiest tongue alive, which will not stop planking against my soft palate while I sleep and occluding my airway with its massive lats (this is also the reason I had to get braces—my tongue BULLIED my teeth out of place!!!).

At some point, my snoring—imperceptibly, with no clear announcement—became a major flash point in my marriage. My snores were at their shrillest when I was at the shit-pit nadir of my depression and things were particularly bad between Aham and me. My snoring became a physical manifestation of the resentment seething between us at night—his anger that I seemed to have given up on youth and life and growth and hope and fun and myself, and my anger that his response to my despair was to pull away.

Our nights unfolded one of three ways: He would "accidentally" fall asleep on the couch and never come up to bed; he would wake me up in the middle of the night in a panic attack, repeating, "I can't do this! I don't know what I'm going to do! I have to sleep! I have to sleep!" and I would say, "I'm sorry!" and he would say, "I'M NOT MAD AT YOU," and I would run to the guest room and cry; or, most often, I would lie awake all night, terrified of sleep, because with sleep came the buzz saw that was vivisecting my marriage.

Snoring felt increasingly like being fat—a thing that I could not help, that I did not do on purpose, that is literally impossible to "fix" in any immediate way, but that people were SCREAMING at me to change OR ELSE. And snoring and fatness felt connected in a physical way too. I was certain that I snored *because* I was fat (society tells us this with confidence, and we accept it unquestioningly, as though thin people never snore), one impossible fix contingent on another impossible fix. The cure for snoring was surely weight loss, the one thing I had failed at for thirty years. Snoring came as yet another reason to bulldoze my fat body, just when I was trying so hard to love her.

COVID hit and Aham and I, in our shaky peace, decamped to my family's log cabin a few hours outside of Seattle. We fell into a routine of all the classic COVID things: baking bread, crocheting blankets, planting a garden, foraging for nettles, taking long walks in the woods, playing HORSE at the community center, seeing a bear, getting to know the neighbors, picking up newts we found on the road and later learned can secrete enough toxin to kill one thousand men,[1] somehow not dying from picking up the newt, and, despite my protestations, walking to the beach and back twice a day.

The cabin sits on a bluff a few hundred feet above Hood Canal, a hook-shaped inlet of the Salish Sea. Our property includes a sliver of wild beach, and to get there, you have to walk about a mile along a dirt road, sloping steeply down to sea level. The most brutal part of the walk to

---

1. The newt said I get to pick which ones!!!

the beach is the last fifty yards or so, when the grade must be 40 percent at least (a number I got by googling "how steep can a hill be before it becomes a cliff"). Coming back up is gruesome. Oh, were you feeling refreshed from swimming? Not anymore! Now you're gross! Sincerely, Satan himself.

Walking up hills sucks. It's like regular walking except as soon as you do it, you start to die. And there's nothing more humiliating than starting to die in front of your friends when you were doing something as ordinary as going out to dinner. When I'm walking flat, I can masquerade as a chill regular person with regular abilities and regular breathing. It's amazing, actually—it's like I'm playing a sport with a bunch of thin people, and I am as good at the sport as them! We can all go the same pace, and sometimes I'm even faster because I have long, strong triceratops legs. But as soon as we hit a slope, I'm Grimace again, a great big sloppy meat wagon hauling an extra 150 pounds of purple pork chop slop up that hill and wheezing and gasping and moving slower and slower and puffing and apologizing and falling awkwardly, inexorably behind. Kill me first!

Drown me in McDonald's Sweet & Sour! Is there anything worse than when your LUNGS HURT just because you ASKED THEM TO DO THEIR JOB? And THIN PEOPLE ARE WATCHING?

I hated that hill so much that, until lockdown, I went years without seeing the beach. My favorite beach. In my twenties, I used to have parties out at the cabin—high school friends giddily home from college—and each day when it was time to go to the beach, I'd say I had cooking to do or cleaning, or I needed some alone time, and I'd sit at the cabin by myself in the quiet while everyone I loved swam and played without me on the beach where I swam and played as a child. I already felt old and defeated by my body, even in my twenties, and I couldn't bring myself to walk back up that hill in the midst of them—my peers who seemed so strong, or at least so "normal"—and let them hear my breathing, see me lag behind. My incapable body felt alien, out of place in the mob of youth, and I hated the thought that they'd pity me or feel some animal alarm at my weakness. One year, someone heard that Hood Canal had bioluminescent algae at night, so then night walks to the beach became tradition too. I declined and stayed home, alone, in the dark, as they ran giggling away in their headlamps.

To this day, I haven't seen the glow.

～～～

Aham and I were right at the precipice, looking over the edge. But the stillness of lockdown germinated some breakthroughs. We were in couples' therapy twice a week, grueling hours of "active listening," a deceptively simple technique in which one person gets to talk and the other person has to listen without interrupting, and then repeat back, in good faith, what they heard. If the active listener gets defensive or sarcastic or shitty or rolls their eyes (my last tether to sanity!), the therapist intervenes. "That's not what I heard him say." Well, fine. We both had to open up to the process and really listen. I hated it, but what else was I going to do—let the therapist be mad at me?? It's against my religion!

We went back to the beginning—every conversation we'd never been able to get through without me melting down and him storming out. Nine years of unfinished arguments, painstakingly dissected and sutured up. My worst vice is avoidance. Aham's is rationalization. It is difficult to get me to engage with hard things. It is difficult to get Aham to engage beyond his own perception. With a little professional help, and all our money, we began to find each other in the dark.

COVID dragged on. The fire of the previous year had burned so much resentment away. We looked at each other with younger eyes. We laughed, cooked, stayed up late, asked each other new questions. And every day, we walked up the hill from the beach.

At first, as I suspected, I could not do it at all. I had to stop and catch my breath three or four times just on that first fifty-yard climb. And once you get to the top of that, there's just more hill! But then, I'd think, *Literally what else was I doing?* The world was frozen. Maybe I could unfreeze myself. What if I could become a person who walked up hills?

Spending time on the beach was an obvious reward. We'd watch bald eagles snatch fish out of the water. Harbor seals followed us and stared, always curious. Once I saw a river otter acting like such a twitchy freakazoid that I emailed the Department of Fish and Wildlife because I thought it might have rabies (they wrote back: "I suspect that what you saw as a funny or odd walk was the otter defecating"). We swam in the cold water. We turned over rocks and snatched up tiny crabs. One summer day, at low tide, we walked for miles along the beach until we came to an oyster bed that must have had a million oysters.

And every time, when we'd had our fill of sun and water, we'd turn and walk up the hill. At first, I went at my own pace. Sometimes Aham would walk behind me, his hands on my rump, giving me a turbo boost like a football player pushing a sled. I'd giggle like a little kid. As I got the tiniest bit better each day, he'd issue me little challenges. Can I make it to the top of the steep part with only one break? Can I make it to the top of the steep part without stopping at all? Can I make it all the way to the field without stopping? The gate? The pickleball court? The creek? It happened so gradually and so miserably, the change was imperceptible, but at some point, I could walk the whole way home without stopping.

This hill that I'd been afraid of my whole life—this great symbol of my torpidity—it was conquered. And my snoring disappeared.

A clear airway and watching an otter defecate were just the icing on the cake: For the first time in my adult life, I *wanted* to use my body. If my fat body could learn to walk up a hill, maybe it could do all the other things that thin people get to do with their bodies. Maybe it could ski, hike, climb, paddle, ride a horse. Maybe I could stay fat and have it all.

That hill saved my life. Not because I was on the verge of a heart attack or whatever, but because over the years I'd lost or rejected all contact with my body as a movable, changeable, capable, alive thing. Life is change. The turnover of cells. Growing, stretching, searching, striving, adapting, even dying. Learning that my body could walk that hill every day was the first brick in rebuilding myself. My primal cells waking up, timidly dividing—in the most direct way available to us as animals, thickening that membrane between me and death.

Once I conquered the hill, I began searching out more lost indulgences: sleepy sex with Aham as the birds woke us, the breathless wait for an exquisite treat that I baked for myself, loud music, long naps, the exhaustion of a hard day's work, an icy swim after a sweaty hike. Aham and I kayaked out into Hood Canal, porpoises bubbling around us, crabs shuffling below. Moving my body stopped being something to check off a list. Exercise wasn't a penance for eating food; food wasn't a reward for exercise. It was like rejoining a lost world.

The truest thing I ever wrote about Aham was hidden in my silliest book, *Shit, Actually*, in an essay about *Honey, I Shrunk the Kids*. The chapter is one long, elaborate setup about a beleaguered wife discovering that, on top of everything else she's had to forgive, her no-good husband has gone and—here's the punch line—SHRUNK THE KIDS??? I wrote it in spring of 2020, between couples' therapy and trudging up the hill, an easter egg for myself.

> The true work of love isn't staying together when things are perfect; it's staying together even when

things are awful, weathering catastrophic mistakes (within reason) because, well, you decided to, and because you know the potential is as real as the now.... You're promising another person not just passion and love but a safety net, some degree of stability and certainty in a fucking terrible world. You're saying, "I promise I will stay with you even if you suck for a while," an almost narcotic comfort that we all deserve.... I dream of dying calloused and wise, of looking my husband in the eyes and saying, "Remember that thing we almost didn't survive? Aren't you so glad we did?"

HWY 2, SWEETWATER, NEBRASKA

Where am I? If you wanted to get here, you would have to fly to Lincoln, probably, and then drive hundreds of miles. I don't even see a regional airport. I mean, I guess the whole thing is a regional airport, if you're good at landing.

I passed a house that had two giant banners out on the fence. One said TRUMP 2020, and the second one said SAVE THE SANDHILLS, which must be those sand dunes that I drove through earlier. So that's a person who's rooted in this place, and they love this wild country that they live in, these empty Sandhills.

And yet their national politics are so destructive and brutal and devoid of real place. Like, Trump has no roots, you know what I mean? Because to have roots, you have to care about something. I used to think, at least George W. Bush could ride a horse. Trump can't do ANYTHING. You think Trump is gonna save your Sandhills? You think he gives a fuck about your Sandhills? That bitch is not gonna save your fucking Sandhills.

Too Big to Fail

When my car was repossessed in the middle of the night because I forgot to make the payments for six months (in my defense, I thought I was on autopay; in my prosecution, I had never set up autopay, and one would think I would know that), Judith suggested that perhaps I should get evaluated for ADHD. This was late 2019, early days for the social media ADHD self-diagnosis boom, a flood of memes and "It me" and "THIS!" that frays the edges of credibility (not *everything* can be because of your ADHD, babe!)[1] but offers a helpful truth at its heart: Many, many people, especially women, are struggling to live neurotypical lives with neurodivergent brains. As my

---

1. "Drinking orange juice is so ADHD!"
"Not wanting to get bit by a dog? Now that's ADHD."
"I heard a study that people with ADHD are more likely to use their stomach enzymes to metabolize food. That's SO me."
"Breathe underwater? Not with my ADHD-ass brain!"

passport was seized by the US government for unpaid taxes, I had to wonder...could I be one of them?

Growing up, I did not have ADHD. I was "lazy." I got good grades because I would get in trouble if I didn't, but I snaked through on charm and the bare minimum. I did as little homework as possible as late as possible so that I could spend the bulk of my time doing the things I loved: reading the same books over and over, making up fake languages with my friends, and hiding in the bushes taking notes on what my neighbors were doing. My room was not clean. I was never on time. My life was an entirely trouble-based economy. I exchanged goods (homework, chores, keeping it vaguely together) for currency (not getting in trouble).

Things got more chaotic when I grew up and was no longer a child with full-time parents / enforcers / administrative assistants: When you're twenty-five, no one gets mad at you if you don't clean your room. No one reminds you that you have to pay your car insurance every month. No one can tell you not to watch TV until after you get this week's column written.

For me, independence was liberating and catastrophic. Until just the last couple of years, everything you've ever read by me—especially the things you've loved the most—has been written between 5:00 and 7:00 a.m. hunched over my laptop on the living room couch while crying. Is that normal? To pull an all-nighter *every time you have to do anything?*

No, I always thought, in my mother's voice. It's not normal. *It's lazy.*

It didn't occur to me until years later that writing a column good enough for *The Guardian* or *The New York Times* in two hours on no sleep is actually really, really difficult. Wouldn't a lazy person want to make things easier, not harder?

When Judith introduced the notion I might have ADHD, a weight of shame I didn't even know I carried was vaporized. Could it be possible that all of it—the chaos, the lateness, the lifelong cascade of fuckups—wasn't a moral failing or a lack of willpower but just something about me, a neutral thing, a different kind of brain?

My primary care doctor referred me to a behavioral health specialist who listened to me sob about how hopeless and incompetent I have always felt, like I was not simply unskilled at administrative tasks but physically incapable of doing them, about how many thousands of dollars I've wasted in late fees and parking tickets and plastering over my own unforced errors, about how I regularly hurt people I love with my negligence, about how I have this suspicion that I might be someone special but undermine myself at every juncture. She nodded and took notes.

We had two half-hour telehealth sessions. Early on, she mentioned that for the evaluation, she needed to call my mom, because ADHD is "classified as a childhood disorder," so she had to verify that my symptoms had presented in childhood. I should have said no. I was nearly forty years old at this point. My word on my own life should be sufficient, and under no circumstances should a medical professional need to call my mommy. But I was a good girl! I didn't tell authority figures *no*.

My mom is not lazy. She is not scattered. She works hard and her house is clean, and then she gestures at her clean house and apologizes for what a mess it is. She always sends a thank-you card. I know that in some ways I am an alien to her, and my failings that she finds so unfathomable also spark her resentment, because they were my dad's failings too. Every task he and I failed to complete was something she had to take care of instead, and in a three-person household, that is—beep boop beep—100 percent of the tasks.

At our third session, the behavioral health specialist—a stranger who had spoken to me for sixty minutes spread out over a month—snapped her notebook shut and said, well, she didn't think I have ADHD because I'm "too successful." They get a lot of people these days, she told me, who are highly successful professionals just trying to get Adderall to "increase their potential." If I "really" had ADHD, I wouldn't have been able to write a book or make a TV show. I was welcome to schedule a follow-up appointment to talk about "tips and tricks" for time management.

That is, um, actually a really mean thing to say? I rarely get my feelings hurt in new ways—generally people hurt me in the old ways over and over. So this was at least novel! I didn't realize until this woman accused me of spoiled millennial pill-seeking that I had a lot riding on this diagnosis. I didn't want her to lie, I wasn't doctor-shopping, but I wanted an explanation. I'd felt briefly free from shame, and now the shame was back, except worse, because I'd also been diagnosed as a liar by a medical professional.

I booked the follow-up appointment, then canceled it. My life was a graveyard of failed tips and tricks. I didn't want any more. A woman whose dysfunction can be fixed by tips and tricks is not disordered, she is lazy, and her failure to fix herself is her own fault. I was right back where I started: There was nothing clinically wrong with me; there were no mitigating circumstances; there was nothing *not-normal* about my failures; I just fucking sucked. And there was no hope. I would never be more functional than this.

A few years later, I was poking around in the online portal for my doctor's office, trying to schedule a mammogram without having to make a phone call, and I noticed that in addition to the standard "Visit Summary" attached to each of my past appointments, there was now a second link called "Notes." I don't know if the patient privacy laws changed or what, but suddenly—without requesting it—I had access to every gossip item that every doctor had ever written about me in their nasty little burn book. I scrolled immediately to my ADHD assessment. (I was still mad.)

Right at the top, she'd written: "Lindy presents today for ADHD evaluation. Didn't complete the questionnaire, and 10 minutes late to visit."

LMAO. I understand that formal diagnosis is complex, but imagine typing that sentence and then deciding "patient is too successful."

It went on: "Lindy Lauren West presents for assessment regarding inattention and anxiety. Symptoms appear to be moderately severe. So afraid of people not liking her or abandoning her, tries to go out of her way to keep people. Overextends herself in ways that are not necessary. Very likable."

Sorry, if there was an absolutely blistering read of my darkest pathologies in there, I'm not aware of it, because I forgot everything she said before "very likable"!!!!!!!!! VERY likable? Okay, queen! Why didn't HIPAA tell me that my patient notes were full of *the highest accolades*? I always assumed doctors were typing, "Fat slut presents with stinky ass disease, advised her to JOG to the garbage and eat shit!" Was it even legal for a doctor to give you a compliment on anything other than weight loss from an undiagnosed wasting disease?

I clicked another link and found the thing I was really after—the recap of the behavioral health analyst's conversation with my mother, the one that I suspected had gotten me fired from having ADHD. This was it. I was sure my mom had sold me out. She's old-school and therapy-averse—did she even believe in ADHD? She probably told this lady that I was just too lazy to manage my time—more propaganda from Big Tips and Tricks.

The window popped open, and I read: "Mother reports that she was a very good student in school. Always the best. Always seemed prepared. Wasn't very disciplined, was a little sporadic but eventually got things done. Described pt as a people pleaser at times. Overall, never suspected any concerns for attention or ADHD. Could read by the time she was 4–5 years old."

Oh, right, I thought as my eyes filled with tears, a little bit embarrassed and a little bit soothed. *My mom loves me.* It's not her responsibility to tell the behavioral health specialist anything but her honest perception, which is that her daughter was a very good student, always seemed prepared, wasn't very disciplined, but was "always the best." It's not her responsibility to ferret out ADHD in a little girl trying desperately to make everyone think she's fine. What a good mom. How could she be expected to know what it feels like inside my head?

And then I got to the big finale, the reason why I don't have ADHD, according to this lady:

> Based on patient report and collateral from patient's mom, there does not appear to be long-term history that would suggest ADHD symptoms in childhood. Patient clearly struggles currently, but these symptoms appear to be more closely related to anxiety and unstructured/unmanageable environmental factors. There is not enough information to suggest ADHD is a concern.

Patient was tearful and anxious upon the conclusion of today's visit. I validated patient in her emotions, provided empathic and reflective listening,[2] and expressed that there are still some options to help her manage, but that these issues do not seem consistent with ADHD, but rather mismanaged anxiety. No further evaluation needed, as patient does not meet criteria for ADHD.

I mean, sure. This lady has a PhD and no agenda against me. I trust that she believes her assessment is correct, and she probably is getting fifty basket cases a day begging for Vyvanse because they resonated with a meme they saw. What I've learned in the years since my tearful and anxious telehealth appointment is this: I don't care what that lady thinks!!! I've been fighting for decades to stop constructing my sense of self based on external feedback, so why would I let any stranger tell me I'm wrong about how my brain feels? Self-diagnosis is a core principle of intersectional disability justice, because not everyone can access formal diagnosis, not everyone wants one, not everyone is made safer by one, and arguably, the whole paradigm is

---

2. This verdict is not unanimous.

tainted. In a culture that allots credibility on a sliding scale based on phenotypic proximity to Chris Pratt, trusting people to know who they are isn't just kind, it's liberatory. If you resonated with a meme you saw, I believe you.

To be clear, I'm not saying that I did a spiritual brain scan (verdict: GOOFY) and determined that I definitely have ADHD and if the pharmacist refuses to give me vibes-based amphetamines it's a hate crime. I was raised to trust medical professionals. I'm on high alert for my own bullshit. I don't know if I have misunderstood-girl ADHD or untreated anxiety or long COVID or perimenopause or a hippocampus full of microplastics or some proprietary blend. I suspect that the mind isn't so cleanly delineated. But I know I spent forty years loathing myself for being a lazy slob, and then one day, I let myself imagine that I might just be different—whether that difference has a label or not—and it was like taking my first breath.

There's SOMETHING wrong with me, and no one can ever take that away.

Precious Moments

June 15, 2021

I spent the night at a motel in Lincoln, one of those cute liberal-bubble university towns, and wished I could stay longer. But I had business in Lawrence, Kansas, so after a breakfast of corned beef hash and a big, frosted sugar cookie and a second big, frosted sugar cookie, I was on the road.

I was going to stay with my second cousin Jill and her partner, Ehren, in their farmhouse just outside Lawrence. Jill and Ehren lived in Washington for a while, so I knew them, but not that well. Our great-grandparents had ten kids who each had ten kids who each had ten kids who each had ten kids (BASICALLY), so our family reunions might as well be San Diego Comic-Con, except Nathan Fillion never shows up.

There's an obligatory intimacy around family

that I'm not sure is justified, and it makes me anxious. I have trouble feeling at ease with people I've been close with for decades. Distant relatives are strangers with unknown politics who I'm supposed to hug and then try to explain what my job is (???), and I haven't yet decided whether or not it actually means much to share small amounts of DNA with people. I act like my Norwegian heritage is this huge part of who I am, but why? Even at family reunions, I'm still basically a tourist. Am I claiming something that isn't mine because I come from a colonized place with a dead soul and no identity? Scientists say MAYBE!!

Sometimes I wonder: Do I actually know how to connect with other people, or am I faking it?

But it's easy to love Jill. She's silly and disarming and she loves talking shit. The night I arrived, she took me swimming in a man-made lake, and I grilled her for all the gossip about the Midwest branch of our family. Ehren made corn on the cob, and the cat fell asleep on my lap.

That night, I had a nightmare that Aham told me he loved Roya more than he loved me. I woke up crying and resisted reaching out to

Aham for comfort. Not that he wouldn't have given it to me, but I didn't want to be that person anymore—fragile, enmeshed, dependent. Instead, I switched on the light and wrote in my journal: "Aham is not my lifeline to emotional regulation. My refuge is inside." It wasn't true, but sometimes in mental health, we fake it till we make it.

Jill took the next day off so we could hang out. We went to an optician in downtown Lawrence to repair my glasses, which had lost a screw and become wiggly. As we waited, Jill said, "This is my COUSIN, and SHE'S FAMOUS," just to torture me, but the girls at the glasses store had watched *Shrill*! They were genuinely excited! I put another tally in the "I do exist" column. "I don't exist" remained in the lead, but we couldn't sleep on the underdog yet!

Jill and I ran around Lawrence, and it was easy. Is that how family feels to everyone else?

My second night in Lawrence, I had dinner with Corissa Enneking, Jay Aprileo, and Meghan Tonjes, three fat creators I know from the internet. We sat outside in the warm breeze and talked about the strange niche of being a public fat person—a defining force in my adult life but something I rarely get to discuss with anyone who understands. These three were just so *there for each other*, and I thought about how easy and healing it was to connect with people if you're brave enough to let them know you.

I said I was trying to figure out how to feel sexy again, and I thought maybe I'd start a secret OnlyFans. But I didn't want to show my face, and I didn't want to be naked, and what would I DO on it? "Anything," Corissa cut me off before I even finished the question. "Men will pay to watch you do anything. You don't understand. They want to watch you do ANYTHING. Vacuuming, playing video games, cutting your toenails."

"I'm not sure if cutting my toenails on camera is going to help me reconnect with my sexuality," I said.

"Maybe not," Corissa laughed. "But you're leaving money on the table."

They walked me out to my van and I noticed Fat Daddy's honey jar still stuck in the cup holder. Impulsively, I offered it to Jay and Corissa as a goodbye present, as though the power of Fat

Daddy might cement our friendship, preserving this moment in its amber depths forever.

"Hell yeah!" said Jay.

"Drive safe," said Meghan. "I gotta go clip my toenails on OnlyFans."

As I packed up to leave the next morning, Ehren showed me how to pick mulberries, apologizing that the birds also enjoyed mulberries and had crapped them all over BAAA. Jill demanded I stop at the Precious Moments Chapel in Carthage, Missouri, on my way to Arkansas, and I promised her I would. I'm only medium into kitsch, but I couldn't live with another Boneyard Creation Museum air ball on my stat sheet.

If you're not familiar, perhaps because you hate your grandma, Precious Moments figurines are collectible ceramic child statues in various poses and costumes, such as "clown," "hugging a goose," "praying," "looking into a wishing well," and "Indigenous baby petting a wolf."

In 1989, at the height of the Precious Moments Company's power, they opened a Christian theme park in the woods of southwestern Missouri. Most of the attractions are now closed, but the crown jewel remains open to the public: the Precious Moments Chapel. It's like a regular church, except that all the murals and frescoes and bronze reliefs and stained glass windows and elaborately carved doors feature Precious Moments babies acting out various scenes from the Bible. Precious Moments Adam and Eve nude in the garden. Precious Moments Cain killing Precious Moments Abel. Precious Moments Israelites enslaved by Precious Moments Pharaoh. Precious Moments Jesus being betrayed by Precious Moments Judas.

Behind the altar, a floor-to-ceiling mural called *Hallelujah Square* depicts "Heaven through the eyes of a child," according to Precious Moments founder and artist Samuel Butcher. Basically, it's a bunch of (dead????) Precious Moments children waiting in line to get into heaven, while a bunch of other (dead?????????) children are waiting inside to welcome them. The woman next to me was crying, but, like, because she loved it. There were thirty-five school shootings in the USA in 2021. Missouri has some of the laxest gun laws in the country. I looked at the mural and thought that maybe it's happier for children to live.

But I get it. I'm happy for that woman. It's important to find touchstones that make life sweet and bearable in the now; perhaps later, we'll all be strong enough to reach for something beyond comfort.

Grenade

I went to the doctor to try to explain what I wanted. Not surgery. Not deliberate weight loss. Not anyone explaining to me about portion size, talking to me about carbs, or otherwise treating me like a fucking idiot who was just born. Is there a kind of person who doesn't believe that thin people are better than fat people but who will just tell me what to eat and when so I don't have to make emotionally complex choices that trigger my traumas all day every day and also build in indulgences that honor my very genuine and well-deserved worship of food?

My doctor is always busy. She is perpetually booked out at least a month, sometimes three. I am not sure I have ever met her. I always tell the clinic that I'm fine seeing whichever provider is available the soonest, because I only make doctor's appointments when I'm having extreme fear or extreme pain. No time to wait for the

WORLD'S MOST POPULAR DOCTOR to be available! For my "I think I'm addicted to yummy muffins" appointment (which I tacked on to a Pap smear), I was assigned a slightly fatphobic but reassuringly no-nonsense nurse practitioner whom I'd seen once or twice before.

The intake nurse asked if it was okay if a medical student observed my appointment. I said, "OF COURSE!" because I care about education and it seemed like the cool thing to say in the moment, but as I waited for them to come in, I realized that maybe I didn't want to tell a random medical student about my debilitating fixation on whipped cream and then let her look at my vagina.

But it was too late, so I sobbed to them about how complicated it is to be a famous fat person who wants to change how she eats without participating in diet culture and betraying all of her fat angels. The nurse practitioner had no fucking idea what I was talking about. The medical student was really sweet and she had watched *Shrill*, which was nice, but almost worse, because I felt like I also had to apologize to her for being a fraud. The LNP listened to my whole monologue and then said she agreed with me that it would be a good idea for me to lose weight and suggested I try Wegovy.

The emoticon is a lost art, but dare I say… linemouth????

:-|

I'm not going to sit here and say that I haven't been tempted by the weight loss industry's magic fixes. It's exhausting to be fat. The world is hard and mean. If you're at a low point in your life when the billionth person suggests you get bariatric surgery, you might say, "Fuck it, I'm not strong enough for this anymore," and make the appointment. In fact, I'd done exactly that in 2019—losing weight is the obvious prescription when your husband suddenly has two new girlfriends. I was booked for a consultation for April 2020 and, well, it got canceled.

Instead, I spent eight months in the woods hiking and swimming and hauling firewood and planting a garden and eating eggs from our neighbors' chickens, and I grew strong and happy and felt intensely grateful that I hadn't risked my life to have my stomach removed for cosmetic reasons, and then I went on my road trip and stretched beyond anything I'd thought my mind or body were capable of and truly felt like I'd reached something close to Nirvana, or what Herman Melville called one's "insular Tahiti."

And eventually, because mental health isn't linear, I crashed and slid so far back into the Hunt's Snack Pack Pudding Blues that I couldn't move or work and I slept on the couch so nobody would touch me or hear me snore and I completely forgot how to eat and I was back on my ten-a-day seasonal pumpkin-shaped Reese's grind and throwing away my empties at the park again, the whole deal, and I'd sit frozen in the car for hours and was gaining weight fast and losing strength and my whole body hurt again and I felt like a dead dog if dogs could feel shame.

But this time, having had some experience with this particular mental meat grinder, I went straight to the doctor and begged for help. And this bitch said WEGOVY.

JUST WHAT MY FRAGILE PSYCHE NEEDED. AS PROMISED, YOU HAVE CERTAINLY DONE NO HARM.

Wegovy is in the same family of drugs as Ozempic—a compound called semaglutide that slows digestion, originally developed to treat type-2 diabetes, but approved in 2021 for weight loss. Pharmaceutical companies quickly began targeting fat influencers, paying them to pivot their body-positivity or plus-size fashion accounts to weight loss accounts. And lots of people took them up on it. It's hard to live publicly in a fat body, and it's hard to make rent in the twilight of empire.

Take the injection, get the surgery, Godspeed—I truly believe in bodily autonomy and I get the temptation and the desperation to be treated well and I wish every fat person peace and healing—but personally, I'd draw the line at marketing weight loss products and procedures to the vulnerable people on whose trust and wallets you've built your career. Is it so hard to lose weight, for any reasons you like, without undermining everyone else's healing by making it aspirational? Diet culture ruined my life in ways I'm still discovering. Full recovery is impossible. You'll never catch me posting before and afters.

Sitting in that exam room in spring 2022, I had five minutes of temptation again until

PRAISE SAINT GUY FIERI I found out this shit is $1,000 a month. I don't have an extra $1,000 a month, but even if I did, I'm not gonna pay $1,000 to hate food! The nurse practitioner said she could probably find me some samples, and she knew about a program that would bring it down to $200, but I'd snapped out of it by then. This wasn't me. Even if it didn't cost $12,000 a year, I didn't want to feel sick every day for the rest of my life to pander to an unjust world. Wegovy has been approved for children as young as twelve, when we don't even know the long-term physical effects, let alone the mental ones. Look how fucked up I am, and I didn't have to live with the knowledge that my parents took out a second mortgage so that I could vomit up everything I ate. Prescribing weight loss to kids is a moral catastrophe.[1] A few months later, a wave of stories about "stomach paralysis" hit the news cycle, and I lit a candle to my financial insolvency. If $1,000 had been loose change to me, who knows where I'd be now! Luckily, my

---

1. Putting this here so it's copyrighted and Big Pharma can't use it: Wee-govy. Mounjunior.

bank account ain't jigglin', so my stomach is still squigglin'. Just like my Grandpa Ole used to say.

I told the nurse practitioner that I didn't want the Wegovy and begged for the thing I had originally requested—a referral to a nutritionist—and she shrugged and gave me a list of practitioners and only one of them didn't mention weight loss on their website, so I picked that one. Her name was Grace.

I found the appointment request form and poured my heart out:

> Hello! I was referred to you by my primary care doctor, and I'm hoping to book an appointment with Grace. I've recently been coming to terms with the fact that I have a disordered relationship with food that feels out of control to me. I use food as my primary coping mechanism, and when my mental health is poor, I am unable to make conscious choices about what I eat—I am compelled to seek indulgence in every moment (to

the point that the indulgence ceases to be enjoyable or satisfying), and if I don't have good/special/high-value (whatever you want to call it) foods in the house, I feel emotionally unsafe.

  I don't feel like I need to lose weight, per se, although incidentally, I do find that when I am in a good place with food/depression, my weight drops, which feels like this heavier body is a physical manifestation of my depression—I am wearing my emotional pain, and I would rather not do that anymore. So maybe that does mean that I want to lose weight. I'm not sure how to navigate that. Five-ish years ago, I got so depressed and gained so much weight that I had some mobility challenges, and through a lot of therapy (and the forced downtime of early COVID), I managed to pull myself out of it for about a year and a half. That was an eye-openingly joyful time. My pain disappeared, and I felt strong and capable and young and alive. But gradually over the past year, I've lost my grip on my authority and routine and fallen deeply into old patterns, which scares me. I've probably gained 40 pounds since last summer, and I am in constant pain again. I just would like to be mobile and active and retain full participation in life. And be able to genuinely enjoy food!

All of this is complicated by the fact that I am a public figure in the fat-positivity/fat-liberation space, and feel a great deal of guilt over somehow betraying my community and submitting to diet culture. But I don't think I am! I think there's space for me to build/repair my own relationship with food in keeping with my values. I've been nervous about pursuing professional assistance on this, so I was relieved to see Health at Every Size among your services.

Adult Braces

> I am worn out from a lifetime of being infantilized and condescended to about food and exercise and was worried I wouldn't be able to find someone with literacy in these issues. So thank you!

Grace wrote back the next day with some scheduling options and then said:

> Lastly, I love your work, Lindy! I did a double take when I saw your name in my inbox. I've learned a lot from you.

I never watched *Jersey Shore*, but during the pandemic, my stepdaughter got hooked on it and exposed me to secondhand *Jersey Shore* (there is no safe level!). In one episode, the guys bring two girls home from a bar. One of the girls is hot, and the other one is a "grenade," which is what the Jersey boys call fat girls. The boys run around the house trying to avoid/distract the grenade so that one of them can have sex with the hot girl, and it's presented as clowny high jinks. But if you really listen, you can tell they're also tremendously angry at the grenade for being there, because she has absolutely no value to them. There's a hostility to the jokes, a rage familiar from my own youth.

None of that was surprising. The part that had me spinning was that this woman was not even fat. I could barely understand the plot of the episode, because I couldn't tell the hot girl and the grenade apart. And that episode came out in, what, 2010? I was almost thirty years old at the time, and that was the state of television??? I didn't remember it being that bad. I was only six or seven years away from making television myself. How much worse must TV have been for fat people when I was an actual child?

Vinny and Pauly D's attempt to smush sent me into a grief spiral. How different might I be now if when I was a teenager I'd had someone to look up to, one fat person I really connected with who was modeling basic happiness and self-respect? I'm still searching for that—I still crave reassurance that I'm okay, that I don't need to change. And then the real horror dawned: *Oh no. It's me. I'm the person. I'm that person that people look to, but I'm not even healed.* It felt like on

Looney Tunes when Wile E. Coyote would climb up and up and up a rope, all the way into the clouds, and he'd get to the top and discover it wasn't tied to anything at all. He would look down, he would look at the camera, and then he would fall. One of the sources my eating disorder therapist used to learn about well-adjusted, self-respecting fat people was me. I taught my eating disorder therapist a lot. I'm holding my own rope.

Grace's email continued:

> I can definitely imagine reaching out to providers feels extra vulnerable given your work/status—so again, thank you for trusting me. We can talk about all of this and more in session, but I also want to validate that it doesn't sound like you are betraying anyone here.
>
> It sounds like you are continuing to do this tricky body liberation work, which includes making space for all the nuances, contradictions, and uncomfortable feelings related to

being in a body, having feelings, and eating food.

I soon learned that what Grace was offering wasn't a meal plan, it was therapy with a focus on food—convenient timing, as my beloved Judith had just retired. After a few sessions, Grace diagnosed me with binge eating disorder. "I don't really binge, though," I protested, and she explained that it doesn't work like that—the salient factor is that I feel a lack of power around food. Then she paused. "Have you ever been evaluated for ADHD?"

I told Grace that a mean behavioral specialist had hurt my feelings and accused me of shopping for speed and being "too successful" to have ADHD, which sucked, because I feel like I'm punching way below my potential due to the fact that I sabotage everything I touch, and Grace was like, "I've never heard of a clinician calling someone's mom. I'm so sorry that happened to you." You're so sorry that *who* happened to *what*?!?! Heaven 911, are you missing an angel??

Grace said that people with ADHD are more likely to have eating disorders in general, but particularly BED. She said there was a lot we could work on to address both at the same time. She was very chill about it, which made me feel like perhaps I wasn't a swirling black hole to nowhere at the bottom of the ocean. And then, just like that, I was in eating disorder recovery.

One of the first things Grace taught me was that it is normal and okay to *want* to lose weight—it is not a betrayal. It's a rational response to the way the world treats fat people. Like any animal, we are not wired to suffer. Of course we yearn for relief. What's not healthy for me, mentally or physically, is to *try* to lose weight. There is no diet that doesn't stigmatize eating, no meal plan that doesn't estrange the dieter from her own hunger. The cure for my eating disorder, Grace explained, was eating.

If you've ever needed a case study for how medical bias harms fat people, let me reiterate: I went to the doctor seeking help with anxiety around food and body, her solution was to put me on weight loss injections, and when I got a second opinion, I was diagnosed with an eating disorder. What if I'd just taken the Wegovy? I can think of few things that would have driven me deeper into disorder than committing wholeheartedly to the narrative that my body needed to be fixed, feeling repulsed by food indefinitely, and losing weight only to gain it back, and then some, after I ran out of thousand-dollar bills.

Man Cave

June 17, 2021

Just over the Missouri-Arkansas border, I stopped at Crystal Bridges in Bentonville, one of the most important museums of American art in the country nestled incongruously in the thick jungle of Arkansas. Bentonville is also the birthplace and national headquarters of the Walmart corporation, and the superstore's billions established and continue to fund Crystal Bridges.

The museum is a marvel, a nearly circular wood-and-glass crescent cradling a still, green, creek-fed pool. I sat by a picture window and ate hush puppies and stared at the water, then wandered slowly through the galleries. An exhibit of preindustrial landscape paintings took my breath away, arrestingly beautiful, a portal to a time when my country's sacred secrets were still untainted and untamed. *Yes*, I thought. *That's the America I'm searching for.*

The museum labels told a different story, as good curatorial work does. These paintings were made by white artists, I learned, well after colonial settlements and even railroads had spread across the continent. These selfsame landscapes, if depicted honestly at the time of their creation, would have been riddled with evidence of human habitation. Instead, the artists painted nature as though humans had never set foot there—perhaps out of nostalgia for something lost, or guilt for actions profane and irreversible.

I thought about the ways that I have wanted to disappear and wondered if all this denial of the damage that white people have done to the earth, all the way up to denying climate change, is some sort of large-scale self-negation. We pine for wild spaces, but instead of protecting them, we paint simulacra that are sick with lies. We erase human impact. Even conservative white people must know, on some level, that we are fundamentally destructive. It would make sense if Republicans in particular had a very deep, unexamined self-loathing, a conviction that they should not and do not exist.

Maybe everything they do is acting out against that feeling—the opposite of "leave no trace." Carve your mark bloody. But then, paradoxically, erase the evidence, paint over it, and say you did nothing wrong. Engineer calamity to prove you exist, and then erase yourself from accountability. Why erase yourself? It has to be because you're ashamed.

~~~~~

It was another few hours to my next destination, Eureka Springs, Arkansas, a Victorian resort town tucked into a fold of the Ozarks. I booked a room at the Crescent Hotel, built in 1886 and allegedly the most haunted hotel in America. Top-billed ghosts include a poltergeist named Michael, a nurse pushing a gurney, a Victorian man looking for the hot woman he saw yesterday, and an entity that tucks visitors into bed if their comforter falls off. I got there early enough to either swim at the hotel or explore the town, nicknamed "Little Switzerland of America," because its picturesque streets are built into the steep hillside. Swimming sounded better than climbing stairs after a long, sticky day of driving, so I opted for the pool.

It was the wrong choice. Tragically, the modestly sized pool had been taken over by a family that was there for... my best guess would be... KKK wedding? The revelers were drunk, loud, and plentiful. They'd brought a Bluetooth speaker to the pool (firing squad) and were listening to a genre of music I'd truly never encountered before, and one I hope to never meet again, some sort of racist Four Loko cowboy death metal. I texted Aham about it and he wrote back, **The difference between Seattle and Arkansas is that in Seattle, the racists listen to hip-hop.** I sat in the shallow end of the pool, as far from the speaker as possible, closed my eyes, and tried to relax.

A kid was screaming at his Uncle Larry to do a backflip into the water. He kept using some slang word—"Uncle Larry, rock a backflip!" or "Uncle Larry, shred a backflip!"—like that, but stupider. Uncle Larry, a steadfastly land-based mammal, did not want to shred a backflip. Uncle Larry was not in a swimsuit. He was busy day-drinking and trying to enjoy the MP3s he'd downloaded straight from Satan's ass. Once in a while, to get this kid off his back, Uncle Larry would be like, "You do it!" and then the kid would yell, "I can't do a backflip. I can only do a front flip!" and then he would do a front flip, and Uncle Larry would be like, "AWWW YEAH," and peace would reign for a time.

But for some reason, this kid couldn't let it go. Summer vacation, and, perhaps, life itself, would be a bust if he didn't get to see Uncle Larry's bodacious moves. Always, he'd start again: "Uncle Larry, Uncle Larry, Uncle Larry, backflip! Uncle Larry!" And Uncle Larry kept yelling, "No, I haven't had enough beers! Tell someone to bring me another beer, then I'll do it!"

Eventually, the kid made his fatal mistake. He started making *bok bok bok* noises at Uncle Larry. I guess he didn't know that nobody calls Uncle Larry a chicken and lives to tell the tale! Our once jovial Lawrence turned hard as stone and said, "HEY. THAT'S IT. You're gonna be BANNED FROM THE MAN CAVE if you don't cut it out. You're gonna have to sleep in the hall. You have to sleep in the hallway. No more man cave. No more man cave!!!" As if by magic, that kid shut his yapper and didn't make a peep for the rest of the night.

I floated on my back, letting the water fill my ears, enjoying the relative calm. I hope he didn't get exiled from the man cave, though. I hope he got to stay.

I slept peacefully, no ghosts, and got back on the road early the next morning. I was driving through the Ozarks on my way to Nashville, listening to a playlist my friend Charlotte made me, when a Linda Ronstadt cover of "Desperado" came on. Unexpectedly, when she got to the line, "You've got to let somebody love you before it's too late," I found myself in tears.

This is one of the great perks of the solo road trip—no one can see you be extremely embarrassing to an Eagles property! Who among us hasn't heard "Desperado" 7,750,000 times in her life? But in that moment, it got me.

For as long as I could remember, I'd felt unloved, and for most of my marriage, I just assumed that it was Aham's fault. He must not be loving me correctly, or else I would feel it. His love was thin and weak, because on some level, it was a lie. No matter how much he poured into me, it drained out the bottom.

But Linda Ronstadt slapped me across the face—what if I'm not a shitty, broken pit with a drain at the bottom but a perfectly intact vessel with a wall around it? What if it wasn't Aham failing to pour enough love into me but me refusing to let it in?

Early on, our couples' therapist brought up attachment theory (a framework for categorizing how humans bond with each other) and suggested that I was experiencing something called "anxious attachment," which meant that my fear of abandonment controlled my whole life and caused me to cling to Aham like a sobbing barnacle. I remember feeling my body flood with light. That was me! That was my diagnosis. As I'd known all along, all this conflict and agony was not my fault—I simply did not feel *secure attachment*. I did not feel secure attachment because Aham was not giving it to me.

But attachment theory is not a diagnosis any more than gravity is the reason somebody jumps off a bridge. Attachment theory is a framework for thinking about relationships and trauma—a place to start, a point of leverage. My job, as the less securely attached partner, was not to point at the concept and say, "See? Soothe me!" but to name in myself the deficit and work to repair it.

I'd never been the kind of woman that men are compelled to save and own and cherish. The fact that Aham *did* want me and *did* feel compelled to rescue me simply did not compute. It went against everything I knew. It felt like a trick. But if him doing it was not enough to convince me that he was doing it, then what could possibly get through to me?

I hadn't understood before how low self-esteem could tank true love, but I see it so clearly now. To ask him to continuously pour himself into me to keep me just barely alive? And I hated him for it? No one can do that forever. *It has to be different*, I thought as Linda came to the end of her song. *I can fix it, and I'm starting to. A great gift, to have that power and the time to execute it.*

When my dad died, I remember thinking, *I wish I could just crawl inside of Aham's body and hide there, so he could carry my pain.* I returned to that image often over the following years; I held it up as my vision of what perfect love might feel like.

How small did I think I was? Not physically small, but how small was my presence that I thought I could fit inside of another person, even if I wanted to? Aham could not contain me. I can't even contain me. I am immense.

US-65, HARRISON, ARKANSAS

The fuck town is this? Harrison, Arkansas. It's Harrison, Arkansas. Ooh, Dad's Donuts. I bet they're good. I cannot believe I didn't get a picture of this, but I just passed a business, and I didn't see a sign that said EXTERMINATORS or anything, it just had a big awning, like a gas station, and crawling all over the roof were these giant spiders. Like, you know, fake spiders, sculptures of spiders, fiberglass or something.

So it was covered in giant spiders, and then it had a banner across the front that just said SICK OF FIGHTING SPIDERS?

And that was it. That's the business. Yeah. I mean, I would be instantly sick! If spiders ever tried to fight me, I'd be sick of it right away. Is that happening around here? Thank you for your service, then!

Hot Chicken

June 18, 2021

Stubborn curiosity wouldn't let me backtrack into Missouri to take US-60, a quicker route to Nashville, so I meandered across northern Arkansas on small county roads, which got me to my hotel close to midnight.

I was staying one night at the Russell, an old church that had been converted into a boutique hotel. It wasn't in the downtown core but on a dark side street in the Edgefield Historic District, a quiet neighborhood of stately homes on the east side of the Cumberland River. I parked the van in a lot across the street and cut the engine.

I sat in the van. The parking lot was pitch-black. The street was empty. The lights in the hotel were dim. I knew from my welcome email that this was an internet-age hotel with no doorman or valet or twenty-four-hour reception; I had an assigned room and a code for the door. I mentally cataloged everything I had to dig out of my fifty-pound suitcase in the back of the van—toiletries, pajamas, clothes for tomorrow—and realized that I was scared.

Literally every person I'd talked to in the past month had asked me about safety, but so far, I hadn't felt unsafe. But that night, some combination of exhaustion and homesickness and too many murder podcasts and good old-fashioned fear of the dark kicked in and whispered: *Somebody's gonna GET YOU! The Killer's gonna SNEAK UP and STAB YOU! Leaning over to get stuff out of a van in the dark is the number one cause of death in women aged thirty-eight to thirty-nine! You'll never make it to the hotel alive!!!!!*

The hotel was maybe twenty yards away. This was not a rational fear. The Edgefield Historic District is not a high-stabbing area (although apparently the outlaw Jesse James once lived there!), and I've lived in big cities all my life. I don't subscribe to baseless NIMBY fearmongering about "suspicious characters," and anyway, *the street was empty*! Empty is the opposite of being stabbed!

I think I was just tired of being alone, tired of self-reliance, tired period, and I wanted someone to walk me across the street and put me in bed. I wanted comfort. I wanted Aham.

I sat in the van, immobilized, for half an hour, trying to reason with myself. It was now past midnight. The stab rate was only going up. I was not going to sleep sitting up in the front seat of my van because I happened to listen to a podcast about the Yorkshire Ripper while recovering from codependency! Eventually, I forced myself to open the door and jump out, and it was like waking up. The real world awaited, like it always did. Of course this parking lot held no dangers, other than the danger of wasting $158 on a nonrefundable hotel room due to mental illness.

I grabbed my stuff and found my way to my room. The hotel is gorgeous—literal cathedral ceilings, stained glass, mid-century furniture—and I immediately regretted only booking one night and arriving nine hours past check-in.

I took a blistering shower and lay naked in the crisp white sheets.

I'd been having intrusive thoughts about Aham and Roya. When I thought about them in the abstract—them loving each other, Aham replacing me with a beautiful, small woman—I felt pain and fear. I felt like screaming and dying. But when I thought about Roya in specifics—her sweet texts, her generosity—I felt...good. I realized that the more contact I'd had with Roya the real person, not the ghost my insecurities invented to scare me, the calmer and safer I'd felt.

Oh no, I thought. *I think I need to meet her.*

I slept a deep, velvet sleep and woke up early, smiling, the sun streaming through the stained glass window high above me. The previous day's fear was gone, replaced by nothing, just space, and I let myself flood in. Me, my body, my trip, my desires, all one piece. I took a shower and blow-dried my hair, a rarity. I put on makeup. I got dressed up in a short plaid skirt and a little white blouse. I felt jubilant and sexy and went to get some hot chicken before my drive to the Great Smoky Mountains.

A couple of hours outside of Nashville, I stopped at a truck stop to pee and get some camping snacks. I took a cute picture of myself in the bathroom mirror, texted it to Aham, and flounced up to the counter. The old guy working the register was chunky and dour, with overalls and a big bushy beard. He looked me up and down. *Oh boy, here it comes*, I thought. *I'm about to get sexually harassed. I am blowing this old gas station guy's mind! Nothing too creepy, please, mister!* I braced myself, a little bit excited.

"What they got going on up at North Campus?" he asked.

This was not the question I'd expected. I guess he thought I was a college student? That was a *little* bit like sexual harassment, maybe? "I have no idea," I said, confused. "I'm just passing through. I'm going camping."

"Oh," he said, losing interest. "I thought they were having the Highland Games or something."

"No..." I said. "I don't know... Well, bye!" I walked outside.

Then I realized: *my skirt*. He saw my plaid skirt and thought I was there to compete in the Highland Games. I was going for slutty co-ed but giving Hafþór Júlíus Björnsson. This man saw me and thought, *That girl throws the caber.*[1]

Not the validation I was fishing for, but no doubt a lucrative OnlyFans niche. Something to think about!

---

1. One time I was at the airport and I had my hair in a little braid crown and I walked past all the livery drivers and one of them had a sign that said, BROOMHILDA. As soon as I came out of baggage claim, he clocked me and followed me with the sign. I kept shaking my head like, *No, I'm not Broomhilda, I swear!!!* And he just kept chasing me and looking at me like I was crazy and pointing at the sign, like, *This is definitely you! You're telling me some other woman in this airport is Broomhilda? You are the most Broomhilda-lookingest woman I've ever seen!!*

I-40, SILVER POINT, TENNESSEE

I want to take some dance classes. I think a deep part of my body insecurity is feeling alienated from my body and not understanding how to move my body deliberately as one complex whole. I feel very disconnected and very fragmented and very self-conscious when I dance. And I'm not even a bad dancer, for a white! But it's still a really deep fundamental problem for me.

So here's my silly little thought—I was thinking about white people in general not being able to dance, and I was like, oh my god, is it possible that the ongoing project of global white supremacist imperialism and white people not being able to dance are symptoms of the same thing? Like, white people globally are so disembodied that they just hunger to take and destroy and claim and eat and they're never satisfied?

It's like trying to fill this void. You know, like, that void is why they can't dance. It's probably self-perpetuating too. You're just full of poison and then you hate yourself and you know you're bad and you... I don't know. It's a big stretch, but it feels completely true!!!

Terrifying smaller thought in that vein: Did I colonize Aham to try to fill my disembodied void? Is that analogous? I'm scared!

What I'm feeling in my body when I dance is that every single part of me is a separate, disconnected entity that's independently shaking around and has no idea what it's doing. Like I'm all portioned up, you know?

Which is a very capitalist thing! We're gonna section this up and make sure the parts don't work together, don't communicate, don't feel in community. It's also colonial in that way, how white people pretend like the world is not one entity. That somehow Tennessee is separate from Argentina.

You know what I mean? Even though you could just, if it weren't for fucking human beings, you could move your body from here to there contiguously. And the land wouldn't change. It doesn't have these stark divisions. It flows and it evolves, and the ecosystem flows and evolves all the way there. Just like your neck flows into your shoulders, which flow into your arms. Decolonizing your understanding of your own body is not unrelated to decolonizing your thinking about the world.

Naked and Afraid

I have always felt like life was a constellation of secret clubs to which I do not belong. In my teens and twenties, sex was the club that tortured me the most. I felt victimized by sex, bullied by sex. When I try to imagine playing, say, strip poker, I simply can't. It would be like getting invited to play "dolphin ball," a sport for dolphins where the rules are in dolphin language and I'm the only one who is not a dolphin and the dolphins only invited me because they felt bad.

As far as I know, strip poker could be an urban legend. But whether it's real or apocryphal, and whether spin the bottle or seven minutes in heaven or never have I ever or truth or dare or any of the other teenage mating rituals are real, the aura that they evoke—that frisson you feel when you remember or imagine them—that adolescent swell of *it's happening*—is some important building block of life. I know it by its absence in me—the body memory of anticipation, the pattering rabbit hearts, desiring and being desired, participating in the hot, electric exchange of gaze and being welcome there. The FUN of it! Your crush looking back at you like a mirror instead of a wall. Anyone, anywhere, looking at you as anything but a blight to be eradicated. It's all I've ever wanted.

There's something about fatness and gender. I often say "I think I'm ugly" as shorthand for whatever the fuck is wrong with my self-image, but that's not right. I don't think I'm ugly so much as unseeable. I identify as a woman, but I'm not quite categorized as one—not that people perceive me as a man, but as some third or fourth category, a pretender in an ill-fitting costume. Is that gender dysphoria? Inside, I feel like a beautiful woman. When I attempt to present as such in public, it doesn't translate. I feel like a clown. Lipstick on a pig. I feel like everyone who sees me wants to laugh. *Nice try, meatball! Get back in the spaghetti!*

I think the day I decided to suppress my sexuality forever was the day they released that publicity still for the movie *Exit to Eden* where Rosie

O'Donnell is dressed in full fetish gear with her foot on Dan Aykroyd's back. It was in every late-night monologue for a month. The world had never seen something so disgusting and hilarious. A fat woman (*was she, though?????????*) in a sex outfit?! Who does she think she is? A regular woman?!?!!?? If she came for Dan Aykroyd's balls, is she coming for *my balls next*?!

Exit to Eden came out in 1994, so I would have been twelve. O'Donnell recognize O'Donnell! Now I'm entering middle age, and I can't even tell my husband which movie stars I think are hot, because I'm afraid he might make fun of me for being horny. I blush when the doctor asks me if there's any chance I might be pregnant, or if I need STI testing, like I don't want her to know that I have sex—even though I have been married for years and had a famous abortion. I can sort of talk about sex with partners, in the moment, if pressed—"Yes," "That feels good," "Don't stop"—but if a partner were to ask me, for example, to recap the sex we had last night, in clinical detail, not even poetic detail, I'd rather die. The discomfort is primal. I do not have the language. The cupboard is bare.

I've had the same friend group since third grade, and I still don't talk to them about sex. It's a bonding ritual that I've never participated in—laughing together to take the sting out of bad partners, sharing advice and little scandals, coping with the shared trauma of being a woman in the world. You don't have to talk about sex to be close with people, but it's a big part of life to be left on the table. Gossip is an exchange of confidences. Why would you tell me yours if I won't tell you mine? This weird sex complex I have steals platonic intimacy from me just as much as romantic intimacy. I don't even like to hug platonic friends that much, because what if they think I'm doing something weird like leather mommy Rosie O'Donnell?!?! My existence itself feels perverted.

To protect myself, when I was younger, I developed a squealing contempt for sex. It was a way to engage without ever being vulnerable—to reframe discomfort as sophistication. I sneered at people who were too public with their sexuality, flagrant and immodest. Not that I subscribed to modesty as a concept, but do I have to see *your whole ass*? Must you drag me, a stranger, into your sex life by making out at the food court? It's profane! I would have hated "WAP" when I was sixteen. Ew, ma'am, I don't need to know about your macaroni!

Most contemptible of all, to me, were cis-het men who used sex drive as an excuse for cruelty and negligence, arguably a foundation of heterosexual dating. They can't help cheating on us, manipulating us, flattening us, disposing of us—the horniness HURTS, their balls literally HURT, they are BLUE, the horniness is in their DNA. Give me a fucking break. How pathetic. You don't even have authority over your genitals and you think you deserve to run the world? Grow up.

And that's all true. My contempt for "men are dogs" / "boys will be boys" culture is earned. In a power structure stratified by gender and whiteness and beauty, sex is a weapon. But it must be possible to acknowledge men's greedy trespasses, to isolate and vivisect that construct, while keeping a soft, sweet place inside for yourself and the ones you love. No need to scour and cauterize *sexuality itself* to punish a population of bad actors who don't deserve your soft, sweet places.

It doesn't work anyway. Abuse of power doesn't disappear if the rest of us cut ourselves off from one another.

Once I did start having sex, there was always something missing—a hollow I hid from my partners—because what was sex but a standardized test I handed out to men to prove I had some value? Or a trinket I could offer to beg them for some mimicry of love? Eventually, when I was married and the validation chase was over, I gave up on sex. I didn't need it anymore for any of the reasons I'd been taught to pursue it before. I had a partner to prove my worth. I had love—the real thing. I felt safe enough with Aham to cherish our sex life, to feel almost normal. I didn't stop having sex, I didn't stop enjoying it, but I stopped being curious about it. I stopped hungering for it.

I see other fat women who know innately how to embody their sexuality—I can tell they didn't have to be taught. I pore over their pictures on social media. I want what they have. But it's not a code I can crack. I've tried. I scrabble at that veil till my fingers bleed. I also know the veil doesn't exist. A solid wall of nothing that I cannot pass through. I cannot do it because I have never been able to do it. An unshakable tautology.

I want to be desirable, but I do not know how to be desired.

Desirability isn't just a passive, aesthetic state. It's something you do. I don't know how to present my body as something to be consumed. It's foreign to me. I don't know how to approach Aham as a gift to be unwrapped, to walk into a room with unselfconscious openness, to hold sexual energy without it dissipating like smoke, to curl myself under his arm so his reaching out to hold me is the only natural response. Instead, I lead with guilt and awkwardness; I clomp in like a Sasquatch and spray him in the face with the hose. *You probably don't want to, but maybe we could have sex later if you're not too busy and I don't smell too bad, I don't know, never mind, sorry.*

What woman, of any size, reaches adulthood without some trauma around sex? I used to get so angry in couples' therapy, when we were trying to hammer out polyamory and Aham would explain that he's *such a sexual person*, he just *loves sex*, he loves *new experiences*, he's *so curious* about human sexuality, there's *nothing wrong* with it, it's *fascinating* to him, he listens to *sex podcasts*, he reads *sex books*, that's just *a unique thing about him* that can't be contained, maybe that's just a way that we're *naturally different.* WOW! MUST BE NICE! Must be fucking nice to have the freedom to think of sex with uncomplicated lightness. Must be nice to have any sense at all of your "natural" connection with sexuality.

It is bad for a person to live forever in an unrequited state. Not saying it's an injustice—I'm not an incel—but it's corrosive, stunting. I know because I'm extremely fucked up. Because even now, over forty, long married to a hot person who wants me more than anything, I approach every sexual experience from a place of "I'm sorry you have to do this." I never have sex without making jokes. I rarely have sex without feeling either disassociated or hyperaware. I struggle to let the moment in.

In the dark times, Aham constantly begged me to try harder, to try to be sexy—for him, if I couldn't for myself. To stop hiding in my clothes, to take a shower, to brush my hair, to move and act my age, to reach out and touch him. But I couldn't conceive of being wanted. I was so ashamed that this beautiful, *alive* man was chained to me but felt like I'd die if he left. One time, in 2018, a lady in a restaurant asked me if I was Aham's mom.

I couldn't imagine that Aham wanted me to come back to life sexually because sexuality is part of being alive. Even asexuality is sexuality, is information, while hiding from sex is just nothingness. Aham wanted me to be sexy not because he thought I was ugly but *because he thought I was sexy*, and watching this chasm grow between my self and my self-perception felt like a steady crawl toward doom. And when he tried to stop me from crawling, I cried and told him he was hurting me.

I listened to "WAP" probably four thousand times on my road trip. I think when it came out, people treated it like a novelty song, but honestly? That song means a lot to me! "Paid my tuition just to kiss me on this wet-ass pussy"? Do you think I have ever valued myself like that? Do you think I have ever felt like I deserved to demand anything from men? Do you think that anyone wants to hear fat women even acknowledge that we have pussies?[1] Let alone pussies worthy of worship?

I didn't stand a chance. Do you know how many times strangers on the internet have joked that Aham must have to throw a handful of flour at my grotesque puzzle of a body to find the wet spot? More times than any man[2] I've actually fucked has told me I'm pretty!

I am just closed. I don't know how else to describe it. I am shut like a vault. Not locked but welded. Most of that is society, but some of it is me. There are things that I do that cut me off from people who love me. I don't know.

Lust is too much like hunger, and I am not allowed to be hungry.

---

1. Me asking Satan to burn me with his fiery whip rather than make me type this.
2. Aham is non-binary he/they, so this statistic holds!

US-321, WALLAND, TENNESSEE

Growing up alone as functionally an only child, and then becoming a lonely adult, I used to find so much pleasure in time to myself. I just relished the feeling of being by myself. No one putting pressure on me, nothing. No one judging me, no one looking at me. And somehow I lost the flavor of that. And now I only know one flavor, which is Aham. And that's really bad. It's really destructive. They want it to be romantic but it's not romantic.

I feel so sick not being able to take pleasure in my own company, be my own friend. It feels like an illness, and I know this trip is part of the cure. I know it. And I think another part of that cure is gonna be, like I said before, I really think I gotta not be in touch with home so much. It's hard. It makes it hard. It's like sticking a big fucking tube through my ear and sucking my brain all the way back to Seattle. My brain and my heart. So I gotta learn how to be where I am and reach out to that feeling that I used to love. Being alone used to be a feeling of being, like, free and safe.

That's what it was. Because you're away from other people's judgments. You're away from other people's needs and other people's expectations, and you just get to be you. And I think that growing up, I felt very judged, and very, kind of, at the mercy of other people. I think when you grow up feeling judged, you try to make yourself palatable to everyone, because you absorbed this idea that you're bad.

Cicada

June 20, 2021

BAAA and I camped at Cades Cove Campground in the Great Smoky Mountains National Park. It was a rowdy campground in the deep woods, kids spilling out of RVs, retirees sipping beers in elaborate outdoor living rooms, frat guys whooping and hollering. The air inside the van was hot soup, but I didn't mind. I had my little fan, my little window screens, my little string lights, all my little things just so. I woke up at 3:00 a.m. and crept past other people's campsites to the bathroom, my phone flashlight catching centipedes and frogs in its beam, and found, with pleasure, that I was no longer nervous. Up until this point in the trip, if I had to pee in the middle of the night, I was holding it. Imagine missing out on seeing a frog because you were afraid of the unknown.[1] I was relieved to be camping again. Hotel rooms are for hiding. Camping is for the joyously exposed.

I ate breakfast in my camping chair with my feet up on the metal firepit. I'm good at building fires—I have a knack for the balance of wood and air, fuel to burn and space to breathe, and an instinct for when the flame needs time to grow and when it needs tending. I didn't have supplies for a real fire, but I gathered some twigs and burned some flowers—rose petals that Rainbow gave me and some Kansas wildflowers from Jill. A little morning sublimation, transforming something into something else and watching it dissipate among the maples and buckeyes. Dissipate but not disappear. Change form and go out into the world to new places, to be new energy for something else.

It's me, I thought, tending my fire. *I'm the flowers, I'm the flame, I'm the smoke, but I'm the pit*

---

[1]. The next day, I found out that a girl sleeping in a hammock at a nearby campsite had been attacked by a bear. But she survived! It was still worth seeing the frog!!!

too. I'm the girl who's good at making fires, and I'm the girl who burns.

I packed up and stopped at the ranger station for advice on a quick hike. I had a long drive to Savannah, but I wanted to experience this wilderness without the security blanket of BAAA. The ranger recommended Spruce Flats Falls, a two-mile out-and-back with a waterfall at the payoff. Short but juicy.

The cicadas had just emerged from their seventeen-year nap and the trees buzzed and croaked around me, giving my hike a historicity that I liked. I was nervous about leaving all my stuff at the trailhead, and I was self-conscious about hiking what was reportedly a popular and well-traveled trail. Unlike my earlier hike in the Badlands, this was going to be all uphill. Even after a year of climbing the hill at the cabin, I knew I would be slow, I knew it would be hard, I knew people would pass me, I knew some of them would tell me "good job" (a horror), I knew I'd "inspire" some of them with my fat ass, I knew I'd be resentful and embarrassed.

But I was trying so hard to say yes instead of no. I wanted to hike in the Smokies, and I wanted to see that waterfall.

Adult Braces

I made my way up the mountain. It wasn't as much gain as I'd feared, just a few hundred feet, and while I did get passed by elderly women and toddlers, I wasn't terribly out of breath, and I felt more kinship than condescension from my fellow hikers. When I was nearly at the top, a woman on her way back down said, "Swim when you get up there! It's worth it!"

My knee-jerk reaction was no. I didn't want to have to hike back down wet. What if there's some extra scramble to get to the pool where you can swim? What if I climb up and can't climb back down? What will I do with my shoes, my fanny pack, my stuff? It's probably crowded. It's probably full of kids. People will look at my body. I'm just here to hike. I've already pushed myself today.

But then I thought: *What if I just said yes? What if I SWIM? What if every day of my life I set fear aside and climb the hill and swim instead of not swimming? What kind of life would that be amplified over years, decades?*

You do have to clamber up boulders to get to the pool at the foot of Spruce Flats Falls. It was crowded, and I had to abandon my fanny pack on a rock and hope for the best. I stripped off my shirt and shoes and socks and sank into the water in my sports bra and bike shorts. The cicadas screamed, and so did the part of me that's tired of being afraid. They screamed with joy at their awakening and I at mine.

There was no cell service in the national park, and when I finally got back to the highway that afternoon, I had thirteen voicemails. Without signal, I hadn't been able to tell Aham I was going on a hike after packing up camp, and when he couldn't get in touch with me for over twenty-four hours, he panicked. This dynamic had happened many times in the other direction—convincing myself Aham was dead because he didn't text me back for a few hours—but it was a power I'd never felt before. I hadn't even noticed it had been that long since we talked. I was busy *doing something*. How long had it been since I was so immersed in my own life I didn't think about him at all?

US-321, TOWNSEND, TENNESSEE

I'm driving through the most beautiful forest. Well, maybe not as beautiful as my forests at home, but an absolutely stunning forest. It looks like a fairy tale. It's not evergreen trees, it's deciduous trees, and they're bright green and there's space between them, you know? Not the kind of undergrowth that we have in Washington. But it's still so thick. The forest is thick, but there's also space in it. My metaphor!

Part Four
SEA LEGS

Jingle Bells

JUNE 21, 2021

I chose Savannah as my stopover in Georgia because it seemed romantic. Live oaks, Spanish moss, architecture, sweatiness, murder, *Midnight in the Garden of Good and Evil*—a book I have not read, but that doesn't matter, because it's really the title that's doing the heavy lifting. You're telling me something's happening at MIDNIGHT in the GARDEN of GOOD and EVIL?! Whatever it is, I want to be there! It had better not just be Kevin Spacey with a mustache!

I had a full day off, so I slept in past breakfast and scheduled a quick mani-pedi before my big (ROMANTIC) afternoon plans of wandering around the city's leafy squares until I was hungry enough to eat a whole fried chicken. I was staying at the Ballastone Inn, a Victorian bordello turned Confederate officer's mansion turned upscale hotel on a sun-dappled boulevard in Savannah's historic district.

I walked to a nail salon, where there was, ominously, only one customer (henceforth referred to as Me) and one employee (henceforth referred to as This Lady). I don't know if this lady was new, or lonely, or bored, or an impostor, or doing a prank, but she took—I am not exaggerating—*four hours* to paint my nails. No wonder nobody in this town could get to the Garden of Good and Evil until midnight!!!

She was sweet, though. She told me about growing up in Honolulu and what brought her to Savannah, and at one point, her fiancé came and dropped off some Chinese food for her. That's my weakness! I can't say, "Hurry the fuck up" or "You are doing a bad job" to a nice person who likes Chinese food, even if they did cut my toenails so short they bled. I asked her what I should do while I was in town, and she said "clubbing." A reasonable suggestion, actually, since that was the only thing still open once she was done with my fucking nails!

My all-day romantic wander had been thwarted, but I still had a couple of hours before my dinner reservation. I was in the historic district already, I reasoned—I could just walk around near the hotel and pick up enough of the vibe. I wore a pink gingham sports bra and matching bike shorts and my new nails were butter yellow and my confidence was high and I felt positively pornographic. A kitchen employee on his cigarette break outside a fancy hotel called out to me as I bounced along.

"You from here?"

"No!"

"You need a tour guide?"

"I'm leaving tomorrow!"

"That's too bad!"

"I know!"

!!!!!!!!!!!!!!!!!

Catcalling is a poisoned well, not generally where a woman on a Liberation Journey wants to be drawing her self-esteem, but it also wasn't exactly catcalling. This was different from the guy at the bar in Montana. Or maybe I was different. This guy picked up on the energy I was projecting and engaged with it. I felt visible, desirable, seen, part of the fabric of life.

You know what that is???

Random
Outside-a-hotel
Man
Asks
Nicely
To
Intercourse
Crindy!!!!!!!!

A block or two after I got hit on, I was walking through a shady square ringed by townhomes and a stately stone church when I saw a plaque that read, tantalizingly, JINGLE BELLS. A certified Christmas-head, I stopped to investigate.

"James L. Pierpont (1822–1893), composer of 'Jingle Bells,' served as music director of this church in the 1850s when it was a Unitarian Church located on Oglethorpe Square."

Cute!!!

"Son of the noted Boston reformer, Rev. John Pierpont, he was the brother of Rev. John Pierpont, Jr., minister of this church, and uncle of financier John Pierpont Morgan."

Very interesting! A notable family! We love a reformer!

"He married Eliza Jane Purse, daughter of Savannah mayor Thomas Purse..."

Congrats, brother!

"—and served with a Confederate cavalry regiment."

A crazy thing about the South is that you'll be walking through the most beautiful park you ever saw and you'll stop to look at a cute squirrel and then BAM! A plaque pops up like, "THIS SQUIRREL WAS DESCENDED FROM SQUIRRELS PERSONALLY TRAINED BY STONEWALL JACKSON TO BITE SLAVES."

When you're from the Pacific Northwest, you simply don't prepare yourself for info like "btw, the guy who wrote 'Jingle Bells' fought for the Confederacy" to drop in your lap at any moment. James L. Pierpont wasn't even from the South! He was from Boston!!! In fact, he came from a famous family of abolitionists, and he estranged himself from them to fight for slavery as a daddy-issue rebellion! Next you'll tell me "Jingle Bells" was first performed in blackface at a minstrel show in 1857! (It was.) More like Shidnight in the Shartin' of Poop and Peepee!!!!!!!!

On my stroll back to the hotel, I posted

a pretty picture of some Spanish moss on Instagram, and someone in the comments let me know that Spanish moss is full of little red mites that bite you and make you itch. *You know what?* I thought. *I've done enough hard truths lately. I can lose "Jingle Bells," but I'm keeping the Spanish moss.*

Tomorrow would be the final leg of my outbound journey. In twenty-four hours, I would be in Kokomo.

I-95, MIMS, FLORIDA

Man, Florida really is Florida. Like, I didn't expect Florida to be this Florida. I don't know what I expected. More pavement and strip malls, I guess, and less swampy jungle. It's just all swampy jungle! And this is the interstate, not some rural highway!

It's so intense. I just got gas and bought some water and went to the bathroom. And it might have the most vibe of any place I've been yet. It just feels like Florida. It feels like anything could happen at any second. Everything is a little bit melted and a little bit decayed. It feels wild here. And I don't mean crazy, I mean untamed. You feel like nature and the elements could take you over. The trees could grab you. The air feels like it could solidify around you and trap you. It's not a bad feeling. It's not a bad vibe. It's just a very, very, very intense vibe.

There's a guy mowing the side of the highway right there. Don't bother! It's gonna grow back in thirty seconds!

Arrival

June 22, 2021

The Overseas Highway departs terra firma just south of Miami and stretches an improbable 113 miles out into the Caribbean, a series of bridges hopping from island to island until it dead-ends at Key West. The longest of these, Seven Mile Bridge, is a concrete box girder bridge that soars over the shallow blue sea for, as the name says, *seven whole earth miles*. The battered skeleton of an old railroad bridge runs alongside, like the Ghost of Bridgemas Future warning you that no infrastructure is immortal. When you're on the Overseas Highway, you feel certain that it should not exist. You are literally driving a car over the ocean in hurricane country and you have not seen land in ten minutes?? Why do you need to do that?! American hubris!!

If the Overseas Highway has one thing to

recommend it, it's the view. I, a genius, set myself up for a ten-hour-drive day (in practice, it was closer to sixteen) from Savannah to the Keys and crossed this wonder of the world[1] in pitch-blackness punctuated by the strobing of heat lightning from thunderstorms on every horizon. Before my trip, I didn't really know what the Florida Keys were. It was one of those collections of sounds that you recognize but that doesn't actually signify anything, like *capital gains* or *Dragon Ball Z*. Crossing the Overseas Highway, I came to understand the deeper history—that the Florida Keys are a series of tiny rocks that God designed to scare the shit out of Lindy West.

That morning, I'd also made the unpleasant discovery of a, let's say, BLOOPER with my budget. Money had been getting tight, but I still had a few thousand dollars, enough to feed and gas myself back to Seattle while having a little bit of fun. Then I thought of something bad. Due to having cotton candy instead of brain, I had been operating under the assumption that I'd paid for

---

[1]. WONDERING WHY IN THE WORLD AM I DRIVING ON THIS.

my Key West hotel in advance. But as I bit into and then threw away my Hardee's sausage and egg biscuit on the outskirts of Savannah, I had to ask: *Had I actually paid for my Key West hotel in advance?*

I stopped to pee at a gas station and searched my email while the thunderclouds boiled in the distance. Hmm, fascinating. It seemed I had not paid for my Key West hotel in advance. And it was, inconveniently, the big splurge of my trip. I would need to find, um, several thousand dollars by the time I got to the end of this highway. Would it literally kill me not to be a fucking idiot all the time?

My sister-in-law, Ijeoma, a successful and responsible homeowner with a solvent savings account, said she'd wire me the money. **Have fun in Key West!** she said. **I would die for you!** I said. **Ha ha ha!** she said. But would the wire transfer go through by the time I handed BAAA off to the valet? Not knowing is the fun of life!

From what I'd been able to discern online, Key West wasn't a beach-swimming kind of place; it was a snorkeling-and-scuba-diving kind of place—low, thick vegetation crowding right up to the water's edge, rough rocks dropping straight and steep into the deep, coral lurking to slice toes and exterminate shins. So when I was looking for a Key West hotel, I knew I wanted something with a big, beautiful pool, a pool I could stay in all day long.

I also learned in my research that Old Town Key West—the recognizable, iconic part that occupies the western half of the island—is, in fact, old, and as they teach you in Architecture 101, old things are small and close together. If you want the charm of a historic pirate cove chockablock with gingerbread Victorian houses painted every color in the SweeTARTS roll, you have to sacrifice sprawling modern resort hotels with swimming pools to write home about. Everything in my price range in Old Town was teeny-tiny and kitschy and precious, but I'd just spent two weeks in a van. I wanted a taste of the finer things.

I chose a resort a few minutes from Old Town, on the other side of the freeway, because it was on the water and had four pools, including a no-kids-allowed quiet pool for elegant women on spiritual side quests. It was expensive, but not as expensive as the hotels that were more expensive, which technically made it a bargain! What they didn't mention on the hotel website was that not only was it waterfront to the west, it was also Walgreens-front to the north, Dollar Tree–front to the east, and Mattress Firm–front to the south. Space is at a premium on a four-square-mile island, and if you're not in the charming core, you're at the mall.

Still, it managed to be beautiful. As I pulled into the front courtyard in BAAA around 11:30 p.m., the palm trees beckoned and enfolded me, sheltering my fantasy from the glare of the Five Guys across the road, and golden light spilled from tall windows in the white colonial facade. I asked the valet if I could grab some things from the back of the van before he took her, but he told me not to worry—there was no space in the garage that could accommodate BAAA, so she'd be right there in the courtyard for the duration of my stay, welcoming each new guest with a friendly "BOING BOING BOING, EAT SHIT, FUCKERS!"

I stumbled up to the reception desk, as tired as

I'd ever been, unsure if I'd be able to get into my room. But—yes!—Ijeoma's money had landed! My debit card worked. I was in. I was starving, but the kitchen was closed, and the bartender was a bitch to me about it, as though I'd asked, "Are you still sucking dick?" instead of "Are you still serving food?" Didn't luxury hotels usually have some kind of all-night menu, even if it's just olives? I would have sold state secrets for some olives. But I was too exhausted to care that much. I flopped onto the white king bed in my all-white room and passed out.

Bodies in the Sand

June 23, 2021

My ground-floor room had doors that opened on two sides: one leading to the interior courtyard with its four blandly identical pools, and the other leading to a sandy corridor lined with deck chairs that faced a hedge, beyond which, allegedly, was the sea. I ignored the two-inch cockroach clinging to the closet door (not my circus, not my monkeys) and slipped into my swimsuit.

At a poolside bar, I ordered coffee, bacon, and "Avocado Toast with Jalapeño and Radish," then settled down to write in my journal:

> My vision for Key West is: 1. Cute outfits, 2. Confidence, 3. Perfect makeup and hair, 4. SEX VIBES, 5. Swimming, 6. Drinks, 7. Talking to strangers at the bar, 8. Writing, 9. Sunscreen, 10. RELAXED BEACH MAN KOKOMO

ENERGY. Maybe I'll go to the Hemingway House today. I could use some Hemingway in my writing. I'm a little florid. Not that that's bad. But it can be self-indulgent. I mean, it's good sometimes. You need a balance.

The arrival of coffee interrupted my train of thought. It was in a squishy Styrofoam Dixie cup and came with two of those little tubs of half-and-half that they give you at your higher-end gas stations. An interesting choice for a "luxury" hotel. Maybe it's because I was by the pool, I reasoned. A lot of hotels don't let you have glassware by the pool. It's actually very safety conscious! Ernest Hemingway probably thought only pussies switched to Styrofoam cups to avoid cutting their feet. He probably stepped on broken glass all the time. *Men.*
 I emptied both tubs of cream into my coffee (not enough), took a sip (bad), and was about to put pen back to paper when I was distracted yet again, this time by an Eavesdropping Emergency: Threat Level Midnight. Two drunk couples in the shallow end were fighting about chickens. My head swiveled 360 degrees like the demon Pazuzu. YOU RANG??

They were classic American tourists, white, corn-fed, a few years older than I was, with accents so powerfully Pennsylvanian that even I could tell—*Whurs my tall? I needa get oudda da wooder!* Their conversation was pure, uncut Lindy-bait.

"A rooster is a chicken," one woman insisted.

Her husband scoffed. "A rooster is *not* a chicken!"

"If it's a chicken, then why would we call it a *rooster*?" said the second man, certain he'd struck a killing blow. The tension mounted.

His wife began typing a search query into her phone, presumably some version of *WHAT IS A CHICKEN*? I wondered if Google sent out medals for questions that no one has ever asked before. "Ohhhhh, okay," she said, interrupting the melee. "So a rooster and a hen are both a chicken, but a rooster is the male."

Both men threw up their hands and bellowed. "No way!" "I don't believe it!" "No!"

"No, that's what it says!"

"So roosters don't lay eggs?"

"No!!!!!!!"

"Ohhhhhh," the other three intoned in

Adult Braces

unison. The tide had turned. Peace settled over the pool.

"Okay, so," one of the husbands said, gears still turning, "*chicken* is the big word at the top when you do the Venn diagram?"

"Yes," everybody agreed.

"So now next time somebody asks," the original wife said, smug and vindicated, "you'll know that a rooster is a chicken."

"Yeah," her husband added, "and also today, we learned that Zachary Taylor was a president."

All hell broke loose again, but this time they were united: "I still don't believe that!" "I've never heard of that person in my life!" "I've never heard that name in my life." "I don't believe it."

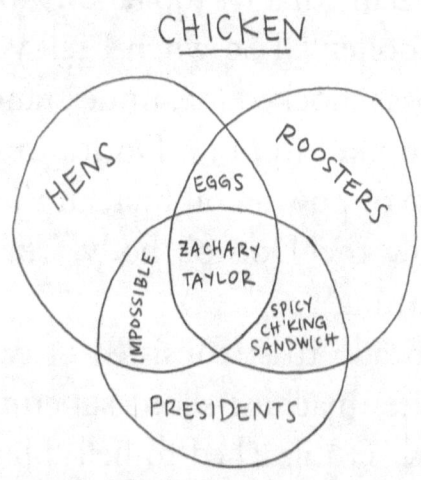

It was beautiful to see—this hunger for knowledge sated in real time, man's vibrant curiosity turned loose in the pastures of Wikipedia—even if it left my feeble mind with more questions than answers. How often was somebody asking these people whether a rooster is a chicken? What did they think a Venn diagram was? Who brought Zachary Taylor into it??

The server appeared and Frolfed my avocado toast at me with a silence that shouted, "I don't care if you live or die." I regarded my plate. First, I need you to understand that I am not a snob about almost anything, food least of all. As the poets say, I love trash, and I love it *because* it's trash. If I ever have a complaint about avocado toast, it's usually that it's too fancy. Nobody asked for fennel pollen!!!!! So when I tell you that this avocado toast shocked me, understand that I'm a person who likes to put a Dorito in my mouth, suck the flavor powder off first, and THEN chew and swallow the Dorito's body. That's the bar! Trigger warning!

This avocado toast consisted of two pieces of cheap, white, machine-sliced supermarket sandwich bread (a bleached-to-hell blinding-white chemical candy bread is one of earth's undersung pleasures, but not for MONEY at a RESTAURANT), imperceptibly toasted, each topped with a smear of packaged avocado spread, like the kind they give you in a little tub at Starbucks and probably aren't legally allowed to call "guacamole" without declaring war on Mexico, and then a handful of desiccated matchstick-cut carrots and broccoli stems picked out of an old raggedy bagged salad, lucky understudies for the role of "radish." It was here that our two slices diverged—sisters, not twins—the left sporting two pieces of bona fide fresh avocado (attaboy!!), and the right four mournful coins of raw jalapeño that looked like they had dried out in the fridge for a month. But "Avocado [*sic*] Toast [*sic*] with Jalapeño and Radish [*sic*]" found unity once more in its topping, a generous (some might say *food-ruining*) pour of bottled honey-mustard salad dressing.

For once in my miserable pandering clown life, I am not exaggerating to be funny. This description of the avocado toast would pass peer review. And it's not that it tasted bad. It tasted exactly as you imagine—like cheap bread and Shelf-Stable Avocado Product drenched in honey mustard. The problem was that it was something I'd throw together at 3:00 a.m. from a bunch of garbage I found in the fridge. It was fridge garbage for seventeen dollars, tossed at me like a throwing star by someone's no-good stepson.

The incongruity between the price of my hotel room and the execution of the avocado toast made me uneasy. I wondered what other corners had been cut, what other components of my stay might have been (figuratively) picked out of the bottom of an expired salad bag. My pillow? My towels? My fire extinguisher? I thought about the cockroach on the closet, then un-thought it.

Having chewed and swallowed my morning food (I can't legally call it *breakfast* without declaring war on god), I stopped by the concierge desk to get some advice. I explained that I had driven all the way from Seattle and was in the market for an excursion—something outside my comfort zone that SCREAMED Key West. Maybe a boat? Dry Tortugas National Park? Night swimming with whale sharks?

The concierge, a middle-aged white man who seemed to have recently been unboxed, said he had just the thing. He may have even said the words *I have just the thing*. The very best snorkel excursion in town just happened to have a shuttle that came right to this hotel! The boat had drinks, food, music, and guaranteed wildlife encounters or your money back. He slid a glossy brochure across the table. A fluorescent reef fish stared at me from the cover.

"A lot of the snorkel excursions in this town are just tourist traps," he said. "This company's not like that. They'll take great care of you."

"Is there anything else I should consider?" I asked, not wanting to take the first offer (isn't that what they teach you in CEO school?). "Since I only have time for one thing, is there anything I shouldn't miss?"

"Nope," he said. "This one is the best. I wouldn't work there if I didn't believe in the company."

"Wait, you also work at the snorkel company?" I said.

"Yes," he said. "But that's not why I'm recommending it."

"Okay," I said.

"That'll be $49.95," he said.

I feel like it should cost more, I thought.

At seven o'clock the next morning, I climbed into the ten-passenger van that would shuttle us to our adventure and slid across the bench seat behind the driver. Some other people got on after me and sat in the back. When we got to the marina, I stood up to exit the van, but the people in back pushed past me as though I wasn't there. I said, "Oh, I'm actually getting off here too," but they didn't say anything. They didn't even look at me. This is something I'm accustomed to, but it felt ominous to head into the open ocean unsure of whether or not others could perceive me. Can pure consciousness sink and drown?

There were seventy-three snorkelers on the boat and four crew members. Every single one of us was white, too revealing a demographic breakdown to occur by coincidence. The Florida Keys are weird like that. They are indisputably the Caribbean—they are Cuba, they are Jamaica, they are Haiti—but they identify as Florida, as something apart from the rest. I once met a woman who lived in Key West and told her I'd recently traveled to Puerto Rico and become enraptured by the Caribbean, its beauty and its tragedy, and she looked at me like I'd called her mother a dog.

White people don't mind having people of color serve them. But I think that what a lot of white people really want is to vacation in white-majority places where the other people being served are white and the government is white. They want the fruits of other lands without ever having to compromise, adapt, leave home, or learn respect, and that's what empire is all about.

We boarded a massive catamaran (NOT romantic) and took seats on the plastic benches that ringed both decks. Captain Jeff got on the loudspeaker to begin the safety announcements: Don't put anything down the toilet, because he's not just the captain, he's also the plumber and the bartender! And we don't want him fixing our drinks after he was just fixing the toilet, do we? Everyone laughed and cheered.

Oh dear, I thought. *I seem to have gotten myself into a booze cruise.*

Captain Jeff handed the mic off to Snorkel Instructor Shawn, who informed us that we would be swimming in a protected nature reserve, so don't touch the coral or it will die. And don't cut yourself on the coral or big sharks will come and eat all of us, and by the way there's one kind of coral that gives you a chemical burn but it looks just like all the other coral. This sounded like not just reasonable advice but important information for both our survival and the ecosystem's. But was anyone listening? I thought it was a tremendous amount of faith to put in both the attention spans and self-control of a group of American tourists at 8:00 a.m.

Snorkel Instructor Shawn showed us the hand signals to use if we "got in trouble" in the water, and promised that he would swim to us and "do my best David Hasselhoff impression," a timely reference that everyone enjoyed. If we signaled distress, he said, "then I'm gonna come get you, pull you onto the boat, and immediately do CPR, so, gentlemen, I don't think you want to get to know me that well. But, ladies, I am single and looking for Mrs. Right!" Huge laughs. I pondered the implication that women should drown ourselves so that we could kiss Snorkel Instructor Shawn.

Look, I would have kissed Snorkel Instructor Shawn. All men in their twenties who work on boats are hot. But I would have felt bad about it because of his personality!

Next, Snorkel Instructor Shawn showed us how to put on our life vests. The life vest had a strap that went under your crotch, back to front, so that the vest couldn't float up over your head. Snorkel Instructor Shawn had a bit about this as well: "Gentlemen, make sure you fasten this when you're standing up, not sitting down!" He meant that if you fastened it sitting down then the strap would squish your dick when you stood up. Everyone died laughing again. "But, ladies," he continued, a twinkle in his eye, "you can fasten this as tight as you want! You're on vacation!" Good idea, Shawn, I will fasten the life vest crotch strap tight for sex pleasure.

Captain Jeff hopped back on the mic and addressed the question that I assumed we were all thinking. "Uh-oh," he said, "looks like we got a thunderstorm coming. Those are normal for this area. We're gonna just skirt around it. It'll add ten minutes to the trip, but we'll still get a full hour in the water." He hit a button on the console and "Blue (Da Ba Dee)" began to play. Black clouds boiled in the distance.

The crew handed out juice, coffee, and

muffins, our complimentary breakfast. The plastic packaging on my muffin read:

CHEF PIERRE
BAKING DELICIOUS SINCE 1922™
BLUEBERRY
NATURALLY & ARTIFICIALLY FLAVORED
MUFFIN

Underneath it had a stamp of Chef Pierre's signature. I took a bite. *No offense*, I thought, *but I simply do not believe that a chef baked this muffin, let alone autographed it*. I finished it anyway. I needed my strength to swim to Cuba after we capsized.

It took about an hour to get out to the reef. The sky was tense, as if poised to attack. There were three or four other boats already there—mega-catamarans identical to ours, each with a different tour company logo painted on the side. As if it hadn't been obvious from the concierge being in league with the snorkel company, the seventy-three-person passenger manifest, the homophobic safety training, and the muffin, I had been had by a tourist racket. A money factory.

But, fine. I was technically on an excursion on a boat in the Caribbean and I was going to be brave and I was going to see a fish.

Captain Jeff tied the boat up to a buoy, and everyone started getting into the water. We had a choice of jumping off the side, going down a little slide, or climbing down a ladder. I'm not a jumping-off-things type, and the slide was about one-half the width of my ass, so I opted for the ladder, along with pretty much everyone else.

Three teenagers, who were clearly not sure about the snorkeling, sat on the stairs that led down to the ladder, giggling and screaming, with no awareness that sixty-five other people were trying to get past them. Perhaps it was doubly triggering to me as a person who's been emotionally abused to deter me from taking up space, but having to squeeze past those idiots in that stressful moment made me throw all my values out the window. I hoped they either got gay-CPR'd by Snorkel Instructor Shawn or DIDN'T get to kiss Snorkel Instructor Shawn, depending on their preferences. I was already stressed about snorkeling. I didn't know what the fuck I was doing. I was the only solo traveler on the boat. I was alone.

I was fat. I was in my swimsuit. I felt simultaneously like everyone was looking at me AND like no one could see me. "EXCUSE ME," I said as I edged along in my flippers, "TRYING TO GET BY YOU." The teenagers didn't seem to hear.

And then I was in the water.

Mortality slapped me in the face. I'd never been swimming in the open ocean before, so I have nothing to compare it to, and maybe it was simply the gathering storm chopping up the waves, but the motion of the water felt chaotic, alien, and dangerous. I'm a cold-water girl, an any water girl, a strong swimmer, a pruned and sunburned ocean floater. If you take me someplace where I can get in the water, I hope you're ready to stay all day, because I will never get out. I'd been pulled by scary tides and hit by giant waves before, but the water at the beach behaves in broadly predictable patterns. It sucks you out in one direction, it glides you back in another, sometimes it tosses you around, but always in ways you expect. You disrespect it, it disrespects you. The open ocean was something different—powerful and ungovernable. This water didn't care whether you respected it or not. Talk about nonexistence.

I put my snorkel in my mouth and ducked my head below the surface, but the storm had churned everything into an opaque nothingness. I thought back to the crystal-clear blue coral paradise on the brochure and laughed. Obviously Captain Jeff can't control the weather, but the magnitude of the failure was funny. This really hadn't worked out. The sea owed us nothing, and it was making that clear.

I snorkeled around looking at nothing, taking pictures of nothing with my disposable underwater camera, kind of as a joke. I came to a shallower area and a couple of small fish (brown) materialized and darted past me. I clicked my camera. The contour of a glob of coral (brown) loomed out of the murk, and I thought, *Yep, there it is. Click.*

The wind had picked up, and the waves were getting bigger. It was clear that we had not, in fact, succeeded in skirting around the storm. Or, if we had, it had hunted us down with prejudice. I'd been snorkeling for about ten minutes, I'd seen four fish, I'd braved the ocean, and that felt like accomplishment enough. I was ready to go back to the boat. A milky gray wave crashed over my snorkel, filling my mouth with seawater.

I thought back to Snorkel Instructor Shawn's "tutorial"—not so much a safety training as a poorly received segue between The Vengabus and The Piña Colada Song. The protocol in this situation, I was fairly certain, was not to panic and sputter for air but, rather, its counterintuitive opposite—to blow out through the snorkel, expelling the water like a whale's spout. What Snorkel Instructor Shawn hadn't prepared us for (besides everything) was the fact that when you tell your brain to breathe out, the first thing it tries to do is breathe in. I inhaled, and the Caribbean obliged, pouring into my lungs with a reciprocity that seemed fair, symmetrical. *You're inside of me, I'm inside of you.*

Was this how it ended? Did I just drive 3,500 miles to drown on a morning booze cruise? Maybe, I thought. But at least I didn't see any fish or coral or anemones or whales or manta rays or make any friends or have fun.

This wasn't what I'd pictured when I left Seattle two weeks before. I'd imagined something charming, human, spontaneous, specific—I thought that if I brought my body to this place, as far away from home as I could get without crossing a border, then the meaning would make itself. The sheer scale of my need for magic would manifest a chance meeting, a wooden sailboat, an oyster, a lover, a revelation, an explosion of color, a moment of eye contact with a dolphin. Not watching seventy-two drunk Trump voters fail at the limbo, followed by a pointless death in twenty feet of churning brown bathwater.

I took a class on *Moby-Dick* in college because my favorite professor was teaching it, a professor I loved enough to later sign up for Intro to Ancient Greek and spend my last semester of senior year memorizing the four moods and seven tenses of τέλος. I was afraid *Moby-Dick* would be boring, or that I wouldn't be smart enough to understand it, but I didn't know myself very well then either. Late into the night after our first class, I sat cross-legged on my dorm room bed, the book on my lap, devouring text rich as marrow, until I reached the moment in chapter 7 when Ishmael encounters a memorial to whalers lost at sea:

> Oh! ye whose dead lie buried beneath the green grass; who standing among flowers can say— here, *here* lies my beloved; ye know not the

desolation that broods in bosoms like these. What bitter blanks in those black-bordered marbles which cover no ashes! What despair in those immovable inscriptions! What deadly voids and unbidden infidelities in the lines that seem to gnaw upon all Faith, and refuse resurrections to the beings who have placelessly perished without a grave.

Tears spattered the page. I had never read anything so beautiful and so sad in my whole life.

That passage returned to me as I flailed alone in the sea. MUST BE NICE! Must be nice to perish placefully with a grave. Must be nice to know for certain you're real, to be killed by the familiar rather than the strange.

What was I even doing out here? Adventuring? Herman Melville had a roving spirit too, and what did it get him? A job at the customs office? *Moby-Dick* was a flop until thirty years after he died!

Instead of flopping and dying, I rolled my island bulk to the surface, spat out my snorkel, and coughed up brine.

I saw nothing but the choppy, dark ocean,

heard nothing but the slap of waves and fat raindrops and the white noise of wind over water. I was lost, at the mercy of the current, my flippers an unfamiliar impediment, snatches of "Axel F" by Crazy Frog surfing the swells like a siren's song, reminding me that there was nothing good waiting for me even if I did make it back. Snorkel Instructor Shawn was nowhere in sight; the Vengabus was decidedly not coming. Not to save my fat ass anyway.

Well, I thought, I came on this trip to be alone.

Only I could save my fat ass. Not Shawn, not Jeff, not Ahab, not Aham.

I knew I hadn't gone far. I made my best guess and struck out in that direction. It was *hard*. I had to fight for every inch, even with flippers. It was probably less than a minute before I crested a wave and saw the boat, not far at all, but that minute of uncertainty felt like an hour. No one else seemed concerned, but that was fine—I wanted the fuck out of that water, and I didn't care to wait in a line at the ladder. Didn't they have barracuda here?

I switched from a breaststroke into a full

crawl—stroke, stroke, breathe—the wind and the current dragging me away from my goal. At last, I reached out to grab the ladder, and my hand closed on air. The ocean had pulled me away again. I gave it one final push, my strong legs working the flippers, and made a wild snatch. Got it. Jesus fucking Christ. There were little tiny kids out there!

Just as I began to climb, Captain Jeff got back on the loudspeaker, sounding nervous: "Okay, well, heh heh, we're gonna have you all come back to the boat now! And, uh, we're gonna get outta here, heh heh!" It was clearly a fucked-up situation. The storm was upon us. But for the tourists, for the *apitalism-cay* (the most important cay in the Keys), Captain Jeff had to make it seem like everything was fine, like we were all still having fun.

I got my shorts back on and took a seat on the upper deck to observe Captain Jeff. He paced back and forth like a captive tiger, leaning over the gunwale to scan the ocean for stragglers. It was obvious that people weren't swimming fast enough, but he couldn't yell, "HURRY UP OR WE'RE ALL GONNA DIE," so instead he kept saying, "HEYO! I think it's time for PIÑA COLADAAAAAAS ON THE HOUSE!!!"

Maybe we weren't gonna die—I know thunderstorms are normal in the tropics, and maybe the piña coladas were simply meant to placate people so that they didn't complain about only getting ten minutes of brown snorkeling. But as the minutes ticked past, Captain Jeff's messaging became increasingly less oblique: "Hey, party people, uh, let's hurry back to the boat so we can pull up those stairs!... Reeeeeeeally need to pull up those stairs!... I'd LOVE to pull up those stairs, if you party animals can all just swim back to the boat!" In the water, Snorkel Instructor Shawn darted back and forth, pulling weaker swimmers toward the ladder.

At some point, Captain Jeff was satisfied and decided to call it. "Okay," he said, "we're all back on board and accounted for! Now who's ready for a MARGARITA?!" Everyone whooped.

We were many things on that boat—cold, wet, Republican, singing along to "Don't Stop Believin'"—but we were decidedly not "accounted for." There had been no head count, no roll call, no little clicker, no buddy system. All seventy-three party people had jumped in the water at random. No one had accounted for me! So how could they know that everyone was accounted for? Everyone else on the boat was with a group, but they never even told people to check that everyone from their group was there. Maybe a family would notice if one of their children was missing, but no one would fucking notice if I was! I guess no one got left behind that day, but then again, I don't know how they would know. Maybe someone was dead. Maybe someone was eaten by a barracuda. Maybe it was me. Maybe I'm a ghost.

Captain Jeff announced, comfortingly, that the thunderstorm seemed to be coming in "from the north and from the south," so we were just going to punch through as fast as we could. We YOLO'd back toward Key West, catching air and crashing down again, piña coladas flying.

Captain Jeff steered with one hand and wiggled his hips to "Limbo Rock" in his little plastic raincoat while the rest of the crew poured drinks as fast as they could. "Remember!" Captain Jeff kept saying over the loudspeaker. "We work for tips, so give generously!"

Sorry. Come again? Keeping us alive on that

boat wasn't even a salaried position? As much as I distrusted the general vibe, the crew was working their fucking asses off. That job was a nightmare—you're running a ship, lifeguarding, making drinks, corralling drunk people, and constantly in danger of being complicit in a mass murder, and you're paid in TIPS that you have to BEG FOR?

A teenage girl approached me. Her family had been sitting nearby for most of the trip, and I don't know what energy I was giving off, but clearly it was some flavor of feeble because she crouched down and said, "Can I get you a water or something? Do you need anything?" in a tone you might address a wandering dementia patient you just picked up on a Silver Alert.

"No," I said, confused. "I'm fine. Thank you, though!"

"Okay," she said. She patted my knee and left.

Well, that answers that, I thought. *I'm not invisible. I'm just a fucking loser.*[1]

Eventually, miraculously, we got back to shore. We disembarked, and I walked a few miles,

---

[1]. Higher Self Counterpoint: Or you could just let people be nice to you!!!!!!!!!!!

salt-crusted and dazed, through the residential streets of Old Town, past men chatting on stoops and an overgrown cemetery overrun with roosters (man-hens), and wished I'd stayed anywhere instead of my fancy hotel, done anything instead of that stupid snorkel trip. A friend had recommended El Siboney for Cuban food, so I walked there in the rain and went buck wild on roast pork, cassava, tamal, and sweet plantain. I bought a bottle of their house hot sauce to bring home to Aham and drank two liters of water. That time between the boat and the hotel, those brief hours of walking and eating, were the closest I'd come to the feeling I'd left Seattle to find: a tactile, autonomous, lived-in place, not a lifeless tourist fantasia. Discomfort is traction on the road to joy, and tourism at odds with true sensuality, but I didn't understand that before my weeks on the road in BAAA. It seemed I was already a different woman from the one who'd booked the trip. All my planning and expectations and wasted money and I found the Key West I wanted in this liminal moment, this crack in the pavement.

 Around sunset, I slipped into the quiet pool and impulsively texted Roya.

Just want you to know that all of our interactions have been really healing for me! Thank you so much!

She wrote back right away:

Our texts have been really affirming for me, too. They've felt so good! I have been thinking of you and hoping your trip has been going well. Congrats on getting to the Florida Keys! I hope you continue to have a safe trip!

Sometimes you get everything you want and it doesn't make you happy. Sometimes you arrive at your destination and realize it never existed. Sometimes you have to adjust your expectations and let the world be what it is, not what you want it to be. Sometimes you can't set your own bar. Sometimes you have to spread your limbo feet, limbo ankle, limbo knee, bend back like a limbo tree, because the limbo stick bends to no one, and there's a limbo moon above, and maybe, just maybe, you'll fall in limbo love.

OVERSEAS HWY, ISLAMORADA, FLORIDA

I made Judith cry in my therapy session yesterday because I told her that I had this moment walking around Key West where I was trying to do what Rainbow taught me, tune in to my heart chakra, and the leaves parted and I had this glimpse of what it would feel like to love myself first, to love myself more than I love Aham. And it was so beautiful and easy. She got really emotional and she said, "You know, it's the most profound thing, I can feel the intensity of your emotions even through the computer."

The Key

If I could give you one piece of travel advice, it would be this: When you go to a place, embrace the thing that the place is famous for. Do not seek out something that the place does not naturally provide, for what you receive will be a poor imitation of what you want, and you will miss out on the true pleasure of travel, which is specificity, and you will regret it.

If I could give you just one piece of relationship advice, it would be this: When you enter into a partnership with someone, embrace the unique and flawed person that they actually are. Do not try to convince yourself that they are someone they're not, or try to shape them into the person you think you deserve. What you find will be a poor imitation of love, and you will miss out on the true pleasure of other human beings, which is what absolute fucking freaks they are, and you will never be happy.

I-75, OCALA, FLORIDA

I used to be the kind of person who would get the giggles with my friends, uncontrollably, just laugh until I puked. And I have gradually frozen up to the point where now I am almost always the type of person who just says out loud, "That's so funny." Somehow I lost the ability to connect with the part of myself that produces that kind of ecstatic laughter. Because it's letting go of control. I think that's the part of me that's starting to come back.

Part Five

HEAL TURN

Jeffie

June 25, 2021

I backtracked up the Overseas Highway, then cut diagonally across Florida, stopping only for a Burger King Spicy Ch'King sandwich in Orlando, heading for the Panhandle as fast as I could scoot. My original plan had been to snake up the Gulf Coast and spend one night in Tampa so that I could avenge a terrible self-own I committed at Bern's Steak House in 2013 (I ate too much steak and was unable to enjoy my bananas Foster). But my friend Jessie was meeting me in Tallahassee, where her friend James lived, and she told me to hurry up and get there because we had a big day tomorrow.

James and Jessie had already set our itinerary: two days of swimming in and around a region of the Florida Panhandle known as the Forgotten Coast. I'd never heard of it. I didn't even know you *could* swim in natural waterways in Florida: I pictured alligator eyes shining in the reeds and water moccasins gliding through chocolate-milk swamps and brain-eating amoebas taking root in my sinuses. But I was on this trip to loosen up. Maybe it would be relaxing to have a little less brain.

Jessie is Sam Irby's best friend from Chicago, so I'd known her peripherally for a few years, but she and I hadn't yet transitioned from gossiping in the group chat to gossiping one-on-one. She still felt like a new friend, and I'm nervous around new friends. I'm always afraid I'm going to lose track of who I am and freeze up and try too hard to be cool, the most alienating thing a person can do.

Coming out of the weeks of isolation on the road and the weirdness of Key West, I was excited to socialize, but convinced that I was going to be awkward. I only knew James from the internet, but it was obvious that he was the most intimidating type of person: a magnetic eccentric who does whatever he wants. Jessie and James are a comedy double act, effortlessly confident in all the ways I'm lacking. They both design knitting patterns for a living—gauzy, lacy dreams in silk and linen—a job straight out of fairyland. They're thoughtful and graceful and they aren't weird about sex and they laugh all the time and always have fun and they're not scared and they have cohesive aesthetics and they know what's good and what's bad without stressing about it and they make beautiful things with their hands. They don't assume that other people don't like them. Their brains never scream, "SAY SOMETHING FUNNY!" in high-stakes moments, and if a person doesn't like something that they do like, they say "Whatever, babe" instead of "Guess I'll die." I was going to be a freak and ruin this. But Jessie was insistent, and she said I could stay at her Airbnb in Tallahassee that first night, so I canceled my motel in Tampa and dove into the choppy brown waters of friendship.

~~~

The last normal thing I did before COVID was go to Detroit for Sam and Jessie's joint birthday. It was February of 2020, and I was at a loss. Aham's chaos was peaking, and we weren't in couples' therapy yet and I felt like I was living with a stranger who hated me—which, in addition to being scary and hurtful, felt *extremely* unfair. He had no right to hate me when this was obviously MY time to hate HIM! The trip fell over Valentine's Day, and I didn't hesitate, and I didn't ask him if he'd mind. I just booked it. Fuck him. He could spend Valentine's Day with someone else since he loved other people so much.

I held it together for the first day, but at a Greek restaurant on day two, Sam's wife, Kirsten, asked about Aham, and I extruded the whole story like one long turd of shit. I hadn't told most of my friends the details of my relationship issues, I guess because I wasn't planning to let the relationship go. It didn't feel cathartic for people who loved me to hate Aham on my behalf. It felt worse. I didn't hate Aham; I loved Aham; that was the whole problem. So Sam knew the basics, but not how bad it had gotten.

They were perfect, of course—appropriately horrified and validating without getting vindictive in my defense. They didn't make me feel stupid for insisting my marriage was special and worth saving, but they were clear-eyed about the ways Aham had fucked up. Jessie set down her gyro (extra tzatziki) and shook her head. "No, babe," she said. "That's not how polyamory is supposed to work."

This is how friendship is supposed to work, though, I remember thinking. *Why am I so private all the time? Why do I keep secrets? Why can't I just let go and let people catch me?*

A switch flipped, and for the rest of the weekend, I felt light as a sunbeam—one whole Lindy instead of half a Lindy-and-Aham. It had been a long time since I'd felt like that. Maybe since our very first date, when malformed instincts told me to make myself into whatever Aham wanted and hold on for dear life.

We drove around Detroit in a delirium: eating square pizza, getting our auras photographed, wandering through Belle Isle Aquarium and picking which fish we were (Samantha, screaming: "BLACK CRAPPIE!"), and half watching *Million Dollar Listing* in Sam and Kirsten's suite while they caught me up on gossip about Chicago people I'd never met. Kirsten had ordered Sam and Jessie each a birthday cake from their favorite bakery, and when Jessie opened her box, the decorator had written "HAPPY BIRTHDAY

JEFFIE" in swirling yellow icing. In case you've been looking for it, this is the meaning of life.

Codependency is a two-way street, and I expected Aham to be pouty and bitter about me leaving him alone over Valentine's weekend to go hang out with Sam (he LOVES Sam). But when I finally had a chance to talk to him, late at night, in bed after Valentine's dinner, I was surprised to discover that the cool distance I'd felt over text had been contrition, not resentment. He had been respecting my space, and now he was excited to talk to me in a pure, kind way. I found it was mutual. He understood why I'd decided to go. He was glad I was having such a great time.

Something had changed. It felt like the fight had gone out of us. *I could leave*, I thought. *I could move to Chicago. I could move to Kalamazoo. I could move to London. I could learn Norwegian and move to Hov and have a whole herd of goats.*

"I miss you," he said.

"I miss you so much," I said, and it was true, but I wasn't talking about the trip, and for once, I didn't cry.

A year and a half later, I was zooming up Florida's Turnpike to see Jessie for the first time since Detroit. I pulled up to the Airbnb around 10:00 p.m. and sat in the van, feeling nervous. But when she answered the door, our rapport snapped back into place. *It's friendship*, I thought. *I'm doing it!*

James picked us up at dawn to beat the rush at Madison Blue Spring State Park. Wooden stairs descended through dense jungle ("Don't think about spiders"—woman thinking exclusively about spiders) and delivered us into an astonishing scene, a fairy glen ringed with ferns and moss, still mostly empty at the early hour. The spring was electric blue and clear as glass: not chocolate milk but Gatorade. The stairs continued straight down into the water, which bubbled up, ice cold, from a cave eighty-two feet below, flowing out over rocky shallows into the slow, warm, red Withlacoochee River.

Cicadas screeched in the trees as we lowered our sweating bodies out of the humidity and into paradise. As we floated, taking underwater photos, kicking our legs out long, and watching mullets and hogchokers dart around our feet, bubbles rose from the unseen depths. Then, an uncanny wonder, a scuba diver emerged from the cave below, waving in slow motion. We draped our bodies across the hot rocks between the spring and the river and warmed up until we couldn't stand it and had to jump back in. Jessie and James were as enchanting as I thought they'd be, and—miracle of miracles—I fit right in.

For lunch, we stopped at Hutton's, a roadside shack that sells deep-fried seafood. Even my arachnophobia couldn't dim the sparkle of crunchy soft-shell blue crab and a Coke at a folding table in the shade, still wearing my swimsuit, feeling sleepy and damp and a little deep-fried myself. This is why budget travel will always be better than luxury: Nothing makes you feel freer and more alive in your body than finding joy amid mild discomfort. Ever eat a peanut butter and jelly sandwich after hiking twelve miles? Contrast is pleasure.

We bought Tupelo honey from some kids in a barn next door and set out through the largely untouched jungles of the Panhandle, hundreds of miles of protected forest. A blessed Sonic at the halfway point bestowed upon us cherry limeades, still sweating in the cup holders when we arrived in a town on the Gulf Coast called, of all things, Panacea. Names matter in mythmaking and, whatever its faults, Florida delivers on names. We parked on a sandy residential street and walked a block to a beach called Alligator Point.

I detest the modern obsession with beaches as mere opportunities for display, water as something to lie next to. To me, beaches are for swimming. The measure of a good beach is how easy, fun, safe, and pleasant it is to get in the water. Saying that "lying out" is your favorite part of going to the beach is like saying that standing in line is your favorite part of going to Six Flags. Centering sunbathing as the primary purpose of a body of water is a sickness that leads to crimes like luxury hotels with three-foot-deep decorative pools. You can lie on the ground anywhere! It's pure brain-eating amoeba behavior, and I will not indulge the fallacy.

Alligator Point couldn't be more of a contrast with Madison Blue Springs: wide-open sandy shoreline stretching beyond sight in both directions, no shade, no people, gentle waves, warm water. We bobbed in the ocean like three fat corks and read our books on the white sand in easy silence. We goofed off about who was the strongest and most elegant swimmer and who was most appetizing to the alligators. We played catch with a Nerf football and called it "tossing the pigskin," a funny thing to call it. We moved from sand to water to sand to water to sand to water for hours, the sacred cycle. The ocean held us like babies.

US-98, MEDART, FLORIDA

We're zooming down the Forgotten Coast Highway to go swimming. I feel drunk from joy, and I ate a soft-shell crab! We swam in the Blue Spring for hours and hours. But we couldn't go in the river. They said you can't go in cuz there's poop in the water right now. And we said we're not afraid! Even though I have an open wound on my toe and I snorted the nematodes up into my brain for sure. But we didn't go in the river.

Alligator Point. That's where we're going now. We're turning left to go swimming at Alligator Point. We went to Hutton's Crab Shack—uh, what's it called? Hutton's Seafood and More. I had fried grouper. I had fried okra. I had hush puppies. I had fricking one fried shrimp. I had one soft-shell crab. Jessie had a fried gator. And I had a fried gator bite or two. It's just been the greatest day of my life.

I'm a Tallahassee girl now. I'm moving here. I'm gonna live in the swamp. The lady at Hutton's said that my name was cute, and she called me Miss Lindy. And we took a million pictures, and we are the most beautiful! Turns out, Most Beautiful People Award goes to us! We're collectively the *People*'s Sexiest Man Alive. Move over, Richard Gere!

It's really nurturing to be with Jessie and James. I really admire their friendship. It's a real friendship, a really deep, special friendship. I have always had friendships like that, it's not that I haven't or don't, but sometimes as an adult, I get overwhelmed and I let them lapse, a thing I really hate about myself. But this time with Jessie and James was the kind of thing that makes you think about what you're doing with your life and your relationships, because they're just so funny and creative and smart and insightful, and they prioritize fun and pleasure in ways that are aspirational to me. It was just really, really fun.

I feel like sky's the limit for the rest of the day. I can't believe I have to leave tomorrow and go to Alabama for no reason. Why? Why am I doing this? Why'd I spend two days in Key West by myself? With ten thousand Marjorie Taylor Greenes? When I could have been here having friends?

Cry of the Limpkin

June 26, 2021

My second night in the Panhandle, I slept at the Lodge at Wakulla Springs, a historic hotel, largely unchanged since the 1930s, located inside the state park where we were having our third big swim the following morning. There was no TV in the room and I was bored and wired, so I stood in the mirror and took pictures of myself in my underwear. Then I lay in bed and flipped through them again and again, back and forth, back and forth.

Could that really be me? It was the same body I'd left Seattle in—same belly, same rolls, same saggy tits—but seemed to be an entirely different person. I looked like a woman at ease, unconcerned with straining to be beautiful, one unified being rather than an itchy consciousness bracing for disaster, hyperaware of every micro-movement, every atom, every danger, every potential mistake. My outside reflecting, I hoped, a new inside. I slept the kind of sleep that only a sunburn and fried foods and seven hours of swimming can provide.

James and Jessie and their friend Alexandra met me for breakfast at the lodge (eggs benedict), and we took a boat tour of the springs and adjacent wildlife refuge. They'd already taken the boat tour when Jessie arrived in Tallahassee a few days earlier, but if I have one life tip, it's that the Wakulla boat tour is worth doing an unlimited number of times, especially if you get Ranger Collin, the Singing Park Ranger. As we putted along, Collin performed his original songs about the biodiversity of the springs[1] and encouraged us to check out his album on Spotify.

---

1. Partial track listing from Ranger Collin's album *River of the Crying Bird*:
"We Eat the Dead Things"
"Without Hands"
"A Little Quirky"
"Floating on a Boat Downstream"
"Cry of the Limpkin"
"The Ballad of an Ancient Tree"

Wakulla's water flows out of a cave system that's 350 feet deep. Moss hangs from every branch in the ancient swamp. Cormorants, grebes, bitterns, and herons nest in tuffets of grass. Alligators go about their business. You can see right down to the sandy bottom, where manatees overwinter among the mangrove roots. You feel certain that if anything ever harmed this perfect place, you would die. I didn't expect to feel that way about the Florida Panhandle. Another thing I was wrong about.

The Wakulla swimming area has a proper beach with a high concrete diving platform and a string of buoys that, supposedly, the alligators are polite enough not to cross (lol). Ranger Collin said they stay away from the swimming area because humans are loud, but in truth, it's just the honor system stopping them from munching you. We trust them to keep their promise.

We were standing in the shallows tossing the pigskin when a tiny little kid in water wings, maybe seven years old, came up to us. "Uh, can I play?" he asked, almost too softly to hear. James threw him the ball, and then he threw it to me. He said he wanted to be in the NFL someday.

We hyped him up while we played catch—complimented him on his tight spiral, told him the NFL was a sure thing. He blushed. Then, abruptly, he said, "I think I want to go dive now," and turned away. As he went, we saw the text on his backward baseball cap: ALL ABOARD THE TRUMP TRAIN.

"He was NOT actually that good at throwing," I said.

"He was a fake friend," Jessie agreed.

James told me the very best way to do the springs is to leap from the diving platform and let the imperceptible current carry you all the way down the beach, then swim back and do it all over again. Alexandra stayed on the ground like a normal person, but Jessie and James and I climbed up the two flights of stairs and walked to the edge. Jumping off something that high feels unnatural. Just like the night before in the mirror, my mind and my body were briefly united: They both said, *Absolutely not*. I am moderately afraid of heights. I have recurring nightmares about falling from a cliff—not about the smash but about the gasp of regret right after I go over, when I'm still whole and conscious and alive but the fatal slip can't be undone. I dream that I am frozen in that moment.

James leapt without hesitation, and I started to panic. It's a two-story drop into a bottomless cave full of alligators. "You don't have to jump if you don't want to," Jessie said. "You can just climb back down." But I was here to feel things, to defy a little bit of gravity, to swim. I knew if I hesitated one second longer, I would never do it. I plugged my nose and jumped.

HWY 27, BLAKELY, GEORGIA

Aham says that I have a very natural sexuality, a natural sexual energy about me, which sounds crazy to me, but it must come through every once in a while. Ever since I've been kind of an adult, talking about sex or being perceived as sexual has felt like an ill-fitting garment. Like, it felt like it was too tight and it itched and it contorted my body a little bit and it just wasn't something that fit. And I assumed that it didn't fit something innate in me. It didn't fit me, you know, who I am. And that became more and more of a certainty, and so I think I tried to put the garment on less and less.

And the implications of that go on and on: It's embarrassing to go out in clothes that don't fit. It tells people something about who you are and what you think of yourself, and it's humiliating. So why would I not avoid it?

I think the reason it didn't fit is because I was already wearing something else. Which is the suit and mask that you wear to try to appease society's opinions of you and expectations for you. I was wearing fat-girl apology cloak, you know? And I think that once that cloak comes off, it might turn out that sex does fit. Not even once it comes off, because I hope to never put it back on. If I could just unravel it like a sweater, pick it apart, and turn it into nothing...

Shy Marshmallow

JUNE 27, 2021

I left my friends in Wakulla Springs and drove northwest across Georgia toward that night's destination, a bed-and-breakfast called Heritage House in Opelika, Alabama. It's not hard to fall in love with the South. Hot, thick air, golden light, potent community. It's naive and condescending for liberal white people to characterize the South as a racist white place to be shunned. The South is a Black place. It is a tremendously alive place.

Leif and Dani, the couple that owns Heritage House, lived in Seattle until they bought the mansion and moved to Opelika in 2020. We knew people in common, and they'd seen Aham play music. It was a comforting link to the life I'd built and cherished, the home I was headed back to, the same home but different.

I don't know all the fancy furniture words to describe a well-appointed parloure, but Heritage House, which was built in 1913, is everything you want a gracious mansion to be. We're talkin' brocades, damasks, rare woods, scrollwork, velveteens, crown moulding, statement sofas, credenzas, tiny tables, big tables, wingbacks, claw-feets, chiffoniers, Biedermeiers, Chippendales, Magic Mikes, the Thunder from Down Under—this place has it all. My room featured a four-poster bed and one of those oval-shaped full-length mirrors on a stand that you can swivel[1] and a pitcher of sweet tea on a doily. And maybe you hear *doily* and you think *grandmother's wet kisses*, but it's not like that. Imagine doilies done right. Imagine doilies designed by Jessie and James. Imagine the very first badass-bitch doily knitted by Jeronica Doily herself before POSEURS gave them a bad name! That's how Heritage House is doing doilies.

---

1. When I had to look up all those fancy furniture words for the previous sentence, I accidentally learned that this is called a *cheval mirror*! I wanted to pretend I knew that, but I am actually TOO honest! Please, no more awards!!! MY CREDENZA IS GROANING.

Adult Braces

I got in to Opelika on a Sunday afternoon, so everything was closed for Jesus purposes. I took a walk around the residential streets and the shuttered main drag and talked to Aham on the phone.

"You should come here," I said. "I think you'd love it."

"I want to," he said.

"Do you still love me?" I asked.

"So much," he said.

"Tell me again what Roya thinks about me," I said.

"Roya thinks you're amazing," he said.

"What would you do if I wanted to meet Roya?" I said.

"You have met her."

"But for real."

"Die of happiness," he said. "But you don't have to unless you really actually want to. I don't want you to do it for me."

"Does Roya think I'm pretty?" I said.

"You know she thinks you're beautiful," he said. "I already told you. She's always had a crush on you, and she's always wanted to get to know you."

"Crush" was new. I felt a teenage kind of thrill, a "something's happening" kind of thrill.

"I like it when you say it," I said.

"Yeah?" he said. "Roya likes you."

"I think you can show her one of the pictures I sent you," I said. "But don't pick an ugly one!"

"None of them are ugly, baby," he said.

I went back to my parloure and lounged on my davenport(?). I thought about Roya and how pretty she was and how safe she made me feel, and I imagined her looking at a picture of me in my underwear in the Florida Panhandle and feeling the same things. I thought about how long it had been since I'd swooned over someone and how doggedly I'd insisted to Aham that I was fulfilled with just him, that I didn't need this feeling in my life. Maybe I didn't need it, but did I want it?

Was making room only for my basic needs the best way to govern my one and only life, my unknowable number of dwindling days? Nothing beyond food, shelter, water, oxygen, and physical safety? That wasn't how I lived my life in any other category. I ate the most luxurious foods

I could afford, I feathered my nest with precious trinkets, I admired doilies the world over, I ran unnecessary 5Ks just to see what my lungs could do. I spent forty-two dollars on an insulated water bottle because they came out with a limited edition colorway called Shy Marshmallow and I'M a shy marshmallow. Was this a woman who was content not flirting with her crush?

What had been the fucking point of all this pain—of stripping my defenses away with a rusted carrot peeler, of learning to let Aham be free—if I wasn't brave enough to taste a little freedom too?

As I lay there pondering the meaning of life, Roya texted me.

> Hi, Lindy! Aham showed me a beautiful picture of you. I hope that's okay. [yellow heart emoji]

Oh boy. If there was one unshakable truth about Aham and me, it's that we share a brain in most of the important ways. We like the same things, we hate the same things, we make the same jokes at the same time, we are brilliant and hopeless in similar ways. I figured he probably had great taste in women.

> Me: I told him to show you! I'm glad you liked it! I think you're so beautiful too.
> Roya: xoxo [kissing emoji]

Can you imagine getting a kissing emoji from a hot girl after a ten-year relationship during which you convinced yourself you were so repulsive that the only way to survive was to make sexuality illegal and zap both yourself and your spouse with an emotional cattle prod if anyone, including just random people on TV, ever said the word *nonmonogamy*??? And then through a combination of reluctant hard work, your spouse being a dick, your spouse being a miracle, yourself being a miracle (and sometimes a dick), and complete mental collapse, you drove from Seattle to Florida to Alabama and you started feeling horny and alive again for the first time since, I don't know, 2005?? And then immediately you get X O X O KISSING EMOJI FROM A TINY GOTH WHILE YOU'RE DRINKING SWEET TEA OFF A DOILY?????? I could have dropped dead, but it would have been a waste.

All that calamity, growth, and intoxication was still preamble, though. I hadn't yet made it real, made the choice, pressed the big red button, and I knew and he knew and she knew that the onus was mine. I was the reluctant one, the fearful one. I hung in midair, frozen in the space between real and not real.

Fuck it. I opened a new text message. I added Ahamefule. I added Roya. I threw myself down on my four-poster and kicked my feet in the air, typing furiously, heart pounding.

HELLOOO, I wrote. **THIS IS LINDY, FROM SEATTLE.**

CLOMP, CLOMP, CLOMP!

The next morning, Leif made me biscuits and gravy and Dani dug an old foam mattress out of a closet to make BAAA's bed a little more bearable. I thanked them profusely, promised I'd be back, packed up the van, and was about to drive off when Dani came running out the back door.

"One more thing!" she said.

She handed me a flower crown she'd woven out of sweet jasmine from the garden. I put it on my head and drove north, my phone buzzing on the seat next to me.

I think that moment—in BAAA, in my flower crown, in Opelika, in the group chat, in my body, in my life—is the most beautiful I've ever felt.

US-280, DADEVILLE, ALABAMA

I just passed a business in a random strip mall where all the other storefronts seemed to be empty. There was only one business in there and it was called Born to Be Sorry. It was written in cursive, and the cursive was rainbow, and it just said *born to be sorry dot com*.

Born to be Sorry. Born to Be Sorry. Like, Born to Be Sorry? Born to Be Sorry. What does that mean? I cannot guess what that means.

Born to Be Sorry. Dot com. Born to Be Sorry. Born to Be Sorry. Is it like conversion therapy? Born to Be Sorry? What is it?????? I think I used to feel Born to Be Sorry. Sorry to Be Born. But not anymore, baby![1]

---

1. When I asked my friend Jen Graves (a 2014 Pulitzer Prize finalist in criticism) for feedback on this manuscript, she called me up and said, "I'm not doubting your experiences, but I have to tell you that there is a business in Dadeville, Alabama, that is called Born to Be Sassy." Born to Be Sassy is a clothing store in a strip mall on highway 280 that sells T-shirts with slogans like "I have separation anxiety from my HUSBAND" and "JESUS, flannels, PUMPKINS, sweaters, BLESSINGS." There was never a business called Born to Be Sorry. I read the sign wrong. Jen Graves, a real journalist, got curious and sleuthed it out, and that's the kind of perspicacity the Pulitzer committee is looking for!

Heat Wave

June 28, 2021

I was supposed to camp at Mammoth Cave National Park outside Brownsville, Kentucky, but when I opened the van door at a gas station near the campground, my glasses went opaque with a WHOOSH like I'd stepped into a dishwasher. It was too hot and humid to sleep in a van, I decided. Plus, important developments were happening in the group chat! If I was stuck in Mammoth Cave with no cell service, then how would I talk to Roya about MY mammoth cave???

I was giddy as I booked my room at the Fairfield Inn & Suites by Marriott in Bowling Green—my favorite kind of mid-market roadside hotel, with clean sheets, a DIY waffle maker, and a little shop next to reception that sells Twix and Doritos. I couldn't wait to get my one-piece on and hop in that kidney-shaped indoor pool.

Bowling Green's historic core has, no doubt, many charms to recommend it, but they decided to put the Fairfield Inn & Suites by Marriott in a different part. Just off Route 231, in between the Hobby Lobby and the Walmart, past the Mattress Firm but if you get to the Best Buy you've gone too far, it sat in one of those suburban sprawls where pedestrianism is punishable by death and the salesmen of Martin Dodge Jeep Chrysler Ram and Leachman Buick GMC Cadillac brawl for dominance like Montagues and Capulets. In Fairfield Inn & Suites, where we lay our scene.

As I pulled BAAA to a stop in the treeless parking lot, a small part of me wondered if it mightn't have been truer to the mission of the trip to stay at a charming campground and explore a historic natural wonder, rather than blast across the Bluegrass State in a haze of horniness, seeing only Chick-fil-As and tasting only gas station pepperoni. But a much bigger part of me said, *LET ME HAVE THIS, MAN!*

It was hot in Kentucky, but Seattle was at the peak of a historic heat wave—three consecutive days over 100 degrees in a city with no air-conditioning, where temperatures had only broken 100 *three times total* since they began keeping records in 1894. That day in downtown Seattle, it was at least 108, so Aham and Roya had decamped to a hotel.

I swam, showered, and settled into bed with my Doritos to watch *Forensic Files* and flirt.

Bzzt.

A heart-eyes emoji.

Bzzt.

A blushing emoji.

Bzzt.

A sweating emoji and a pink sparkly heart emoji.

Bzzt.

A tongue-sticking-out emoji and a RED heart emoji.

Bzzt.

A red lips emoji and a two-cat-girls-in-leotards emoji and a water droplets emoji and a shooting star emoji and a chili pepper emoji. [*I don't know what I'm doing!!!!!!*]

Bzzt.

A laughing emoji and three red heart emojis.

We were in uncharted territory, but with me two thousand miles away, it was unclear what we were supposed to do now. Phone sex? Cyber-as-a-verb? What was this, the '90s? I was happy to take it slow. The slower the better.

Bzzt.

A selfie of Aham and Roya at the hotel bar, right at that moment, in each other's arms, faces pressed together, no longer just an idea but two bodies, hot and tipsy and red and sweaty and in love and together and I was alone in Kentucky and I was his wife and I was his wife and I was his wife and he was supposed to love me and she was so beautiful and she was so small and I wasn't ready. Why did he always move so fucking fast?

Bzzt.

We miss you! We wish you were here with us!!!!

Bzzt.

Girl elf emoji. King emoji. Girl genie emoji.

Bzzt.

Three candy emojis. Three little sweeties. Not two and one apart, but three.

I felt like I'd swallowed every Montague and Capulet in Bowling Green and they were hacking away at my insides, a thousand knives in my neck, a thousand swords in my gut. But I didn't have time to lash out in my old, cold ways—go silent and punish—because moments later, before they could have even noticed my lack of response, my phone blooped, a FaceTime from Aham. I let it ring while I took a deep breath. I wasn't ready. Fuck him for never making sure I was ready.

But then: What was ready? Was a person always entitled to "readiness" for life to move forward? What about the pathologically hesitant, the clinically fearful? Should the world always wait for us who cling to stillness most of all? Had I been "ready" to jump off the platform at Wakulla? Hadn't it been the opposite—that the longer I waited, the less ready I became? I could at least try. If it felt wrong, I could hang up and make Aham feel guilty later.

Who did I *want* to be?

I pressed Accept.

I-65, ELIZABETHTOWN, KENTUCKY

I just noticed that I was having this impulse to ask Aham if Roya knows that I'm ugly and disgusting and hideous and gross, and, like, um, a hell to gaze upon? And it planted this little question in my mind, like, am I like holding on to that as a weird point of pride almost? A part of my identity? Because some part of me knows that it's not true, but believing it makes me interesting and tragic?

To be clear, a huge part of me genuinely believes that I'm ugly, and it causes all kinds of disordered behavior in my life. But is there also a part that knows it's not true, but hangs on to it because it's an effective way to communicate to people the depth of my pain and disordered thinking about myself? Specifically because on some level I know I'm pretty, maybe by insisting "I'm ugly," I think I can prove how warped I am. I don't want people to respond by reassuring me I'm not ugly, I want them to think, *Wow, she's really fucked up. She's in a lot of pain.* Which I guess is just me wanting people to understand what it feels like to be fat.

Lost and Found

June 29, 2021

Aham and Roya stayed on FaceTime with me till I fell asleep, the glow of my phone mirroring a new glow inside.

In the morning, I drove north toward Kalamazoo, where I'd be visiting Sam and Kirsten, a welcome, crucial chance to snap back into independence. I was still full of bubbles, but I refused to lose myself in Aham again, not when I'd traveled so far to stake my own edges. Love is never, ever making yourself disappear. Love is staying yourself even if it costs you, and wanting nothing less, in turn, for the people who love you.

It crossed my mind that I might be sidestepping something important here, merely sliding from one coping mechanism to another. It was probable, not just possible, that I was making Aham's polyamory feel safe by inserting myself into it, rather than doing the real work of accepting that there were parts of him I was not entitled to know. But, on the other hand, Roya. Sweet, stable Roya with green eyes and long, black hair who thought I was beautiful, who made Aham happy and soft again, who was generous and silly and ethical, who had a giant brain and a pure heart, who I didn't even know yet but who'd somehow brought peace into our lives just by breathing, and who seemed to need us too. Even me.

Was I *actually* concerned that I was sidestepping something important here, or was I just anticipating the criticisms of friends and strangers who were hurt, or angry, or projecting some wounds of their own, who wanted Aham and me to get a divorce? It wasn't lost on me that, at the turning point of this mission, the thing my "true self" discovered she wanted looked an awful lot like what Aham had been angling for since the beginning. Was I actually attracted to Roya, or was I just relieved to find a loophole that let me stay in my fucked-up marriage because I was too scared to be alone? Was this situation healthy or sick? Real or fake? Progress or regress? Was I strong or pathetic? Straight or queer? A woman who could discern her own feelings or a baby who needed to be told when to get a divorce? Am I happy in a different dimension? Is there ethical consumption under capitalism? As the poet Yasiin Bey once wrote, "Why do I need ID to get ID? If I had ID I wouldn't need ID!"

I don't have fixed answers to those questions. *Here's an idea*, I thought as I raced north on I-65, out of Kentucky and into Indiana. Maybe I don't know and I'll never know and I don't actually need to know right now whether there are red mites in the Spanish moss. Maybe I've done enough thinking, and maybe I could spend a moment in the fucking moment.

Maybe the lesson isn't that I finally learned whether or not I wanted Aham, or Roya, or polyamory, or monogamy, it's that, for once, I ran toward the thing that scared me the most and leapt into an unknown that caught me and made me feel alive again, taught me to trust my instincts again, showed me that what I desire is to feel desire, to feel unafraid, to feel more of everything, to be hungry. Maybe that's its own accomplishment, worth celebrating, or at least worth granting some space to breathe, and maybe it's all I can do to take one step at a time deeper and deeper into life.

Yes, it was singularly, spectacularly unlikely that I would—in a wholly uncomplicated, non-disordered way—connect with my husband's girlfriend and she would like me back and we would go on to have really fun sex at least one time (that much was clear) and maybe more. But, I don't know, crazier coincidences have happened!

Haven't they?

The quickest route to Kirsten and Sammy's, according to Google Maps, was to get on I-69 at Indianapolis, then pass through Fort Wayne and head straight up to Battle Creek, approaching Kalamazoo from the east. I was so wrapped up in arguing with the voices in my head that I missed the interchange completely.

I'm going to be late for dinner, I texted Sam as I pumped gas just north of Indianapolis. **I missed my exit. I'm so sorry!!!!!**

Shut up! she wrote. **We don't care!**

Then, a second later: **Kirsten wants to know if you have a name for your road trip or a motto or something.**

I thought about it. When I first conceived of this trip, staring into my dog's single brain cell, I'd called it "Driving to Kokomo" (aware, on some cynical level, that that might make a great book title someday). But Kokomo had ruined the bit by not existing—my beautiful metaphor about searching for peace and independence became its own dark inverse, the vast and unforgiving un-Kokomo of life, a symbol not of my rebirth but my disillusionment. *Kokomo wasn't real, just like happiness, just like my marriage.* I was over the whole Kokomo thing at this point. Key West had sucked anyway.

However, I'd posted a selfie on Instagram a few days earlier that, due to some kind of red-hot erotic energy I didn't even know I had in me, inspired the artist Lisa Hanawalt to comment, "Loving your Horny Baddie Summer." Me? A baddie??? No one in my life had ever called me a "baddie"[1] before! I'd been saying it to myself over and over as I drove, as I jogged, as I took

---

1. If you aren't familiar with this term, GRANDMA, Urban Dictionary defines *baddie* as "a girl who looks great even on her off days and is always on fleek." ME! A BADDIE!

pictures in the mirror—*Horny Baddie Summer, Horny Baddie Summer*—but I was too much of a repressed freak to say as much to Sam.

I've been calling it "Feeling Myself Summer," I typed. **I'm trying not to be such a repressed freak anymore.**

LOL, Sam wrote.

Google had put me on US-31, a small rural highway that wasn't as fast as the interstate but would only set me back forty-five minutes or so. The landscape was flat and drab and agricultural, the vibe authoritarian. Corn, corn, Baptist church, corn, corn, corn, antiabortion billboard, corn, Baptist church, corn, Baptist church, bumper sticker about shooting liberals, corn, corn. I don't know if it was a fair assessment or just my impatience to get to the dinner table in Kalamazoo—Sam had made me a casserole—but I found central Indiana hard to like. And I LOVE corn!

I was zoned out, submerged in my thoughts again, when the uncanny tapped me on the shoulder. I'd just passed a road sign so cosmically unbelievable, so on the nose, that it could only have been my wandering mind playing a trick. I'd simply misread the sign, and that had to be that, because to accept anything else would necessitate belief in a living god—and I was NOT going to let Indiana win that easily.

But indeed, after a few moments, there it came again—rushing up to meet me out of the brown midsummer haze, a shiny green ghost, its impossibility belied by cold aluminum sheeting and steel.

EXIT 156
KOKOMO
1 MILE

I'd driven five thousand miles across this ludicrously large country, through Washington, Idaho, Montana, Wyoming, South Dakota, Nebraska, Kansas, Missouri, Arkansas, Illinois (wrong turn), Tennessee, North Carolina, South Carolina, Georgia, Florida, Alabama, and Kentucky, on freeways and turnpikes and scenic byroads and little dirt tracks, over mountain and valley and desert and sea and swamp, and by pure chance—I swear on Mike Love's future grave I did not know this town existed—I missed my interchange and was rerouted through Kokomo Fucking Indiana.

I know now that Kokomo, Indiana, is notable for two things: 1) On July 4, 1923, they hosted the largest Ku Klux Klan rally (or "Konklave")[2] in history, attended by over two hundred thousand racists, a natural fit because at the time *over half* of Kokomo's population belonged to the Klan; and 2) it's the town where they kicked Ryan White out of middle school for having AIDS and then terrorized his family until they moved.

I'd gotten my metaphor all wrong. Kokomo was real. So was happiness. So was love. So was hate. So was the moss, and so were the mites. So was my marriage in all of its complexity.

Kokomo is real. It just might not be where you think.

---

2. Violence is the last refuge of the corny.

Horny Baddie Summer

JUNE 29, 2021

I pulled up to Sam and Kirsten's house and launched myself at the front door. Dinner was on the table—the promised casserole, a big salad, and the reason why Kirsten had asked about my road trip motto. She'd baked me a layer cake, my favorite, vanilla with vanilla frosting (I know what you're saying—*That's cannibalism!*) and in marigold icing, it said, "Feelin' Myself," and then a drawing of a sun.

After dinner, I left to check into Kalamazoo House, an aquamarine mansion built in 1878, when Rutherford B. Hayes was president and my family hadn't even left Norway. It's not as fancy as Heritage House—more like staying with an eccentric aunt than PRINCESS FREAKING DIANA—but I *am* an eccentric aunt! I would summer in Kalamazoo every year if I could, like the gays go to Fire Island.

I crept up the creaky stairs and unlocked my room, a simple affair with a queen bed, two tall windows, lavender drapes, lavender floral wallpaper, and a painting of a guy in a straw boater hat sitting in a boat and painting a painting. In one corner, beneath a carved wooden mirror, sat something incongruous—two bulging paper grocery bags. It seemed to me some fine things had been laid upon my table. Sam and Kirsten had swung by the B&B earlier that day and dropped off the following:

- a bouquet of flowers
- a card that said *Feeling Myself Summer*
- a six-pack of Faygo Rock & Rye (bottles)
- a six-pack of Coke Zero (mini-cans)
- a four-pack of Topo Chico (bottles)
- a bag of Better Made Red Hot! barbecue potato chips
- a bag of Spicy Sweet Chili Doritos
- a box of truffles and three bags of chocolate bark from Confections with Convictions,

a shop that teaches formerly incarcerated people how to be chocolatiers
- a bag of rugelach and a box of pastries from one bakery
- three bags of shortbread and two granola bars from a different bakery
- a second, smaller version of the cake Kirsten had already given me

I dumped it all out on my bed and looked at it—such a silly, extravagant gesture. Maybe I was Princess Fucking Diana! I took a joyful, tearful selfie, my face red and scrunched like a newborn. I definitely couldn't shut the love out this time. They broke into my room and left bags and bags of it.

Sam had to work in the morning, so I ate a pastry and a granola bar and went for a run around downtown Kalamazoo. In the afternoon, we drove to Benton Harbor and had burritos at a picnic table overlooking Lake Michigan. I got a horchata and a dipped cone, and then we went home and Kirsten barbecued while Sam and I petted the cats and watched game six of the Western Conference Finals—Clippers versus

Suns. Chris Paul scored thirty-one points in the second half! He really wanted that ring. It's weird that a person can play the most phenomenal basketball you've ever seen and still be labeled a loser. It's like when a couple divorces after ten, fifteen, twenty-five years of marriage and we call that a "failed marriage." Sounds like a successful marriage to me.

I was supposed to leave the next morning to camp for two nights in Michigan's Upper Peninsula, but leaving Kalamazoo was impossible. I could stay one more night, I reasoned. I'd still have one night to camp by Lake Superior before I had to head west for North Dakota.

Here's what I like about Kalamazoo: It's normal. It's not flashy. Nothing's more than twenty minutes away. Wherever you want to go, it's got parking. It's got fat people. It's got coffee shops and bookstores. It's a nice, normal, livable place where normal people are living nice lives thirty minutes from the white sand beaches of Lake Michigan and they have a thriving soft-serve culture and they've never once been charged fourteen dollars for a doughnut. As long as your friends lived there too, why would anyone over thirty-five want to live in a city bigger than Kalamazoo? It's not like I'm going to the club! And if you do need a hit of something, such as hustle, bustle, fine art, or arena rock, Kalamazoo is two hours from Chicago AND two hours from Detroit! My rent at my last place in Seattle was $3,600 a month, and it was a good deal. Do you know what you can rent for $3,600 a month in Kalamazoo? CITY HALL.

In the morning, I checked out of my B&B and raced back to Sam and Kirsten's—I needed to do something impulsive and permanent on my extra day, something that would pin that version of me there forever, a glittering beetle under glass.

Sam's up for anything, so she and I went to get septum piercings. The place opened at noon and we got there at 12:30, but it was still dark and shuttered. A confused line was forming outside. At 12:45, two dudes—crust-punk-lite dorks—strolled up with coffees and a real cop energy, like, "All right, all right, give us a minute, people, clear the area, please, I need you guys to give us a few minutes."

They opened the door and we dutifully

re-formed our line inside. Despite being seemingly a two-man operation, this piercing shop was rigidly hierarchical. The boss, whom I'll call Jimmy, was the taller of the pair, with a weird little beard, and he ruled over the modest storefront like a petty tyrant. His henchman, a smaller man, whom I'll call Donny, was constantly fucking up and getting absolutely reamed to hell. I wanted to feel bad for him, but when Jimmy was out of the room, Donny mimicked his mentor's swagger like a baby lion pouncing on dandelion fluff. So, fuck him.

They had this weird system, almost like a ritual: When Donny signaled that you could approach the counter, you told him what kind of piercing you wanted, and he wrote it down on a tiny scrap of paper that he tore off a bigger piece of paper. Then he carried your paper to Jimmy in the back, who emerged like an oracle from a cave to inspect your piercing site. In our case, that meant he looked up our noses and said, "Um, okay?" like he'd never been so bored in his life, told Donny what diameter of ring we were allowed to get, and disappeared again.

We'd just started picking out jewelry with

Donny when Jimmy, who'd apparently been hovering, sighed and stomped back over. "You don't just get to pick ANY jewelry," he said as though Donny had told us that we just got to pick any jewelry. I said I wanted something small and unobtrusive. Jimmy rolled his eyes and said, "YEAH, that's what EVERYONE WANTS."

Then he broke into a smile and grabbed Sam's hand. "SICK," he said, examining her tattoo of Ursula the Sea Witch. "I used to have such a crush on Ursula." The shift in his demeanor was so Joker-esque, it triggered my fight-or-flight response. Sorry, are you yelling at us for being bad girls who tried to trick Donny into giving us forbidden jewelry, or are you gabbing with your BEST GAL PALS about wanting to fuck a squid with tits?? I can't live in a universe this unstable!

I tried to get things back on track.

"Can I get...this one?" I pointed to a plain rose-gold ring that Donny had recommended.

"Yeah, sure," Jimmy said, annoyed again for no reason. "Donny"—he snapped his fingers—"autoclave."

Donny scampered off, and Jimmy looked up at the line of customers with a sort of paternal loathing. "Sometimes we pierce forty people a day," he said, in the same tone Lieutenant Dan might say, "We lost a lot of good men over there." I wasn't sure how to respond. *Oh, WOW, that is SOOOOOO many people to pierce!* Man, I don't know how many people is a normal number of people to pierce!! Didn't you *pick* this job?

When it was finally our turn, Jimmy beckoned us to the back room. Sam tried to wait in the lobby while I got pierced first, but that violated one of Jimmy's Secret Laws. "HEY!" he yelled. "COME ON!" She followed, and we listened while Jimmy yammered a mile-a-minute Tarantino monologue about how the piercing was going to go. He stopped mid-sentence and turned to Sam, whose attendance he'd demanded mere moments before.

"Okay," he said. "I need YOU in the corner because I'm gonna be using ALL OF THIS SPACE." He gestured to the entire room.

"Okay," she said, squeezing her body tightly against one wall.

Jimmy told me to sit on the piercing table.

"Yes, sir," I said, trying to be obedient. For no discernible reason, this caused Jimmy to go absolutely batshit. He stormed around the room, rummaging through drawers and slamming cupboards. I filed back through everything that had happened since we entered the shop, trying to troubleshoot what I'd done to ruin this man's life. I recalled that in the lobby there was a huge trans flag and nothing else—no rainbow flag, no Black Lives Matter flag. Had I possibly misgendered this person? It seemed as good a theory as any.

"Hey," I said gently, "I'm sorry I called you 'sir' before without asking your pronouns first."

"HUH?" he said, looking at me like I'd called him a naughty baby frog who needed to be spanked. "I don't believe in any of that shit! I'm a man. I'm an alpha male. I mean, I respect everyone, but you don't need to ask my pronouns. I'm an alpha male and I used to be a bouncer. I don't drink and I don't womanize. I'm not one of those people from California."

Then he approached me with a big needle.

"Great." He sneered, looking down at the rose-gold ring that he'd recently helped me choose. "Of course he gave me the smallest possible jewelry for you. He ALWAYS does this."

"Oh," I said. "Do you want me to go pick a bigger one?"

"NO!" he said. "Everything's fine. I wouldn't do it if it wasn't fine. That's not the kind of business that I do. It just makes your piercing as difficult as it can possibly be."

"I'm ... sorry?" I said.

Jimmy shoved the needle through my nose, and it didn't hurt at all. I suspected that Jimmy was, in fact, good at body piercing, even if he sucked at being a guy in ways heretofore unknown to science. He stepped back and admired his work. He looked pleased for a moment, then homicidal.

"Yep," he growled, throwing up his hands. "Ring's too small. Ring's too small. I knew it. I knew it. He did it again. He always fucking does this. Every fucking time." We followed him out to the lobby where his idiot sidekick was helping a pair of teen goths. "THAT RING'S TOO SMALL! THAT RING'S TOO SMALL! SHE NEEDS A BIGGER-DIAMETER FUCKING RING!"

"You approved it, man," muttered Donny

as he pulled a different box out of a drawer and handed it to Jimmy.

"THAT'S THE SAME SIZE," Jimmy yelled. Donny shrugged and handed him another. "THAT'S THE SAME ONE. THAT'S THE SAME SIZE YOU ALREADY GAVE HER." Was this true incompetence? Or Donny's quiet revenge? One might as well ask the sun why she shines.

Desperate to survive this day, I piped up and said I'd be happy with a different ring, if they didn't have that one in the right diameter. I pointed to one at random, plain stainless steel. Donny grabbed it and headed for the autoclave.

"Can you believe that guy?" Jimmy said, grinning, once we were back in his chamber. He was breezy now, amused, as though he hadn't been screaming moments before, as though he were describing a silly goose, a rascal, and not his mortal-enemy-slash-best-friend. He swapped out my first ring for the bigger one, did Sam's piercing lickety-split, and we were done.

As Donny checked us out at the till, I asked if I could buy a single earring for Aham. Donny sighed. "I'd advise you to bring him in so he can get fitted."

"Get fitted?" I asked. "For earrings?"

"Every earlobe is different," said world-weary Donny. "I can't ethically sell you an earring if Jimmy hasn't seen the earlobe." He said it with pride, maybe even with love.

"Oh," I said. "We live in Seattle."

"Oh well," he said.

Even after all we'd witnessed, Donny was loyal to Jimmy to the last. It struck me that Jimmy and Donny had their own strange kind of marriage, one that didn't have to be legible to outsiders to be legitimate to them.

We turned to leave, and I smiled at the girl behind us in line—a dorky brunette dressed like a Christian camp counselor, with a septum piercing the size of an onion ring. Safely back on the sidewalk, Sam and I walked toward the car in silence, processing. Finally, she broke. "Oh, EVERYONE wants a little tiny ring???" she screamed. "Meanwhile, there's literally an Amish woman standing two feet away from us with a fucking DOOR KNOCKER?"

"What should we do now?" I asked Sam.

"What do *you* want to do?" she said.

"I don't know," I said. "Get a tattoo?"

We walked into a random shop near Sam's house and were assigned to a lady in a steampunk top hat who said *awesome sauce* a lot. Sam was getting a clip art of a Chicago hot dog on her non-Ursula hand. I'd hoped to find a piece of flash that spoke to me, but it seemed like everything on the walls was a zombie geisha or a black widow spider with huge boobs.

This would be my very first tattoo, at thirty-eight years old. Up until that point, I'd thought my hesitancy around tattoos was because I was indecisive and claustrophobic. When I imagined having a tattoo on my body, it felt like a big, clinging insect that I couldn't brush off—it made me feel trapped. But when presented with the opportunity to get my first tattoo with my precious Sammy, to have one of those carefree bonding experiences I'd always thought were for other people, to be truly impulsive for the first time in my life, a truth dawned on me: Had I spent thirty-eight years not getting tattoos *because I was afraid my mom would be mad at me*???

I didn't know what to get, but I didn't want to ask anyone for suggestions, especially not Aham—I needed this decision to be mine. I searched inside for how I was actually feeling in that moment: juicy, exhilarated, alive, electric, in love with the world, nearly in love with myself. It was my Horny Baddie Summer! I thought *Horny Baddie Summer* would be a good Horny Baddie Summer tattoo, but I wasn't *that* liberated yet. I wrote *good girl* in tiny cursive letters and handed it to Awesome Sauce, showing her where I wanted it, on my left side under my bra band. "Awesome sauce!" she said. "Let's go!"

In the most obvious sense, *good girl* is (to some people) a sexy thing to hear, and I was in my Horny Baddie Summer, and I imagined sending a picture of it to Aham and him getting a big boner about it and, sure, I liked that. But *good girl* represented more than that. It wasn't about Aham. *Good girl* affirmed that I was good, and it affirmed that I was a girl, two things that I often had trouble believing. And it was an attempt to reclaim myself from the prison of being a terminal Goody Two-shoes, which is just fear recast as propriety, and fear had ruined my life. A tattoo that said *good girl* said I was a good girl for being bad because bad is actually good, and I didn't need anyone else to tell me *good girl*, because my own erotic affirmation is the most primal one, so primal I wrote it on my skin.

A thing people don't tell you about tattoos is that getting a tattoo feels exactly like a person cutting into your flesh with a knife. It's not stinging or burning, but distinctly SLICING, which is hard to ignore. Everyone always says tattoos "don't hurt that much" or "don't feel like what you expect," but in my experience, getting tattooed hurts MORE than you think and feels MORE like what you expect than you expected. It is exactly what it is! Tattoos are honest.

When we got back to Sam's, I went in the bathroom and looked at my finished dumb little nasty tattoo and felt pure euphoria. The fact that you can just pay a hundred dollars and claim your own body?! You can change it and write who you are on it?! Permanently?! A permanent record of a moment in time. Proof that I was here on Earth, at least once, for sure, and I was in charge. That beautiful day in Kalamazoo was real, and I could prove other days were real too, as many as I wanted.

I think, if I'm being honest, I didn't get tattooed for so long because I was still waiting to be thin, so I could see my body in her "perfect," untouched state just once. But, to my surprise, "good girl" made me feel more perfect, not less.

Maybe if I cover my entire body with tattoos, then I'll never forget how to love her.

My third morning in Kalamazoo, I was absolutely, definitely, 100 percent committed to getting up early and driving to Lake Superior to camp. But then Sam ordered us Dunkin', and I was having my coffee and eating my breakfast sandwich, and we were talking and watching Wimbledon and then it was noon, 1:00 p.m., 1:30…

It was a six-hour drive to the Upper Peninsula. I did some math. At that point, I would arrive on the cusp of sunset and sit in the van all night, only to wake up early for a ten-hour drive to Bemidji. I couldn't even swim in Lake Superior if I wanted to because of my tattoo (good girls, even bad ones, don't violate hygiene rules). Or, second option, I could stay on Sam and Kirsten's couch one more night, then skip the UP and drive nine hours to Duluth. It was no contest. *We're being impulsive!* I thought. *We're being impulsive, and we're investing in friendship.*

Sam had some work to do, so I went and got my nails done—a baby pink, almost white, called Fancy Princess. While I was at the nail salon, I got a text from the proprietress of Kalamazoo House.

Hello Lindy, it read. **Our housekeeper found your massager/vibrator. Would you like us to mail it to the address on file?**

Or, instead of that, you could shoot me with a gun!

Lindy: **OH NO. SORRY.**

Proprietress: **Not a problem!**

Lindy: **I am so sorry.**

Proprietress: **No need to apologize, we all have one.**

Could it be true? All of us? Fancy princesses, B&B proprietresses, horny baddies, and good girls? This lady didn't seem to think that me owning a sex toy violated any municipal, state, or national statutes. Her grammar and syntax didn't indicate active retching. *We all have one.* What a generous thing to say, to reach out and save me from my misery, to so casually and easily turn me into us.

KALAMAZOO, MICHIGAN

I'm listening to this book, *Buddha's Brain*, that Judith recommended, and he keeps talking about the parasympathetic nervous system and the autonomic nervous system, except he's shortening them to PNS and ANS, and the way that he says it, he says it really fast and kind of slurred together, and it just sounds so much like *penis* and *anus*. Like, he just said that your penis and your anus have to work together to regulate your mood. Okay. He literally just said that every time you calm the anus you're stimulating the penis! I can't. Why did he say it like that? Sir, stop! Can't you see I'm sex-negative?

I Just Work Here

I hate writing about sex because I am a tortured cold-weather prude who's afraid of people finding out that I like sex because—as, if memory serves, we've already discussed!—I have a lot of trauma around growing up in a reviled and desexualized joke of a body, and my nervous system warns me that people are going to make fun of me if they catch me trying to be sexy or find out that someone once touched me and I liked it. How could I write about sex if I can barely think about sex? I always assumed the case was closed—the only barrier between me and sex-writing was my weird, anxious sexuality, and that was that. But something struck me recently like a big rocket of sperm from a climaxing red penis, and it's that maybe the *real* reason I hate writing about sex is that I hate doing things I'm not good at (see: first part of sentence). Maybe the barrier between me and sex-writing is actually my ego.

The problem is, I always assumed that writing about sex was supposed to be sexy. And when I write about sex, it's awkward. Because I do have weird shit about sex! Sometimes when I imagine two people having sex, my brain goes, "That's bad and they should stop." Ha ha ha! Insane! That's not what my conscious mind believes; however, I am a trained dog raised by Norwegians in Puritan hell! The neural pathways are strong! There's no version of me that's someday going to turn out a paragraph like, say, Jeanette Winterson in *Written on the Body*:

> She arches her body like a cat on a stretch. She nuzzles her cunt into my face like a filly at the gate. She smells of the sea. She smells of rockpools when I was a child. She keeps a starfish in there. I crouch down to taste the salt, to run my fingers around the rim. She opens and shuts like a sea anemone. She's refilled each day with fresh tides of longing.

A filly at the gate!?!?!? Infinite Lindy Wests with infinite typewriters could never!

If you (me) are operating under the

misapprehension that sex-writing has to be sexy, and you've also been conditioned to believe that free and public sexuality is forbidden to you, then the only way you can write about sex is to pretend you are someone else—to mimic, to disembody, to lie. I shape-shift into a desperate, spiraling hack the second I try to write something earnest about fucking. And so I avoid it! It's poison! Such dishonesty isn't just fatal to good writing. It's fatal to good sex.

But perhaps there's a spectrum of sex-writing from analysis to memoir to erotica to pornography, and sex-writing that isn't sexy is just as valid as the hot stuff. Maybe I'm allowed to write about sex the same way I write about everything else: like a dork who's trying to say something funny and real. The worst thing you can do as a writer is try to be a different writer. You will only ever be good at writing like yourself, just like you will only ever be good at fucking like yourself. I do not have to be embarrassed if my sex-writing doesn't come out like poetry. I am not a poet. I am a potato. And I fuck like one too! Just kidding. Or am I??

On the other hand, maybe it's okay to want to

sprout, to grow. Even a potato, bit by bit, tries to touch the sun, and it doesn't even know what the sun is! Maybe, just like in everything else, healing lies in the direction that scares me the most. What am I afraid of? I love reading other people's writing about sex. There's so much joy, a jewel-green jungle of life and death. I love watching other people flirt, find themselves in their pleasure. When I was just postpubescent, sex was fascinating and beautiful, free from pain, for a minute, maybe a month, maybe a year. I wanted to know everything about it. Now that that pain is so far in the rearview, why do I wall myself off? Why do I insist that I don't deserve to change, to live in my body?

Fear is a map. So I'll try.

Here's what's true about me and sex: I am a soft princess who loves to be praised, who wants to be thrown around a little but not in a scary way, who might act scandalized by sex talk in public but only out of insecurity, who privately thinks that pretty much everyone's kinks are soooooo interesting and cute. I am curious and shy and brave and an average level of perverted. I think people who are more perverted than I am are exciting and impressive. I love freaks! They're so free! I'm jealous! I like to have sex one to five to zero times per week, depending on vibes. I like to have sex in a bed. Don't lick my foot or my ear!!! I also think sex is bad and no one should have it or talk about it, but hey! Pobody's nerfect!

I really don't want to write about this—it feels crazy and scary and way too private—but I'm trying to get to something true and it's an important part of the story. In early COVID and early couples' therapy, when despair was the only color left on my palette, when I was slogging through each day in what I can only describe as "panic, but make it tired," when the best ten-year plan I could come up with was to get frozen into a glacier, I asked Aham to tell me what to do.

As I struggled through that overwhelming onslaught of days and nights unfortunately called life, with a sharply diminishing grasp on how to navigate money, career, food, body, friendship, marriage, parenting, nonmonogamy, sleeping, being awake, getting older, and, suddenly, a global pandemic, I had nothing left. Why did I have to make all the choices? Couldn't I outsource that? Abdicate the throne of life to someone who knew me best, who, at least at that point, believed in my potential way more than I did?

The versions of Dominance/submission that make it into the mainstream are typically limited to: mean-mommy dominatrices in vinyl standing over Dan Aykroyd; corny Tinder "Doms" looking for girlfriends too young to discern what losers they are; and resplendent, mustachioed leather gays. But there's also me, a sweetie with depression who just wants her husband to make her a sticker chart so she'll remember to drink water!

One big conflict in our marriage was that I was constantly worried and I felt alone. I wanted Aham to be worried with me, or at least curious about the to-do list gnawing at my skull. I wanted him to help me make the list smaller, without my having to delegate. But he wasn't worried, which annoyed me, and he was annoyed by my worrying, in a way that felt gendered.

We were standing in our bedroom, and I was sobbing and spiraling about my list, all the bills on the horizon, all the work we'd lost to the pandemic, all the chores that needed to get done.

Aham interrupted me and said, "Why don't you try letting go and trusting me?" and I said, "Because you won't do it," and he said, "How do you know?" and I realized that I didn't know, because I'd been so certain that my worrying was the chewing gum holding our life together. Suddenly, I saw that control is just fear, and in a great act of will, I let go of it all and Aham was there.

If you are a spiraling control freak, relinquishing control of the minutiae of your life to someone who welcomes that control with horniness feels better than those TikToks where the husband lifts up the wife's pregnant belly. It wasn't an instant fix, but it was a step toward trust that provided each of us a legible framework for understanding the other. Life felt like a set of labeled containers rather than a mountain of rotting laundry. I was able to transfer my mental load to Aham, and he was invested in our life in a new way.

Our power dynamic wasn't particularly lurid. My required daily tasks were essentially all the things I'd been writing on lists titled "LIFE OVERHAUL" or "MANDATORY DAILY SCHEDULE" and then failing to complete for twenty years: wake up at the same time every day, shower, water the garden, write in my journal, work on my book, walk to the beach, eat three solid meals, do something nice. The self-discipline that had felt out of reach was suddenly effortless, because I had handed over authority to someone I actually respected (i.e., not me). Responsibilities that had been asphyxiating last week were now a cute, sexy game.

A ton of people are in de facto Dom/sub relationships anyway—they just don't know it, and it's not consensual, healthy, or customized for her pleasure. I told Aham the kind of person I wanted to be and the kind of life I wanted to live, and he set up guardrails so that I could not fail. He chopped wood and did the dishes without my having to ask. I made coffee in the morning and brushed my hair every day, which made me feel better and more alive. He had his tasks and I had mine. Now when he went out of town to see Roya, he could say, "Be good while I'm gone," and I was. It was easy, because the unregulated part of me wasn't in charge anymore. A D/s dynamic is a game where you get lavished with kisses for doing basic things that you would have been resentfully doing anyway. It's like a life coach whose D you sometimes S.

We went on like this for a while, and in the space where my worry once squatted, spreading and pressing and noxious, some old, forgotten version of myself could breathe. Finally, in the fresh air of a safe and structured life, I got curious about who I was; I tried to remember.

The freer I became under Aham's instruction, the less I found I needed it. Once I started reconnecting with my own internal authority, I was intoxicated by the fun of wielding it—of pausing in any given moment and thinking, *What do I actually want right now?* It was a brand-new game, my whole life a fogged map waiting to be uncovered.

I watch a lot of wildlife rehab videos, and there's a moment where an injured animal, a weasel or a fox, will stop being docile and handleable and start trying to bite their caretakers. It's good news, the sign the rehabbers are waiting for—it means they're getting strong enough that their natural instincts are coming back.

I started to get indignant when Aham would tell me to do stuff—the stuff that I'd asked him to tell me to do—and I realized that was the feeling that I'd been searching for. I said I didn't want to do the dynamic anymore, so we stopped. It'll be there if I need it again. But I had graduated from something. I wanted to swim in the mystery of my own desires—discover what shape my life would take with me at the helm. Not a construction of me that I thought would please or empower other people, not my best guess placed into the hands of someone else, but the real me.

Part Six
BEING THERE

HWY 194, FOND DU LAC RESERVATION, MINNESOTA

I checked out of the hotel in Duluth, and now I'm on the road. Northern Minnesota is exceeding expectations, which were already high. It's so beautiful. Duluth was cute and weird. I'll go back. I'm sad to leave Lake Superior behind, and I'm sad I didn't get to swim in it. I went for a run by the lake, but I didn't swim.

I'm taking a route that's an hour longer than it needs to be because I want to go through northern North Dakota. I'm driving west through these gorgeous forests thinking about my great-grandparents heading west in 1913. Obviously, they didn't travel this route, this exact route, in a novelty van. I'm sure they took a train from New York to Fargo or something, and then they took a...horse? I don't know. But it's still the same region, just heading west with no idea what they're gonna find there or what life's gonna be like. They're just shooting their shot, you know?

Meanwhile, I'm scared to even move to a different neighborhood. The idea of making such a monumental life change when you're still basically a teenager. No kids yet. Just, *Bye, we're going to Ellis Island.* That's crazy. Just my great-grandparents heading west and passing these same ponds.

It's Fourth of July, which is an interesting day to be visiting the place where my family's colonial participation began. What does it mean to be an American? Nothing good, really.

All the shit we brag about all the time—voting, democracy, freedom, justice, whatever—is being deliberately destroyed in the name of voting, democracy, freedom, justice. The physical landscape is beautiful. But the physical beauty, the landscape, that's literally the thing that white people stole. That's the thing we built the least. So I don't think "America" deserves credit for the landscape. All America as an entity has done is make the landscape worse.

    Anyway, I'm making this westward journey much as my great-grandparents did. I just wanna go there and see what it feels like. I know it's gonna be an Arby's and a Dollar Tree, like everywhere else, but you can still usually get, like, the smell of a place.

New Town, New Me

July 4, 2021

My grandmother Clara was born at the home hospital in Barton, North Dakota, in 1914, the eldest of ten siblings, and when she was eighteen, in the thick of the Depression, her parents sent her back to Norway in charge of two of her little sisters, to ease the burden on the family. The girls were only supposed to be away for two years, but in 1934, Clara met and married my grandfather, Ole, and there was no one to take Boya and Elinor home again. Soon, they were all trapped by war; Norway was occupied by the Nazis; they were active in the Underground; Boya was thrown into Grini concentration camp; Grandpa Ole skied out under cover of night to pick up the Allied weapons drop; that whole thing.

The family was never reunited. After the war, Boya and Elinor stayed in Norway, got married, and had Norwegian children. Clara and Ole had five children, moved to Seattle in 1947, and then had two more, starting with my mother.

As I drove across the wide prairie of eastern North Dakota, I thought about Clara's choice to stay in Norway and get married—a shout of self-determination. She hurt her sisters and surely her mother, trauma that cascaded through the generations as trauma does. But was Clara the source of that calamity? What about Clara's childhood, working on the farm with a baby on her hip when she was still a baby herself? What about Clara's young womanhood, an American teenager shipped across an ocean to parent two little girls in a foreign land? Had Clara ever had any control over her own life before this one blinding moment when she fell in love and chose to stay? I wonder if calling it a "choice" is even fair. Maybe it was just survival.

It's brave to stay true to yourself even when it costs you—when it hurts someone you love, when you know people won't understand. As I drove toward home, I thought about choices: Clara's, Aham's, all of mine past and present and yet to come.

I camped at a state park on the shore of Lake Sakakawea, somewhere near my great-grandparents' homestead. In 1956, the federal government built Garrison Dam on the Missouri River and created the lake, flooding several towns along with a huge swath of agricultural land on the Fort Berthold reservation, an economic disaster for the Three Affiliated Tribes. Our homestead was also on former reservation land, thanks to the assimilationist Dawes Act, which parceled out tribal land to individual tribal members who agreed to adopt European farming methods. Previously, reservation land had been held commonly by the tribes as collective entities, but after Dawes, once individual allotments were distributed, suddenly there was "surplus" land that could be "given" by the US government to European immigrants like my great-grandparents. It's estimated that Dawes, in concert with the Homestead Act, facilitated the theft of over ninety million acres of tribal land. The violence of bureaucracy.

And so my family split into three factions: the descendants of Clara, in and around Seattle; the descendants of Elinor and Boya, in Norway; and the descendants of the seven siblings who stayed on the farm, their children and grandchildren still largely rooted in North Dakota. My Norwegian relatives have always been more legible to me than my Midwestern ones—in our values, our politics, our cultural interests. I suppose every nation has its chasm between right and left, Norway too, but it still feels like an indictment of America's internal sickness. Parceling the land, parceling ourselves.

I pulled into my spot in the evening on the Fourth of July, and I'd never seen so many vehicles in one campground. Every site seemed to have a fifth-wheel RV, a truck, a second truck, an ATV, a boat, a Jet Ski, everything plastered in flags and bunting for the holiday, white people thanking the nation that stole this land for them. For us. I thought again about how conservatism correlates with fear, and how fear feeds on isolation, disconnection, not knowing what's out there. And I wondered whether my affinity with the Norwegians wasn't actually about left versus right but about the siblings who were pushed out into the world versus the ones who were kept at home.

The lake itself is huge—it's sometimes called "North Dakota's ocean"—and I'm sure some parts are beautiful, but Lake Sakakawea State Park isn't a tremendous looker. It directly abuts the dam, so the beaches have an industrial cast: sparse trees, brown grass, coppery mud, low earthen bulwarks, and inscrutable concrete fossils of infrastructure long removed. The campground is less a portal to nature than a glorified boat launch for people who want to drink and catch fish on their pontoon boats all day, then drink and grill fish at their RVs all night. Fine pastimes, to be sure, but a locals' paradise, not a destination. That was great for my purposes—I was there to understand the locals, because in another timeline, I might have been one.

There's always beauty to be found, of course, as I'd discovered in every inch of land I'd traversed on this trip. Miles of golden grass waved in golden-hour light. A white-tailed deer grazed in the shade of a fluffy cottonwood. A vine bearing small bell-shaped flowers, tiny morning glories, crept through the grass, and I wondered if my grandma had picked those same flowers as a little girl, maybe woven herself a crown.

Was Clara ultimately happy with her choices? I didn't really know. She died when I was three months old. I don't even know if this version of her story is true. It's what one relative told me; another said I had it all wrong. I know I'm writing Clara's past to suit my own story, as children always mine and sap the ones who made them.

I lay in bed in BAAA, listening to the patriotic revelry all around and considered life's ongoing puzzle of going or staying, leaping into the unknown or sheltering in place. Maybe it wasn't a clear dichotomy—for me, leaping into the unknown meant staying with Aham, the person who was my truest home, while sheltering in place meant venturing out to find, presumably, a comfortably monogamous partner.

It was clear something was going to happen with Aham and Roya and me when I got home in a few days. I didn't know what, and for once, I let myself not care.

US-2, WOLF POINT, MONTANA

Finally here driving the Hi-Line in Montana. It's more beautiful than I thought it was gonna be. People said it's just really boring, but it's so pretty. It's really, really wide, flat, bright green prairie, and then a river and some hills in the distance, some little groves of trees, you know, just what I like, just the stuff I like.

Long, straight road. I'm three days from home. One thing this trip has really changed for me is that it's gotten me back into the habit of just getting up and doing stuff. There are so many hours in the day when you treat your time like that. That's how I want to treat my time when I get home.

Drip Droop

I noticed one day that when you look at my *good girl* tattoo backward in the mirror it says *drip droop*.

*drip
droop*

*drip droop!
drip droop*

I repeated it, a singsong spell, or the name of a little friend. All this time, I had been two people in one: a good girl and her mirror self, drip droop. I named my depression *drip droop*, and she became smaller, sweeter, softer to handle, a natural appendage, a swirl of internal weather. Sometimes I am drip droop, for a day or for a season.

drip droop.
drip droop!!!!!!!!

It is easy to forgive drip droop. It is easier to care for drip droop than for myself.

US-2, GLASGOW, MONTANA

I'm going through this really beautiful wetland, with these big ponds on both sides of the highway. Super picturesque. And I'm just such a fucking city idiot that I'm sure if I was like, *Wow, I love your beautiful wetland,* they'd be like, *Oh yeah, that's the slurry pond for the pig shit milkshakes that we feed to the worm barrels.*

Life Finds a Way

July 5, 2021

The Hi-Line is a colloquial name for US-2, the northernmost east-west highway in the Lower 48. The Montana section is famously desolate and, by extension, mysterious—the kind of blank space on the map I used to stare at in my mom's *World Atlas* and think, *What's happening up HERE?* There are no cities on the High Plains and few intersecting highways. It's a place people go to be alone, which felt right for my final days on the road.

I drove six hours from Lake Sakakawea to Sleeping Buffalo Hot Springs, a rustic campground next to a central lodge—the small complex an island in a vast, flat sea of lonely agriculture. There was a TRUMP 2024 flag flying above the lodge door, the first I'd ever seen (we weren't even to Biden's midterms yet), and I marveled at the confidence. They definitely knew who their clientele was. It said a lot about the place: who drives this road and who feels comfortable here and who is welcome and who is safe.

The sweet teenage girl working the desk was mortified to inform me that I had booked my campsite for the previous night. The campground was nearly empty, praise Trump; otherwise, I would have been sleeping in the van on the side of the highway—this wasn't the kind of place with a Marriott just up the road. She was soooooo sorry, but I'd have to pay the fee again, a rather shocking fifty dollars considering the facilities I'd observed so far.

My campsite was a treeless patch of gravel with a rickety picnic table next to a drunken plywood bathhouse that looked like a serial killer's toy box. But once I'd parked and returned to the lodge, the girl showed me through a door and into a vaulted, timber-framed, sulfur-smelling atrium. A 3,200-foot-deep artesian well, discovered in the 1920s by an exploratory oil drilling rig, pumps hot, slippery mineral water into one of the largest indoor swimming pools I'd ever seen. One corner of the lukewarm pool was sectioned off for a 50-degree cold plunge, and in an adjacent chamber, like a Roman caldarium, an oblong, tiled hot tub burbled away, fed by the spring's unadulterated 108-degree water. It was no more glamorous than a community center, but it was clean and empty, and to me, it was Mar-a-Lago. The fifty dollars suddenly seemed a bargain.

After swimming, I took a shower and wandered around the quiet campground. I saw a rabbit. I saw a train in the distance. I ate some dinner at my picnic table. I swatted a mosquito on my arm. I didn't feel like putting on bug spray right after my shower, so I lay in bed in the van and talked to Aham on the phone until the sun went down and I started to doze off. My body begged to succumb to a post-swim sleep, but I had a few more things to do—change into pajamas, get a tampon out of the back of the van, find some clean panties, brush my teeth.

I hopped out, using my phone as a flashlight, then circled around to the passenger-side door to dig through my suitcase for some underwear. I heard it and felt it at the same time—the whine and the pinprick stings of mosquitoes. They were, suddenly, everywhere, swarming all over my body and into the van. And these weren't regular little liberal cuck mosquitoes like we have on the West Coast. This was a well-regulated militia. Was it a different species of mosquito that I'd never encountered before? Or could mosquitoes from different regions exhibit different learned behaviors? Did mosquitoes have culture??

I waved my phone flashlight back and forth, trying to lure them out of the van like the lawyer in *Jurassic Park* distracting the *T. rex*, but it didn't work for me either (he died). I said *fuck the panties* and slammed the door, but I still had to find a tampon. That was nonnegotiable. I ran to the back of the van, threw open those doors, and dug wildly through my bags from the drugstore. Squadrons of mosquitoes were invading the van while their comrades feasted in a thick mat on the backs of my legs. A roll of paper towels fell on the ground and rolled away. Diva down. I fumbled the tampon box, and tampons flew everywhere. I didn't have time to put them back—I couldn't spare one more second with the door open. I jogged to the bathhouse, and these fuckers CHASED ME, sucking my blood while

I ran, while I peed, while I brushed my teeth. *Fuck the tampon!!!* I said. *I am not getting devoured on this toilet like that lawyer in* Jurassic Park*!!!!!*

I sprinted back to BAAA, threw the door open, and threw myself in, shoes on, everything in chaos. I'd meant to clean up the remnants of my dinner (a Lunchables and a hummus cup and some Oreos) that I'd left on the picnic table, but this was life or death. I figured if bears came in the night, the mosquitoes could fight them off.

But rather than being safe in my sanctuary, I was now trapped in a metal coffin with one hundred bloodsucking intruders. It took me an hour to hunt and kill them all. Blood spattered the ceiling when I was done, and wispy corpses rained down into my bed, but I got them. I sanitized my hands, put my tampon in, sanitized my hands again—good enough!—and went to sleep safe but swollen, mottled, itchy, a Pyrrhic victory.

I woke up early to the screams of a seagull war over the dregs of my Lunchables. How the fuck did seagulls end up in northern Montana? Are they migratory? Maybe they fly over and stop if they see some unattended hummus and that's part of their life cycle. Maybe there are just seagulls everywhere, no matter how far you get from the sea.

They sold something at the front desk called "Pancake in a Cup," but I couldn't stay to probe its mysteries. This place wanted me gone.

US-2, MALTA, MONTANA

I felt so distinctly, when I was in Kalamazoo and I was impulsively saying, *You know, let's get tattoos, let's get pierced*, it was such a distinct feeling of owning my body, in a way that I maybe have never felt before, ever.

It's what I want to say I felt when I had my abortion, but I think I was too wrapped up in emotions, you know? That felt too complicated emotionally, not because of the abortion itself but because of my life circumstances. But this was so clear. It's my body. I can do whatever I want with it.

Even with my hair, I've always just told Jenny to do whatever she wanted. Which was fun, but what do I actually want? I think that some of these small cosmetic gestures that fat girls are allowed to make—getting our nails done, getting our hair done—it's hollow. It's a substitute for the real thing, for real ownership over ourselves. We do it to feel something, but it's not enough. Not to say that everyone has to get tattoos and piercings, or start running or lifting weights to get stronger, but I think that there can be something really powerful in those things, in making deliberate alterations to your body from a sincere, internal place. Whatever is, for you, the opposite of letting everyone else decide who you are. If you're exercising to be smaller because society told you you're ugly, then that's not it. That's not what I'm talking about.

Anyway, I finally get it. I get what it means. Ownership over your body. I didn't get it before. It's so fun. It's so exciting. It's the most exhilarated I felt since I was young enough to be experiencing things for the first time, you know? When I experienced things for the first time, it was from a really disempowered, scared, wounded place. And maybe I get to do it again. I just can't wait.

Bird Box

July 6, 2021

My penultimate night, I booked a deluxe tent at a glamping resort on the outskirts of Glacier National Park. I just wanted to relax. I was tired. Maybe I was anemic from blood loss. Eastern Montana had been a little stressful. I needed twenty-four hours of adult summer camp in a place close enough to the Pacific that I didn't feel like an alien.

A team of photogenic youths checked me in with rosy-cheeked vigor and a level of choreographed, white-glove customer service I'd only experienced on my honeymoon at the Waldorf Astoria Amsterdam. They informed me that in order to prevent "wildlife interaction," absolutely no food was allowed in the tents, insisting conspicuously that this was a squirrel-centric policy only. I followed their lead and didn't mention the obvious, which was that we were in a famous grizzly bear area surrounded by a wall of electrified steel.

I dropped off my luggage and wandered down to the "bird demonstration" at the firepit, where a pair of women named Gwen and Barbara were taking various birds in and out of tiny boxes. They showed us an owl. They showed us a hawk. They showed us a falcon. The boxes were small and dark, solid aluminum sides with only a few small holes for ventilation. That's how the birds feel safe, Gwen explained. I raised my hand and told everyone about how I accidentally hit a barred owl with my car, and ever since, there have been barred owls sitting on my fence watching me, even in broad daylight. Okay, said Gwen and Barbara, the bird demonstration has ended.

I got a root beer and some hummus from the office and texted Aham, then remembered that he was in Portland because Roya's parents were visiting. I was alone in Montana, my husband was meeting his girlfriend's parents for the first time, and in two days, I'd pull up to our old house and find out what my new life looked like. Anxiety flared; I coaxed it back into my bird box.

At 8:00 p.m., a staff member dropped off s'mores supplies and left without lighting a fire. I got the fire going, and then a Mormon father and son took credit for my fire, and then the guy's Mormon wife acted like I was trying to seduce her husband because I was wearing a crop top. *Sister Elmira, I am self-actualized now! I'm not flirting with a city slicker who tried to light a campfire with just a log and a match!*

I ate two s'mores and was asleep by sunset, a cool breeze snaking through the canvas tent flap, raising goose bumps on my skin, just an animal in the world, all one piece, safe, loved, and alive.

Determined to be a participator, I got up at 6:30 a.m. and trudged up the hill to forest yoga. As we stood around waiting for the class to start, a woman asked me, "Are you the teacher?" Ma'am, no!!! I have been accused of many things in this life, but being a yoga teacher has never been one of them! Did you mean *yogurt teacher*???

The real teacher arrived and we spread our mats on the wet, springy turf. I am not flexible,

Adult Braces

and I cannot really do yoga, and a daddy long-legs walked on my mat, and I got a million more mosquito bites, but none of that matters when you're stretching your body toward the sun in a forest clearing at a perfect seventy-three degrees with birdsong all around you and you're on your way home.

Switchback

> The great flood-gates of the wonder-world swung open, and in the wild conceits that swayed me to my purpose, two and two there floated into my inmost soul, endless processions of the whale, and, in mid most of them all, one grand hooded phantom, like a snow hill in the air.
> —Herman Melville, *Moby-Dick*

When I was twenty-two, my mom took me on a hike called Snow Lake, one of the most popular trails in the Cascade Mountains. I wasn't yet a hiker, but I wanted to connect with my mom, and I wanted to want to hike.

The first two miles are a gentle but steady slope up to about six hundred feet, an elevation gain that was tough but doable for me. I felt tired but proud of myself, beat but unbeaten, and I started wondering when we'd see the lake. Ready to wrap up this successful day! Hiking wasn't so bad! What I didn't know was that the third mile of Snow Lake is all switchbacks, another one thousand feet of elevation gain in one brutal push.

The Snow Lake switchbacks are in full, blistering sun. There is no tree cover. I cannot remember ever feeling so tired. My legs were jelly. Elderly Seattleites blasted past me, smiling, with their trekking poles, just a casual morning hike. It felt like it would go on forever. My mother was patient but, I think, worried? I did not think I could do it. There was always another switchback, and another, and another. No swim was worth this. But I kept going, step after step. I stopped, I sat, I wheezed, I whined, I got up again.

And then we were at the top. The trail crested the saddle and the lake spread out before us and I understood for one brilliant moment why people do this horrible thing. The trail continued in a four-hundred-foot descent to the water's edge and then a four-hundred-foot climb back up to the ridge. My mom and I opted to just enjoy the view and turn back without going down for a swim (science may never know whose idea that was).

On the way home, we stopped at McDonald's, and my first french fry was the best fucking thing I have ever eaten in my life—the exhaustion, the fat, the salt, pure animal satisfaction. But Snow Lake had been so embarrassing. It didn't feel like a success, even though I succeeded. I could only see it as a failure. I had been so weak, so tired. For the next twenty years, I hiked rarely and reluctantly, until the hill at the cabin awoke my confidence and my road trip delivered me home with memories of waterfalls and frogs.

At my therapist Grace's suggestion, in the spring of 2023, I started going for a solo hike every Wednesday with my dog, Barry. I'd get up predawn and pack my little backpack: peanut butter and jelly sandwich, an apple, two water bottles, a water bowl for Barry, poop bags, hand sanitizer. A satisfying ritual. I'd lost some conditioning, but my body remembered the routine from the hill at the cabin, from Gourdon, from Spruce Flats Falls. One foot at a time, just keep going, slow as you want.

Barry bopped along like a little idiot. I'd listen to British detective novels on my AirPods. We'd scramble over rocks and roots in the central Cascades while, in the outskirts of Norwich, forensic archaeologist Dr. Ruth Galloway used carbon dating to identify the mysterious bones of a suspected Victorian baby-snatcher. I let hiker after hiker pass us, and I wasn't ashamed. This wasn't about them. When you're by yourself, you're never behind.

On each hike, eventually, I'd reach the top and behold the view—never a rare view, but rare to me. A small venture into the interior of things that I thought I'd never see.

I wanted to see everything. I wanted to touch every fucking place in the world.

Snow Lake haunted my Wednesday hikes like a white whale. The stats looked comparable to my other hikes—maybe a little longer, a little higher, designated "hard" instead of "moderate"—but I couldn't shake the memory of failure from last time, when I was twenty years younger and stronger.

I kept Snow Lake bookmarked and opened and closed and reopened it constantly, flipping through pictures and worrying over microscopic details of the trail description. What exactly did "a few tough scrambles" mean? I'd done other hikes with scrambles, but what's a *tough scramble*? What if a tough scramble for a seasoned hiker was an impossible scramble for me?

Maybe next summer, I thought as we rounded the corner into September. I had two, maybe three, Wednesdays left in the mountains before I had to switch to muddy lowland hikes for the winter. *That way, I can train a little more and be ready.* I already had a plan for my hike that day—something sensible and unspectacular—but when I woke at 6:00 a.m., I knew I was going to do Snow Lake.

I was surprised by how much of the trail I remembered and by how much more I appreciated it now that I had a dossier of other hikes to compare it to. Snow Lake really is a stunner. Views the whole way, crags and boulders, chipmunks and pikas, Douglas firs and western hemlocks. My trail-conditioned body handled the switchbacks so well that I was halfway up before I realized I'd gotten to the hard part. I took it slow. I stopped to rest and give Barry water. And then we were cresting the saddle again, just how I remembered it.

Of course I thought about turning back there, like we had the last time. I'd conquered the switchbacks, which was what I'd set out to do, wasn't it? But what kind of an ending was that? Quitting again because I'd quit before?

Barry and I descended four hundred feet to the shore and followed the path as it wrapped around the glittering lake. My forty-one-year-old joints were screaming, but I had made it this far and I was going to see the end of this trail if it turned my ankles to mush. The trail left the lake and wound deeper into the interior, eventually (after intersecting with a different hike) dead-ending on a little ridge with a view of seemingly endless wilderness. The dog and I sat and shared our ritual PB&J.

At this point, I realized that I had overshot the official terminus of the Snow Lake trail by a significant distance, turning this 6.7-mile hike into a 9-mile hike. I was wrecked, I was running out of water, and I still had to walk 4.5 miles back out. Snow Lake, you got my ass again!!! Nothing to do but the usual: one foot in front of the other, slow as you like.

Barry and I retraced our steps out of the woods, along the lakeshore, up the tough scrambles, to the foot of the ridge, back up the four hundred feet to the saddle (absolutely brutal). Even my deranged golden retriever was over it at this point. He started to lie down on the trail and stare at me resentfully unless I bribed him with peanuts to keep moving. I gave him most of the rest of the water, because even though I was thirsty, I knew for a fact I couldn't carry a ninety-pound dog out of there.

We were still over a mile from the trailhead and I was in a trance, getting lightheaded and trying to stay in autopilot. A woman passed us and stopped. She was around my mom's age, and she had my mom's vibe. "Do you need water?" she said. Not friendly, exactly—more like she was some deputized steward of the trail, out there making sure ambitious fat girls don't die. *Just doing my job, ma'am.*

My pride reared up. I hated it when thin

people assumed I didn't know what I was doing. I wanted to say no, but the answer was yes. *We are not fetishizing our dignity anymore. We are not rejecting help. We are letting the world in.*

She poured a whole liter of water into one of my empty bottles. I protested that it was too much.

"I always bring extra," she said.

"Thank you so much," I said. "You saved us."

I babbled to her about my little triumph—my return to Snow Lake after twenty years. I said it was my first "hard" hike. She wasn't that interested. Not in a rude way, just a self-possessed way, like someone who has other things to do and doesn't owe chitchat to a stranger. "I do this trail all the time," she said. "This is an easy hike for me. I've been doing this for forty years." Then she left.

The last liter was gone by the time we got back to the car.

The french fries were even better than I remembered.

~~~

That same fall, Aham and I returned to Lummi Island an entirely different couple and completed Lummi Peak with victorious whoops, discovering that on our first try—four years prior—we'd turned back just before the end, just before the trees opened up to an incomprehensible vista of the San Juan Islands, Washington, the Salish Sea, the wonder-world, our home, stretching beyond sight. So close and yet so far.

CURLEW LAKE STATE PARK, REPUBLIC, WASHINGTON

I'm here in the van in my bed on the last night on my trip. I'm at Curlew Lake State Park. There's not too many people here, but enough that it feels good, not scary. My mom said that we came here once when we rented the RV when I was a kid. I forget how old I was. I was young, though, not a teenager yet. I guess we came here. I've been walking around trying to remember. It feels familiar, especially when I don't think about it too hard.

It feels familiar, and it makes me think about what we must have done here. We probably had a little fire and maybe we had hot dogs. We probably went swimming off the little dock. I wonder if my dad held my hand and walked me to the bathroom because I was scared at night. I'm trying to think about myself as a little person here in the same place. What was I like? I remember I was so excited to sleep in the bed over the cab because it was a secret little nook and I could have all my stuffed animals up there and all my books. It's what the van feels like now. I'm still after that feeling. Maybe I should try to create something like that for myself at my house.

It's almost too sad to think about what life was like before everything got so bad, when you could just go on vacation and not wonder if or when this place is gonna change and end. Or if it can be saved or if there's gonna be a fire or if all the wildlife is going to die. I think about being here with my parents and just being free and not scared.

It's almost too much. Maybe it's possible to feel like that again.

The only thing we can do is keep trying, to not give up and not be despairing. Some things are gonna change, but not everything. Not the way that we love each other. I'm really sad sometimes. Just really sad. Sometimes. I'm really happy, though, too. So I think a constructive thing is to try to stay there. Be realistic about the world, but don't despair. We can have hope. We can have optimism as long as we work. You can't just stop life. You can't stop living just because things are scary.

You just can't. I love so many people. I'm so lucky.

It's gonna be okay. It's gonna be okay.

It's gonna be okay. It's gonna be okay.

It might be too late to save everything, but it's not too late to save what we can save. So many beautiful things are still here.

Yay or Neigh

July 8, 2021

I pulled up to the house in the late afternoon, and Aham was waiting outside to meet me. He was the same, but different too—lighter, sweeter, like a muscle unclenched. Me too. We hugged in the street, clinging to each other, each on our own two feet.

I cried as I dismantled my little home I'd built in BAAA: the string lights, the fan, the lantern, the cooler, the aux cord, the photos, the crystals, the blankets, the pillows, the stuffed animals, the windshield visor, the yoga mat, the citronella candle, the Bugzooka bug vacuum, the baby-pink Bluetooth speaker, the GoGirl urination funnel (sadly unused), the swimsuits and towels drying on the back of the passenger seat, the bud vase that clipped on to the AC vent, the mosquito netting I painstakingly secured over

Adult Braces

the windows with magnets each night. I drove BAAA, my good girl, back to the van office while Aham followed in our car. I handed over the keys and the woman at the desk took them chirpily, without ceremony, like I was any other traveler back from vacation. She didn't know that I'd had all my little things just so. She didn't know that I was born in this van.

Aham was turning thirty-nine in a few weeks, and I surprised even myself by suggesting that Roya come up for his birthday weekend. We could get a hotel, and if it felt right, I'd stay there too. If it didn't feel right, I wasn't sure what would happen. I'd stay at our house alone? Roya would stay at the hotel alone? That was a problem for Future Lindy. The days passed in a blur of mutual disbelief—were we really going to do this? Were we insane? Except it didn't feel insane. It felt like the only logical thing.

The day arrived. Aham was playing a show that night, so I dropped him off at sound check and went to pick Roya up at the train station by myself.

It's been my DREAM that maybe by my 40th birthday you and Roya would

be civil enough to sit at the same table and have dinner with me, Aham texted me while I waited. **If you'd told me last month that you'd be going to my show together on my 39th?**

Hold your horses, buddy, I said. **We haven't even met yet. Maybe I'll hate her.**

Then I saw her coming in the rearview mirror, smiling and waving as she jogged toward the car. She was black-haired sunshine, the most beautiful thing I'd ever seen.

Okay, I thought. *The horses are free to go.*

Triple-Double

I got my braces off a year after my road trip. It's funny—since the correction wasn't cosmetic, to the naked eye, my teeth don't look any different. But structurally, everything is different. A healthier smile. A chance at a fracture-free future.

Did you know that after you have braces, you're supposed to wear a retainer every night for the rest of your life? Otherwise your teeth gradually drift back to where they started, or worse. My teeth are doing fine, but as for my life, I haven't managed to retain all my progress. I still binge eat off and on. I stopped running, just fell out of the habit, and I miss it a lot. I still have depression. I can be disorganized and insecure. But there's one thing that hasn't drifted an inch: I do not want to go back to the marriage I had before.

Some people say that I'm delusional, that I couldn't possibly be happy with two partners.

They lose their minds when confronted with the idea of nonmonogamy, and I am sympathetic. I used to share that lost mind. I hated polyamorous people for giving my husband this stupid idea. My skin blistered when I imagined Aham having sex with someone else. It felt like I was dying at just the thought of it. Now I hear Aham having sex with someone else at least once a week, and my reaction is, "Could you jabronis keep it down?"

When we came out as a throuple[1] on social media, the backlash from strangers was deafening and vicious, particularly toward Aham. But the harder thing was seeing a subtle shift in the way people looked at us, people we knew in real life, like suddenly we were something a little unnatural, not to be trusted. Monogamous people don't just project their relationship insecurities onto nonmonogamous couples—they're afraid of us. It's palpable. We're something sinister, sexually deviant, possibly contagious, or worse: the reanimated bones of a Victorian husband-snatcher.

I don't know how a three-person marriage

---

1. There is no good word for this.

works! It just does! This wasn't my plan! But why shouldn't it work? Every day, I wake up and someone has made coffee and someone has done the dishes and two people are happy to see me instead of one, and that's not *that* different from my two-person marriage except that I am not stressed and scared all the time and now I do fewer dishes. When we told our couples' therapist about our new situation she beamed, unfazed. "Three is more stable than two, if you think about it," she said. "You can't build a table with two legs."

If you think I have been brainwashed and I am secretly miserable, I simply do not know what to tell you. Also, it shows me you haven't met Roya. She's so good. Just over five feet tall, she zooms around the house on tiptoe like a spring foal, like she doesn't have time to set her heels down because there's too much life to live. She's a listener and a poet and a scholar, a whirl of big black curls and slutty jean shorts and tattoos. She's so fucking thoughtful. She sends thank-you cards to people for coming to *her* birthday. She brings an energy to the family that lifts us all to new levels of productivity and creation. Her childhood nickname was Moosh, which is Farsi for *mouse*. She's my little house mouse, and she makes everything better.

Did you know it's possible to open a bill the day it arrives in the mail and then pay it immediately and not get sent to collections? Roya does that. Did you know that real people—not just in magazines—date and label leftovers with little pieces of masking tape so you know what's in there? Roya does that! And yeah, I guess technically I have more threesomes than anyone I have ever met, but when you're in a three-person marriage, that's just regular sex! Sorry!

What am I supposed to do—*not have Roya*? Because some strangers are convinced I'm secretly unhappy and they know better? Because I've written candidly about having complex feelings? Because these two skinny devils must be conning me since I'm obviously too ugly for them to actually want me? That's what my "defenders" on the internet say. Are you sure you guys are on my side? Because it doesn't feel like it!

The truth that no one can imagine is that I am—exclusively—the one who pushes my partners away. The more I excavate myself, the clearer it becomes that I still have baggage around sex. I didn't wait until I was fully cured to write this book, because I never will be, and feeling like an impostor in sex is one thing I haven't solved yet. I freeze up when I try to talk about it in therapy. When I'm depressed, and sometimes even when I'm not (Zoloft helps the depression but annihilates the libido), there are long stretches of time when I do not want to have sex at all. I reach for it and my old wall is back.

Aham especially, after all these years, can become desperate for my affection and lust. Sometimes I just don't know how to give it to him. There are broken synapses in me that I'm not sure I can rewire. But now there are three of us! During my fallow periods, Aham and Roya can have the fulfilling sex life they want while giving me space to come back to them.

Three people is too many to sleep in one bed every night, so we rotate in and out between two bedrooms. Way back when I was a mentally ill codependent snore machine and Aham would flee our bed so he could get a good night's sleep, I used to lie there alone and sob. I could only receive it as a rejection. It meant something symbolically to share a bed with a man every night, a signifier that I was "normal," and having to sleep apart underscored our brokenness.

Now? Getting to sleep in the guest room? Sometimes Roya and I fight over it! Keeping the window all the way open all night long[2] with my audiobook playing while hugging my stuffed cat Esmerelda? Not waking up at 5:30 a.m. to Aham info-dumping the history of the San Antonio Spurs' consistently excellent number one draft picks (David Robinson once got a *quadruple double*)? Embracing the pure pleasure of sleeping alone feels like a distillation of this whole journey. It's what I want. I like it. It doesn't have to mean anything more than that.

I love our nights together too. I love to big-spoon Roya and little-spoon Aham. I love sleeping in the guest room and crawling into bed with them in the morning. I love when they tuck me in and leave me to play on my phone as late as I want. I love being physically close to them. I would keep Roya on my lap all day long if I

---

2. AHAM LIKES THE SPACE HEATER AT EIGHTY.

could. I would ride around on Aham's back like a koala.

More than anything else, our life is wholesome. We got priced out of Seattle, and in 2023, we moved to the cabin. Roya left her job in Portland and moved in with us. The dog has space to run around. I am closer to the mountains, so Barry and I can hike as much as we want.

When I was little, I begged my parents to move to the cabin full-time and turn it into a farm; I drew elaborate blueprints showing where we'd keep the pigs, the donkeys, the pumpkin patch. They said no, of course—we weren't farmers—but I think it's beautiful that I ended up here anyway, in the closest thing I have to a childhood home. As I've said, I'm a sentimental person; I rely on the things I love to tell me who I am. My earliest memories are of loving this place, and when I'm here, it's easy to be her again. A hyperbaric chamber of me-ness, a well of bravery, a home base from which to venture out. I have my office up in the attic, all my little things just so. As soon as I can afford it, I'm getting a van of my own.

I know as well as anyone that life comes at

you fast—that everything beautiful I've built in these pages could collapse in a blink, rendering this book an artifact, a husk, a humiliation. But that's okay. A younger version of me might have held back on some of this love, some of this joy, for fear of losing it later and hearing the gallery say "We told you so." But I'm not afraid of hindsight anymore. A life isn't a book. Change doesn't make the past a lie.

For now, I just want to let the soft animal of my body love what it loves, and what it loves is FARTING ALONE IN BED.

Acknowledgments

I'd like to acknowledge ME! I have never worked so hard on anything in my life! This book took me four years to write, and if I have to type the word *nonmonogamy* one more time, I'm shot-putting my laptop into the Pacific Ocean trash gyre.

Thank you to Ahamefule J. Oluo, a true genius who makes me laugh every day, even when I'm mad at them, and lets me steal their jokes, and believes I can do anything, and has always treated me like a real artist. Thank you to Roya "Moosh" Amirsoleymani, who is the easiest person to love. Thanks to you both for letting me share so candidly about our life, and for taking patient, impeccable care of me while I wrote this book. I love you. If anyone is mean to you about any of this, I will exact foul revenge.

Speaking of patience, thank you to my literary agent, Gary Morris, who's been my agent for almost twenty years! Air horn! The best to

Acknowledgments

ever do it! Thank you to everyone at Hachette Books (RIP) and Grand Central Publishing who worked on this book, past and present, especially Jacqueline Young, Brant Rumble, Colin Dickerman, Lauren Marino, Carrie Napolitano, Maddie Caldwell, and my queen Michelle Aielli. Thank you to Elizabeth Banks, David Wain, Jason Richman, Allyson Chung, Liz Zook, David Wain's lawyer Hannah, and an unknown number of attorneys and Business Affairs executives, for helping me secure Netflix's permission to print the phrase "Pizza is really yummy for me" in the epigraph.

Thank you to Mom, Dad, Penelope, Charley, Sue, Ijeoma (I paid you back, right??), and everyone else in my beautiful, weird, funny family. Thank you to all my best friends, whom I'm scared to try to list in case I forget someone—you are my reason for living. I will have more time to hang out now. Thank you to Barry, my son, my pumpkin prince. Thank you to all the cats I've ever met, but especially Bootie, Cocoa, Jackie Brown, and Carrots.

Thank you to the friends who gave me essential feedback on this manuscript: Angela Garbes

Acknowledgments

(who read it TWICE), Megan Stielstra, Meagan Hatcher-Mays, Jessie Mae Martinson, Samantha Irby, Ali Rushfield, Rafil Kroll-Zaidi, Morgan Proctor, and Jen Graves. This book was sooooo scary to write, and I couldn't STOP sending chapters to people with the question, "Is this pure puke??????" and for some reason all of you said no! I love you!

Thank you to everyone who appears in the book, including but not limited to: Rainbow-Renee Manier, Jill Rohde, Ehren Coleman, Jenny Slay, Fat Daddy, James N. Watts, Collin the Singing Ranger, Kirsten Jennings, Corissa Enneking, Jay Aprileo, Meghan Tonjes, Isaiah and Julia Zagar, the guy who thought I was in the Highland Games, Leif and Dani, Lisa Hanawalt, the nice lady who returned my vibrator, Zachary Taylor, Captain Steve, Herman Melville, Martha Plimpton, Tom Lehrer, and all my dentists except for the evil one.

Thank you to professional cartographer Kadin McGreevy for the most beautiful and useful map ever drawn; to Jenny Jimenez for my dreamy adult braces photo shoot; and to Sara Deck for the cover art of a lifetime. Thank you to Devin

Acknowledgments

Gordon for editing the Panhandle chapters and adding the gorgeous phrase, "Names matter in mythmaking." Thank you to Judith, Liz, Grace, and Niki. Thank you to Dillon and Liann. Thank you to the Rowland Writers Retreat. Thank you to Scrivener, SelfControl, and Virtual Cottage, three pieces of software without which this book would not exist. Thank you to video games. Thank you to everyone who is brave. Thank you to all the fat people!

And thank you to Escape Camper Vans! You truly changed my life! Long live BAAA!

About the Author

Lindy West is the author of the *New York Times* bestselling memoir *Shrill: Notes from a Loud Woman*, as well as *Shit, Actually: The Definitive, 100% Objective Guide to Modern Cinema* and the essay collection *The Witches Are Coming*. Lindy is a former contributing opinion writer for *The New York Times* and a columnist at *The Guardian*, and her work has appeared in *This American Life*, *Cosmopolitan*, *GQ*, *Vulture*, *Jezebel*, and others. She is the co-founder of the reproductive rights destigmatization campaign #ShoutYourAbortion. Lindy was a writer and executive producer on *Shrill*, the Hulu comedy adapted from her memoir, and she co-wrote and produced the independent feature film *Thin Skin*. Currently, Lindy co-hosts the popular comedy podcast *Text Me Back* and writes the email newsletter *Butt News*. She lives in Washington state.

RAISING READERS
Books Build Bright Futures

Thank you for reading this book and for being a reader of books in general. We are so grateful to share being part of a community of readers with you, and we hope you will join us in passing our love of books on to the next generation of readers.

Did you know that reading for enjoyment is the single biggest predictor of a child's future happiness and success?

More than family circumstances, parents' educational background, or income, reading impacts a child's future academic performance, emotional well-being, communication skills, economic security, ambition, and happiness.

Studies show that kids reading for enjoyment in the US is in rapid decline:

- In 2012, 53% of 9-year-olds read almost every day. Just 10 years later, in 2022, the number had fallen to 39%.
- In 2012, 27% of 13-year-olds read for fun daily. By 2023, that number was just 14%.

Together, we can commit to **Raising Readers** and change this trend. How?

- Read to children in your life daily.
- Model reading as a fun activity.
- Reduce screen time.
- Start a family, school, or community book club.
- Visit bookstores and libraries regularly.
- Listen to audiobooks.
- Read the book before you see the movie.
- Encourage your child to read aloud to a pet or stuffed animal.
- Give books as gifts.
- Donate books to families and communities in need.

Books build bright futures, and **Raising Readers** is our shared responsibility.

For more information, visit **JoinRaisingReaders.com**

Sources: National Endowment for the Arts, National Assessment of Educational Progress, WorldBookDay.com, Nielsen BookData's 2023 "Understanding the Children's Book Consumer"

www.ingramcontent.com/pod-product-compliance
Lightning Source LLC
LaVergne TN
LVHW031535060526
838200LV00056B/4501